The Body Myth

Adult Women and the Pressure to Be Perfect

MARGO MAINE, PH.D.
AND
JOE KELLY

WILEY

John Wiley & Sons, Inc.

Published by John Wiley & Sons, Inc., Hoboken, New Jersey
Published simultaneously in Canada

Design and composition by Navta Associates, Inc.

For general information about our other products and services, please contact our Customer Care Department within the United States at (800) 762-2974, outside the United States at (317) 572-3993 or fax (317) 572-4002.

Wiley also publishes its books in a variety of electronic formats. Some content that appears in print may not be available in electronic books. For more information about Wiley products, visit our web site at www.wiley.com.

Library of Congress Cataloging-in-Publication Data:

Maine, Margo.
    The body myth : adult women and the pressure to be perfect / Margo Maine and Joe Kelly.
        p. cm.
    ISBN-13 978-0-471-69158-7 (cloth)
    ISBN-10 0-471-69158-5 (cloth)
    1. Eating disorders in women.   I. Kelly, Joe, 1954–   II. Title.
    RC552.E18M32 2005
    616.85'26'0082—dc22

                                                                            2004025686

Printed in the United States of America

10 9 8 7 6 5 4 3 2 1

To my brave patients who decide it's never too late
to overcome their body myths
—MM

To Heather Henderson, for the countless people
she helped in her short life
—JK

Contents

Acknowledgments

Many people listened to us discuss this book and helped us refine its ideas. We particularly thank Carol Dohanyos, Lin Druschel, Gail R. Schoenbach, Kitty Westin, and other friends who prefer to remain unnamed for deepening our understanding of how women experience their bodies in our culture, even when they do not have eating or body image disorders.

Our colleagues Michael Levine, Ph.D., Rosalie Maggio, and Diane Mickley, M.D., were a tremendous help in tracking down and clarifying important data in the book.

We are especially blessed to have Robin Dellabough for our agent and Teryn Johnson as our editor for this project. We encountered surprising resistance to *The Body Myth* in some publishing circles, where people seemed somehow threatened by its simple message. However, from the beginning, Robin understood the importance of what we wrote, as did Teryn and her associates at John Wiley & Sons. We are grateful for their collaboration, support, and strong sense of self.

Many other colleagues have listened, taught, and encouraged us through this and previous projects, including Hollie Ainbinder, Francie Berg, Bruce Brody, Joan Jacobs Brumberg, Doug Bunnell, Jeanine Cogan, Leigh Cohn, Carolyn Costin, Bill Davis, Steve Emmett, Sandra Friedman, Mary Gee, Judi Goldstein, Lindsey Hall, David Herzog, Craig Johnson, Marilyn Karr, Kathy Kater, Ann Kearney-Cooke, Michael Kieschnick, Jean Kilbourne, Sondra Kronberg, Lise Lunge-Larsen, Paula Levine, Beth McGilly, Sam Menaged, Mary Pabst, Judith Rabinor, Meri Shadley, Brenda Alpert Sigall, Anita Sinicrope Maier, Rob Weinstein, Dina Zeckhausen, and Steve Zimmer.

Our spouses George and Nancy continue to encourage our passion for writing, even though it often takes us away from them (or maybe because it gives them a break from us!). Either way, we are deeply grateful to them for their support—and for so much more.

Finally we thank Margo's adult patients, who have been brave enough to ask for help and gutsy enough to change their relationships with their bodies and their worlds. You are an inspiration to us and, through your contribution to *The Body Myth*, an inspiration to women and men you will never know. Thank you.

Introduction

In the relatively short history of eating disorders treatment, the overwhelming majority of patients and clients have been young women in their teens and twenties. In most cases, a young woman's mother makes the first call for help, arranging therapy, medical attention, and other treatment for her daughter.

Nowadays, adult women still make the initial calls to an eating disorder or body image professional. But more and more, these women call to get help not for their daughters—*but for themselves*.

Over the past few years, the national press has periodically asked me to discuss the growing number of women over thirty seeking treatment for eating disorders. Each time a news story appears on this subject, I receive dozens of calls from additional reporters and producers. I also hear from many ordinary women who say, "This is every woman's secret. It's about time we started talking about it."

This buzz of media interest reflects the mounting number of women in their thirties, forties, fifties, sixties, and even older women who suffer from seriously disordered eating or body image problems. The Renfrew Center, a national leader in eating disorders treatment, reports that one-third of its residential patients are now over thirty, a historical shift. Eating disorders therapists around the country are seeing steady increases in the number of adult women on their caseloads. On the outside, most of these adult women seem successful in their careers and appear to have their lives under control. Inside, however, they spiral through frightening and dreary stages of severe dieting, bingeing, purging, and obsessing about their weight.

What's happening here? The prevalence of eating disorders and body image despair isn't contagious or a matter of inverted heredity, spreading from young women to their mothers. Who are these adult women? And why do they need help?

They may be women struggling with body image loathing that arose during their youth and never really abated.

They may have suffered from anorexia or bulimia in their teens but pulled out of the downward spiral for decades—only to relapse when they are older.

They may have been preoccupied with food and weight for years but never been incapacitated—until now.

They may be women who, faced with the challenges of adulthood and loss of status in a youth-oriented world, develop eating obsessions or a steadily distorted body image for the first time in their lives.

As adult women, we have come to live under the terms of a widely accepted Body Myth: that the answer to life's meaning and challenges lies in our body's appearance. We believe that our self-worth (and our worth to others) is (and ought to be) based on how we look, what we weigh, and what we eat. This book reveals why and how body image, appetite, and hunger have become so central to women's lives. The voices and stories of real women in this book expose the deep pain and disruption brought on by body image crises.

But I also make clear how adult women with eating disorders and other serious body image problems are truly *different* from their adolescent counterparts. The myth that these problems are limited only to teenagers often results in adult women with body and food issues feeling even more abnormal than they would otherwise. Many see no place to turn and no sign that others share what seems like a "girl's" problem. Feeling ashamed that she hasn't gotten beyond such problems isolates a woman, which in turn makes it more difficult to seek and accept help.

I wrote this book as a practical, jargon-free guide to the signs of eating disorders and self-loathing—and how to get help. It has concrete strategies to address other, related problems—like yo-yo dieting, problem eating, and body image distress—that also drain an adult woman's sense of self-worth and distort her life.

For too long, body image suffering (and the body myths that feed it) have remained a big secret that many women feel too afraid to reveal to one another, or even to ourselves. Once that silence is broken, women can see how body image hatred fails miserably to help us respond to adult challenges like loss, guilt, regret, aging, and mortality. *The Body Myth* aims to help women rethink how we look at our own bodies, reshape how other people think about adult women, and discover positive alternatives for measuring women's self-worth. It taps the great hope and inspiration in the voices of adult women who have overcome body image despair and eating disorders.

The Body Myth is also a resource we can share and discuss with other people, or use as a support in the privacy of our homes—a kind of "biblio-therapy." Together, its stories can help women, men, and our world discard body myths, get off the body image merry-go-round, and take the first steps toward recovering the lives each of us is meant to live.

Instead of women making a venture of changing the shape of their bodies' exterior, I want us instead to focus on shaping our lives into adventures we can embrace. May this book be a first step on that adventure for you.

Throughout this book, you'll read stories of adult women struggling with body image and other issues in adulthood. All of these women are real, but their names and some of their identifying characteristics have been changed to protect their privacy.

Body Myth Terms

When discussing the complex and emotionally charged issues of body myths, we face the problem of what words to use. For example, the word *diet* can have different, almost opposite, meanings. Most of us think of a diet as a "plan for restricting the amount of food someone eats." But diet can also describe the simple act of eating itself, or the common food and drink of a person or culture; for example, "Milk is a staple of the American diet." So, to cut down on the confusion, I've come up with simple descriptions of what *I* mean when I use certain important terms in *this* book.

adult A person who has reached full physical growth, development, and maturity. In this book, *adult* means anyone over thirty, *young adult* means people twenty to twenty-nine years old, *teen* covers ages thirteen to nineteen, and *child* is anyone younger than thirteen.

aging   The normal process of growing older that everyone (including infants) goes through. In this book, aging is not a disparaging or negative concept—it is a fact.

appetite   The psychologically triggered craving for food (as opposed to the physiological trigger, see **hunger**, in this list); a healthy desire to eat food and drink liquids. Appetite comes from the Latin word meaning "to long for."

appetites   Psychological desires to feel, experience, take in, accept, deserve, connect, risk, comfort, be comforted, and be free. Becoming fully adult means addressing these metaphorical hungers. As Caroline Knapp writes in her book *Appetites*: "a woman's individual preoccupation with weight often serves as a mask for other, more intricate sources of discomfort, the state of one's waistline being easier to contemplate than the state of one's soul."

bingeing and purging   A dangerous practice of eating beyond the point of being or feeling full (bingeing) and then forcing the food out of our body (purging) with vomiting, laxatives, diuretics, and so on. People binge and purge in an attempt to relieve emotional stress and/or pain.

body   The physical home of the heart, mind, movement, passion, searching, satiation.

body image   One's personal perception and judgment of the size, shape, weight, and any other aspect of her body that relates to body appearance—from hairstyle and makeup to skin tone and clothing. Body image is different from how the body itself actually appears to an outside observer. Notice how there is no innate negative connotation in this definition.

Body Myth   The mistaken belief that life's meaning, our self-worth, and our worth to others are (and ought to be) based on how our body looks, what we weigh, and what we eat. When you see *Body Myth* capitalized in the book, this is the concept I'm referring to.

body myths Commonly held misconceptions about appearance, weight, food, and how the body works. For example, it is a myth that dieting is a successful strategy for losing weight.

culture Our collective way of life: all the ideas, objects, and ways of doing things created by the group. It includes the arts, beliefs, customs, institutions, inventions, language, media, technology, and traditions. We shape our culture through the attitudes and behaviors we encourage—and those we allow to pass unchallenged. Culture also shapes us (especially as kids).

diet Most people use *diet* to mean a method of restricting food intake in an attempt to lose weight. That meaning has subsumed the primary definition of the word in the dictionary: "the food and drink that an individual or group usually eats." In this book, I will use *diet* to mean "dieting to lose weight" or restricted intake of food. Dieting to lose weight can easily disrupt the hunger-cue system (see **hunger** in this list) and lead to other serious problems.

disordered eating/problem eating Aberrant behaviors (like continual dieting) that tend to break the natural connection between eating and nutrition. While disordered eating may not rise to the diagnosis of a full-blown eating disorder, it does cause both psychological and physical harm and can lead to eating disorders. Even short periods of disordered eating can send a woman into emotional tailspins as she wastes precious time and energy obsessing about food and weight. Disordered eating creates an imbalance in the metabolism and brain chemistry, which can cause depression, anxiety, and irritability.

eating disorders Complex, diagnosable illnesses triggered by behavioral, emotional, physical, psychological, spiritual, interpersonal, and cultural factors. People with eating disorders often use food and the control of food in an attempt to compensate for feelings and emotions that seem painful and overwhelming. Eating disorders ultimately damage a person's physical and emotional health and can lead to premature death. They include anorexia nervosa (which has the highest mortality rate of any mental illness), bulimia nervosa, and binge eating disorder (BED).

exercise abuse   Exercise is abusive when a person cancels or avoids other activities and obligations in order to exercise; exercises incessantly, whether ill, injured, or exhausted; or bases her self-worth on how much she exercises. Exercise is also abusive when one always pushes herself to do more than is healthful for her body; becomes angry, anxious, or agitated when she cannot exercise; or when she uses it to compensate for calories eaten rather than for health and enjoyment.

fat (substance)   A type of cell in the human body (as well as in other animals and some plants) made primarily of carbon, hydrogen, and oxygen; it does not dissolve in water. Fat is essential for human survival, especially for a female's ability to give birth, lactate, and pass through menopause.

fat (shape)   An adjective (like *short*, *tall*, *redheaded*) that describes someone's body. A fat body is larger and fleshier than a thin body. Our current culture uses the word *fat* to insult or belittle, but throughout history (and in other cultures), the fat figure has deeply attractive and sensual connotations (see the paintings of Renoir). This book uses *fat* (rather than *overweight*) as a purely descriptive, nonjudgmental adjective. *Overweight* is an inexact term that reinforces harmful body myths about weight and diet.

health   The state of one's body and mind. Weight and body shape *may* be signs of good or poor health, but our culture's body myths tend to make them the primary or *only* signs of health. Contrary to popular belief, one can be thin and not healthy, or one can be fit, fat, and in excellent health. Genetics, lifestyle, activity level, and nutritional intake predict health much more accurately than weight does.

hunger   The physiologically triggered craving for food; pain or discomfort in the stomach that is a cue for a person to eat (as opposed to the psychological trigger of appetite; see **appetite** in this list). Hunger is the body's response to its need for food and nutrition.

liminal times   Periods of transition between one stage of life and another. For example, the period of going through a divorce or menopause is a liminal time.

midlife The time of life when a person becomes more conscious of her mortality and experiences major life changes, like children moving away from home or a parent dying. Midlife usually refers to our forties and fifties. The average life expectancy for a woman in the United States is seventy-eight years, so a woman's average midlife is thirty-nine.

normal eating Normal eating is flexible, rather than perfect, eating. It is a *range* of different behaviors at different times and in different circumstances. Normal eating responds to internal cues regarding hunger or emotional needs (wanting a comfort food or celebrating an event with a favorite food). At other times, it responds to external cues, such as a food's availability, aroma, appearance, or place in religious and family rituals (like weddings and funerals). Normal eating includes sometimes eating too much just because we feel like it! A person who eats normally is not afraid of food.

normal weight Normal weight is a range (not one set point) primarily determined by our genes (just as height and skin color are genetically determined). If we eat well, are physically active, and don't have a chronic illness, we will settle into a weight range that shifts over the course of life but continually reflects our genetic heritage.

nutrition How a person eats and how her body uses food once it is ingested. Nutrition also means supplying or receiving food for nourishment. Both nutrition and nourishment come from the Latin word meaning "to feed" and refer to making something grow or keeping it alive and well with food.

thin An adjective (like *short*, *tall*, *redheaded*) that describes a body that is less wide and fleshy than a fat body. As with *fat*, this book uses *thin* as a purely descriptive, nonjudgmental adjective.

1

The Changing Shape
of Womanhood

Jennifer is attractive, successful, and well liked. She is a Super Mom, Super Employee, Super Wife, Super Daughter, Super Sister, Super Aunt, Super Niece, Super Cousin, Super Volunteer, Super Neighbor, and Super Friend. People are awed by her; she always looks perfect, pretty, stylish, and thin—like she has it all. But inside, this forty-something Superwoman is exhausted, depressed, and running on empty.

Jennifer and her husband, Bill, have a preteen daughter and teen son. Bill is deeply involved in his work and is a high-profile volunteer in their community. He isn't very available with his time or emotions, so Jennifer manages most details of family life, including the schedules for Bill, their marriage, their kids, her parents, and Bill's parents.

Her parents and in-laws are getting older and starting to have health problems. They all rely on Jennifer's aid. She wants to help them more but feels guilty if she can't be there for them. In fact, Jennifer feels besieged while trying to hold the home front together in the complex, accelerating rush of twenty-first-century family life, while also working outside the home. Despite the burdens, Jennifer projects a cheerful attitude, seeming to easily juggle the families' needs and manage her career.

Jennifer doesn't know how to stop doing everything for fear that her world will fly apart and she'll let down the people she loves.

While she knows it's impossible, Jennifer keeps trying to be perfect and rarely asks for help. She tends to be a control junkie, attempting to micromanage the minutiae of her life and her family's life because she feels so little command over the larger forces affecting her world and her family.

Jennifer's body is also complex, and its rhythms and shape change as she moves through adulthood. Despite this, she has been led to believe (by her upbringing, the culture, and the media) that she can—and should—control her body's shape, weight, appearance, and aging.

So when she feels overrun by life's requirements and uncertainties, Jennifer fights determinedly to make her body obey her commands. This helps her feel more in control than she does when facing the overwhelming demands of her overall situation, the ambiguity she feels about her life, and the daily comments she gets from other people about her body.

Years ago Jennifer learned to assess her self-worth on the bathroom scale and to translate her negative emotions into what body image educator Sandy Friedman calls "the language of fat." That's why Jennifer has been dieting and struggling with body image issues since she was a teenager, and adult stresses regularly rekindle those struggles. Jennifer kept her problem well hidden, and no one seemed to notice.

Because she had difficulty getting pregnant, Jennifer underwent fertility treatments that made her gain weight. Her pregnancies brought even more concern about weight, and she dieted severely after each birth. Jennifer feels that postpartum crash diets were essential to keep Bill interested in her. Jennifer would rather change her body than explore the mistrust simmering just below the surface of her marriage. She finds it scary to ask why she is afraid that Bill would leave her if she wasn't physically attractive enough.

Her postpartum diet goal was for her to return to her original weight, but she overshot each target, becoming thinner after each pregnancy than she was before it. She likes how people frequently compliment her on her appearance and emphatically praise her weight loss. But while her OB/GYN never addressed it, she still worries about how and why her periods became wildly irregular after her second postpartum diet. Now that she's entering menopause, Jennifer feels even less control over her body and everything else in her life. Afraid that she will gain weight during menopause, she restricts her food intake more strictly and combines periodic vomiting with hours of intense daily exercise to fight the pounds.

Now Jennifer's facade is beginning to crack. The weight is coming off, but she isn't getting the same boost to her self-esteem that dieting used to deliver. Instead of feeling more satisfied, Jennifer feels more anxious. She's always been very close to her kids but now feels left out of their adolescent lives. Her son, Jerry, is less communicative, and she deeply misses their former closeness. Her daughter, Mandy, reminds Jennifer of herself at age twelve: rigid, competitive, and always pushing herself. The familiar way Mandy criticizes her body and obsesses about dieting frightens Jennifer. She is afraid Mandy will replicate Jennifer's own decades of struggle with her body image.

Watching Mandy, Jennifer decides she can't leave this painful legacy to her daughter. Jennifer admits to herself that she has some kind of problem but is ashamed that it has lingered so long into adulthood. Convinced that being obsessed about body image is a teenager's problem, she thinks she should be over it. But finally Jennifer gathers the courage to bring her concerns to her gynecologist at her next checkup.

Before she can even mention her concerns, however, the nurse enthusiastically compliments Jennifer on her appearance and asks how she was able to keep all that weight off and look so good. The doctor is just as flattering when he enters the exam room. Feeling misunderstood and confused, she never asks him for help or tells him the truth about her fluctuating periods and the dangerous ways she manages her weight. Jennifer goes home frightened, ashamed, hopeless, and uncertain about what to do. From what people tell her, she looks better and better on the outside, but she feels worse and worse inside her pretty little body.

The Shape of Womanhood

For Jennifer and many other women, maintaining their body image becomes the answer to all angst and seems to provide concrete answers to abstract questions such as, How am I faring as a person? The answer to that and other major life questions may be elusive, but a woman *can* measure pounds, calories, hours of exercise, and clothing size to judge her performance as a woman today.

Like Jennifer, some adult women slip over the edge into eating disorders and severe body image despair—problems normally identified primarily with adolescent girls. Adult women and adolescents with these problems do share some characteristics, like using body obsession to cope with developmental challenges and identity development. They share the tendency to translate difficult feelings into the language of fat and play out their distress on the canvas of the body. Likewise, younger and older women live together in a culture rife with body myths that are toxic for women's body image and self-image.

However, there are significant differences between the two populations. Grown women don't believe that they should have such "teenage" problems and feel that they should know better. They tend to be more embarrassed and ashamed about body disturbances, feeling that these disturbances are less legitimate and not a worthwhile reason to seek help. Adult women have more serious everyday responsibilities than girls, and consequently, they have more people to disappoint if they fail. For all these reasons, it feels much harder to make the commitment to take the time to address eating and body image disorders.

Jennifer's story probably comes as no surprise to you. She is not unique. Millions of adult women in the United States struggle with being obsessed about their weight and dissatisfied with their body image.

Extensive studies reported in the *Journal of the American Medical Association* and data from the 2000 U.S. census indicate that forty-three million adult women in the United States are dieting to lose weight at any given time—and that another twenty-six million are dieting to maintain their weight. Most of this dieting is of the "yo-yo" variety, where the "lost" weight is regained, often with additional pounds, triggering yet more rounds of dieting. The yo-yo label aptly describes the ways women's lives and sense of well-being spin up and down with the success or failure of their diets.

Women today have inherited a multigenerational fixation with weight. For more than two generations, U.S. women have been preoccupied with weight. A 1983 *Glamour* magazine survey of 33,000 readers showed that 75 percent thought they were overweight, while only 25 percent of them actually were overweight. In other words, *half* of the survey respondents had severely distorted images of their own bodies. Meanwhile, 42 percent of readers said losing weight was the thing that would make them the happiest—twice the percentage of those who chose being successful at work or dating a man they admired.

Twenty years older now, this generation of women is still saddled with a distorted body image and body dissatisfaction. Unfortunately, the passage of time isn't helping aging women feel more at peace with their bodies—or making things better for younger women following them into adulthood. The legacy of being overconcerned about body image and weight is passed down from one generation to the next and is reinforced for women of all ages by the body myths of our youth- and appearance-oriented culture.

The Body Myth

These figures illustrate how many North American women have come to live under the terms of a widely accepted Body Myth: that our self-worth (and our worth to others) is (and ought to be) based on how we look, what we weigh, and what we eat. We look for life's meaning and the answer to life's challenges in the shape of our bodies.

Myths are not inherently bad things (think tooth fairy!). They are stories that help us make sense of our lives and of the meaning of life itself. Myths grow from, and are bound to, the culture of the family and/or the culture of the larger society. Because they are so rooted in culture, myths tend to reinforce our perceptions of reality, rather than to question those perceptions. That's why traveling to another country so often produces culture shock—the anxiety and disorientation of not knowing how to communicate, or what is "normal" or appropriate, and where we fit in. Multicultural psychologist Dr. Carmen Guanipa writes that culture shock produces feelings of discontent, impatience, anger, sadness, and incompetence.

If myths help us make sense of life and hold off feelings of anxiety, small wonder that they are so important to us! But just because myths are not inherently bad, that doesn't make every myth good for us. For women, the Body Myth is deeply embedded in our culture and our psyches. It reinforces a false reality that says: changing my body equals changing my life.

In the Body Myth "reality," the desire to change our shape overwhelms the desire to *be in* shape—in other words, looks trump health.

Paradoxically, being on a diet is seen as intrinsically healthy and good—something to be admired and imitated. However, the most common diets (of the yo-yo variety) undermine, rather than promote, proper nutrition and well-being. They increase the risks for cardio-vascular disease, type 2 diabetes, osteoporosis, eating disorders, and some cancers. (More on how and why this is true in chapter 2.)

Most of us have not heard about those risks. Or if we have, the Body Myth kept that information from sinking in enough to let us feel okay about giving up dieting to lose weight. Many of us have huge blind spots when it comes to the causes and conse-quences of a woman's obsession with her body image because we look at women in Weight Watchers and Jenny Craig programs as being dedicated and committed. They are the good women, doing something positive about their problems, well-being, and sense of self.

However, research finds that up to half of women using commer-cial weight-loss clinics have significant symptoms of depression—a sign that they may obsess about body image in a futile attempt to feed or soothe much deeper hungers. They may be using the clinics to change how their bodies look rather than making peace with the inevitable, natural, sometimes painful changes of aging—and the rapid evolution of women's roles.

Living as Immigrants

Our lives—and the ongoing importance in our lives of how our bod-ies appear—are substantially different from how our mothers lived at our age. The new opportunities open to us, and the new expectations given us, are considerably wider than those of previous generations. The meanings of *success* and *good enough* are light-years beyond our foremothers' definitions.

I think of it as analogous to being an immigrant to a new world. Most mature women started their journey through adolescence expecting to arrive in a world of womanhood very much like the one their mothers inhabited. But today's world has radically different expectations for women than our foremothers' world had for them.

In a sense, we are suffering culture shock. The "Superwoman" script that Jennifer is trying to follow is relatively foreign to her mother and mother-in-law. The stories (or myths) that we use to attempt to make sense of our lives today are markedly different from the ones our mothers and/or grandmothers used—especially when we consider what those stories told each generation about cultural and family expectations for women's roles and women's bodies.

In the span of a generation, the modern world's idea of womanhood has changed radically. As a result, our foremothers often can't guide us through this new territory, and the road maps they supply are faint, if they exist at all. Since they didn't immigrate to this changed world, they weren't able to fully prepare us for our life as women.

Like newly arrived immigrants, many of us aren't prepared for this new culture's mores and can't quite grasp its requirements and demands. We are pioneers with few role models or directions for navigating this novel culture of womanhood, with its new stressors, opportunities, freedoms, and advantages. Ours is a transformed world that is unfamiliar to us, since such a culture never existed before.

Although many of the physical surroundings of this new world may look the same, we have moved into virgin, often unfamiliar territory. Like geographical culture shock, this transition is emotionally trying and confusing. Among other challenges, we experience cognitive dissonance between what our female ancestors expected of themselves (and what we grew up expecting to expect of *our*selves) and what modern culture expects of women.

Feeling uprooted from the world of our foremothers, we crave familiarity and security. In response, many of us grab for the mythical chimera of our culture's narrow standards of beauty as the way to acculturate ourselves and organize our lives. Rather than unlocking all the potential in this new land of opportunity, as successful immigrants do, we cleave to the Body Myth and measure our success by how strictly we manage our bodies and restrict our eating.

Keeping Herself Up

As we grow up, we form our identity, at least in part, by defining ourselves in opposition to someone or something else. Since young girls identify strongly with their mothers, we must differentiate ourselves from Mom to become separate (eventually adult) people. For women born after 1950, this differentiation often centers on the body because the ways our mothers looked and aged are not good enough for the mores of the Body Myth.

We don't dare "let ourselves go," as so many in our mothers' generation did. We cannot abide salt-and-pepper hair or other signs that the aging process is taking its natural course. We are today's women and are supposed to be in control of everything. We feel like a failure if we detect Mom when we look in the mirror.

As our mothers aged, they still cared about appearance and often criticized a woman for not "keeping herself up." But such criticism was likely to be aimed at a contemporary with questionable taste in makeup or a color-blind fashion sense. When it came to body shape, the parameters were pretty broad.

Today we criticize an adult woman because she no longer has the body of a sixteen- or twenty-year-old; any weight gain, no matter how natural it is for the adult female body, is considered wrong. We scrutinize any gray hair, any wrinkle, any sign of natural aging—in others and in ourselves.

Our mothers did not have as many medical technologies at their disposal to help manage their bodies. Today, keeping ourselves up is more of a full-time job than ever before. While our mothers wore girdles and makeup, we undergo cosmetic surgery, experiment with the latest diets and weight-loss products, and hire trainers to sculpt our physique. We have manicures, pedicures, false nails and eyelashes. We wax hair off our eyebrows, legs, and bikini line and go tanning, or we use chemicals to get the bronzed look. Collectively, U.S. women spend as much on cosmetics every five days as George W. Bush raised to become president in 2000.

Another huge but seldom discussed difference between the generations is how much more visible modern women's bodies are in public. Most of us are more active in careers and public life than our mothers were or ever dreamed of being. Therefore, we are exposing our bodies to new kinds (and frequency) of scrutiny. Meanwhile, sexualized images of female bodies saturate everyday media, fueling the Body Myth and distorting our idea of the ideal female form. We don't have the body image sanctuaries our mothers did; today's women are always on display, endlessly criticized for transgressing that ever-shifting fine line between being too sexy or not sexy enough.

While the fashion world urges us to display more flesh, we are simultaneously pressured to hide and control many of our body's natural processes. We are expected to camouflage or chemically alter signs of PMS, menstrual periods, or menopause. Mothers who breastfeed in public still elicit disapproving glances or outright scorn, while breast-revealing bustier fashions and pornographic advertising are celebrated. Navigating among these mixed messages is a challenge.

We have immigrated to an appearance-obsessed culture, where it is considered normal to work out our insecurities in and on our body image—how we think we look. We struggle to live up to (and make sense of) bizarre cultural norms like: "what you see is what you get," "you are how you look," or "you can never be too rich or too thin."

The Shape of History

Let's be clear: the body is an essential part of anyone's identity, because we literally wouldn't be alive without it. For millennia, humans have pondered the relationship between mind and body, flesh and spirit, psychology and physiology, or body and soul. One of the very few areas approaching consensus across the history of spiritual, philosophical, medical, psychological, and religious thought is this: the body is not the sole source of our identity and purpose.

Western tradition often conceptualizes the body as being in opposition to (and baser than) the spirit, which leads to an either/or way of seeing things. But the most enduring philosophies posit that body and spirit work in concert, influencing each other to move toward either growth or regression. For example, Judeo-Christian tradition calls the body a "temple," which we should keep open and clean to help our souls flourish, and thus be helpful to others. St. Francis of Assisi uses a similar metaphor in his famous prayer that asks God to "make me an instrument of Your peace." It is helpful to think of the body metaphorically as a vessel or tool that holds, nourishes, and conveys our essence (or whatever other spiritual metaphor best helps us understand the spark of life).

The body gives us the means to think, speak, touch, feel, listen, taste, smell, and sense both ourselves and what is around us. It enables us to express our self and shape our relationships with our self and those we love. We are in the body when we reflect on life's ongoing difficulties and joys, and when we grow in response to them.

But *we are not our bodies*. You are not your body. Your body is only the vehicle; it is not the journey or the destination.

Even in the most woman-friendly culture we could imagine, the body—and our relationship with it—would be only *a part* of how we experience and respond to life's transitions. Unfortunately, our culture is not so woman friendly. Its distorted view of female bodies and body image becomes central to (rather than merely one part of) how we react to life. This off-kilter perspective presents our bodies as the principal (and sometimes only) canvas on which we paint our future. But if we follow that warped thinking, we paint ourselves into a corner instead.

The Shape of Adulthood

Remember the intense concern you felt about how you looked when you were a teenager? It seemed that popularity was rigidly meted out based on who was cutest and had the coolest clothes. This competition for acceptance fed on and intensified the insecurity of adolescence, a time of major transition from a childhood identity to an adult one.

Identity is central to a person's sense of self. Our identity integrates the different parts of ourselves (for example: daughter, sister, student, friend, mother, childless, single, girlfriend, volunteer, employee, Iranian Sunni, Irish Catholic, or Russian Jew) into a cohesive whole. Ideally, a self-perception feels firm and stable.

But identity is multidimensional and continues to develop throughout life. For example, you may be single, then married, and then divorced. This fluid, lifelong process builds identity on a foundation constructed from:

- family dynamics
- early experiences
- ethnic, socioeconomic, and cultural background
- emotional and mental capacities
- temperament and personality
- physical attributes
- body image (especially for Western women)

Adolescence and childhood are *not* the only times in our lives when our identity is developing. Adulthood is also filled with change, some dramatic, some subtle, and others mundane. A modern woman's development isn't anywhere close to being over when she becomes a legal adult at age twenty-one. A woman traveling through adulthood deals with ongoing developmental issues—an aging body, motherhood, mortality, being an empty nester, and more—which can be just as tough (or tougher) than the challenges she faced in adolescence.

However, many adult transitions lack the rituals that mark signal moments of childhood (our first steps or first day of school) and adolescence (our first bra or first period). There are few grown-up equivalents of confirmation ceremonies, proms, or graduation parties, which help us remember, recognize, and celebrate the transitions between one phase of life and the next.

It may seem odd to think that adults have developmental issues. But while adolescence requires that we synthesize our childhood self with the new demands of puberty and future adulthood, adult development also requires synthesis of past and emerging identities. Even from the earliest years of adulthood, we move from one role to the next: student, career woman, wife, homemaker, full-time mother, volunteer, and possibly student or career woman again— frequently juggling multiple roles at the same time. We experience regular transitions: first full-time job, first time living on our own, serious relationships with significant others, marriage, and leaving the people and places of our youth. Our roles in relation to our parents may change from being the child to becoming a mutual friend, and then shifting to caretaker as we parent our aging parents. Adulthood also brings significant bodily transitions like pregnancy and menopause.

Each one of these transitions can be as intensely challenging as the difficult transition from junior high to high school. At our adult crossroads, we may feel unsure of ourselves because old beliefs and assumptions are being severely tested or rendered obsolete. We may choose any number of paths, reorganizing how we think, see the world, and live in relationships. These transitions can affect our personality and bring major shifts in social roles—what our family, the community, and the culture expect from us.

Indeed, we pass through many developmental changes while we take on more adult responsibility. Managing jobs, family, money, community, and other obligations leaves little time to pay attention to what is happening inside us, let alone to reflect on the impact of all these events and transitions.

Nevertheless, the impact remains. Essential questions stir inside as we move further away from our youth and closer to old age and, ultimately, death. In her book *Passages: Predictable Crises of Adult Life*,

Gail Sheehy describes the sensation of moving through the midpoint of our lives: "Deep down a change begins to register in those gut-level perceptions of safety and danger, time and no-time, aliveness and stagnation, self and others."

A sense of "deadline" springs from our ticking biological clock. If we are childless, we may feel a growing urgency to get pregnant. If we are already mothers, we may sense that a career path is closing down. If we juggle both home and career, the "what-about-me?" clock may sound its alarm. Because family nurturing still falls primarily to women, men are less likely to feel the same sort of crisis. Thus, our deadline concerns may put us out of sync with our partners, a problem in its own right.

Adult transitions do share one quality with childhood transitions: they don't usually happen with a flash or a snap of the fingers. It usually takes time to move from one developmental stage to another. Storyteller Lise Lunge-Larsen calls this threshold when you pass between phases of life "liminal" time. She says that fairy tales in most cultures view these in-between times as periods of simultaneous risk, opportunity, stress, and growth—openings for new, sometimes magical powers and insights to enter characters' lives, no matter what their age.

Fairy tales are stories that reflect important realities: for example, the reality that developmental transitions are times of potential, whether satisfying or upsetting. Such major changes in our relationships, how we think, or our place in the world are likely to turn our own world a bit topsy-turvy, just as they do for a fairy-tale protagonist. A new perspective may be valuable, but we sometimes lack the internal mechanisms or social support to easily meet these new challenges. When our sense of personal identity is shaken up, it places us at risk for anxiety, depression, and other unsettling feelings. Pile these challenges atop our experience of always having to recalibrate ourselves to the values of modern culture, with its evolving expectations for women, and it's no wonder women struggle to keep a cohesive sense of self.

Through it all, our search for identity persists and affects our relationships with ourselves and with our loved ones. But that process is clouded by the Body Myth. So, like Jennifer, we often use our body image as a way to play out our adult developmental anxieties and search for identity.

Shaping Adult Development

The misconception that only teens have problems stemming from body image and eating disorders leaves adult sufferers overlooked by family, friends, and health care professionals. While a young anorexic draws ready attention and sympathy, eating disorders and body image despair are still heartbreaking and dangerous at any age.

Naomi, a New York public relations executive, is no teenager. She was forty-five when she began addictively using laxatives and compulsively dieting to control her weight. Soon, things spun out of control. Naomi had full-blown bulimia and carried just over a hundred pounds on her five-foot-nine-inch frame. She told the *New York Times*, "My whole life was shaped by this. I didn't want to take trips with people or visit my in-laws because they had only one bathroom. I couldn't control my husband's drinking, and I didn't feel as though I could control anything."

Naomi was looking for a way to control the profound challenges and changes facing her. Desperate to gain a hold on some part of her life, she turned to controlling her weight. Bingeing and purging became a pernicious, self-soothing strategy.

Eventually Naomi began to realize the risks of what she was doing. She became desperate to avoid a heart attack or other life-threatening illness. But it took six scary years of suffering before she finally sought therapy. She began to see how the natural stresses and losses of midlife conspired with our culture's notions of "beauty" to plummet her into the deadly cycle of eating disorders.

During life transitions a woman can often feel that her life is out of control. When everything feels ambiguous and looks uncertain, we seek something tangible to latch onto. We instinctively grasp for things that seem either stable or within our realm of control. The Body Myth tells us that our bodies will fit the bill.

We use our bodies to answer the difficult questions of womanhood like:

- What is feminine?
- What is adult?
- What kind of woman am I?
- Am I good enough?
- Who am I as a female in this culture and in this body?

- Am I living up to the standard I'm supposed to?
- What example of womanliness am I setting for my children?

Because our world is fast paced and driven by performance and image, we have few opportunities to explore such open-ended questions. Our liminal paths aren't always clear, the answers not always obvious, and the solutions not easy to grasp. But a woman's body is obvious and concrete. We know our body is here, no matter what else happens. And so, baffled or frustrated by life's hazy transitions, we often seize upon our body as the obvious and concrete thing to shape, force to behave, manipulate, and figure out. In a sense, we use (or misuse) our body's outside shape as a way to process or silence the feelings, doubts, indecision, and insecurity that adult development stirs within us.

Meanwhile, our culture consistently supports beliefs that value women for their bodies, and it sells the fairy tale that women can and should be in complete command of their bodies. So it is not unusual for us to judge the shape we're in by how well we "control" our bodies, especially when everything else (including, sometimes, our bodies themselves) feel out of control. We may feel uncertain about being up to life's tasks, but we believe that we can feel or look like we have control if we can just achieve the "right" body or appearance. That belief is mistaken.

Step Back Exercise

Do this alone, with a friend or in a small group of women you trust. Take time to talk about your feelings and insights afterward.

Stand comfortably, preferably without shoes so you can feel the ground or floor, with enough space around you so that you can move backward and forward several feet. Close your eyes and relax. Take one step back and imagine that you are stepping into your mother's body. Take a few minutes to get used to being in her body and mind.

Take another step backward and step into the body of your mother's mother. Again take time to get used to being in your grandmother's life and in her body. As your grandmother, ask yourself these questions:

What are my major concerns or worries in life?

What are my primary sources of satisfaction? Of comfort?

What is my position in my society: what are its limitations, opportunities, privileges, responsibilities?

How do I feel about my body? How important is it to my sense of self?

What are my worries about my health? About my body?

What pressures do I feel to prove myself?

Do I feel I must be Superwoman to survive or succeed?

What do I feel I must be to survive or succeed?

Take a few minutes to absorb these insights and then step forward to being your mother. Ask yourself the same questions. Again take some time to absorb this experience, then step forward to being yourself and ask the same questions once more.

What are the common threads in these experiences? What are the differences? How did concerns about body or beauty evolve throughout these generations? What do you feel about this experience? In what ways do you feel connected to the past? In what ways do you feel alone, disconnected, like an emotional and cultural immigrant? What surprised you as you traversed these bodies and generations?

Talk about your feelings and insights with friends. Take some time to write these perceptions down in a journal so you can reflect on them over time.

2

Fact versus Fiction

How Survival Shapes the Body

Every woman's physical shape has major implications for her survival. But these implications are quite different from what many of us believe.

We live in an era of intense concern about weight and, paradoxically, widespread myths about the importance of weight to our health. Even more problematic, most of us also hold misguided notions about a person's actual ability to alter and control her body's shape. So before we can go any further, we have to learn the facts (and debunk the common fictions) about the connections between weight, the body, and body image.

For example, few of us would argue with the notion that a diet is the logical, necessary response to a desire to lose weight or to eating too much. However, scientific studies indicate that this conventional wisdom is completely backward, reflecting the exact opposite of reality. For example, J. Polivy and C. P. Herman observed that bingeing does not cause dieting, but rather it is dieting that causes bingeing.

Such an assertion may seem absurd, but only because our cultural body myths ignore biological and genetic reality. However, our personal experience bears it out—when we skip a meal or try to eat very little, we usually end up eating more later on. Hunger, left unsatisfied, doesn't go away; it grows.

We hear constantly that being "overweight" is risky to health and that everyone should lose weight. However the truth is much more complex. Showered with beauty images that get leaner and meaner each season, and with body myths equating health and thinness, most women simply do not understand the connection between the shape of our bodies and the shape of our health.

In the next few pages, I'll knock down some of the most harmful myths by looking at scientific research about body shape and survival.

How Our Bodies Survive

The human body is (and has been for millennia) hardwired to respond quickly when confronted by starvation. The reason is simple: during the long history of the human race, starvation has always been the greatest threat to our survival. Starvation was a threat for our agrarian and hunting ancestors, as it remains for millions of people around the world today. In order for the human species to survive, the body had to develop ways to survive as long as possible during famine and other food shortages.

When our bodies are deprived of calories and nutrition, they respond as if they are starving—because they are. Instinctively and almost immediately, the body responds to food deprivation by slowing down its metabolism, the rate at which it consumes energy and calories (calories are units used to measure the energy supplied by food).

The deceleration in our metabolism is a natural, primeval, and unstoppable preservation response to *any* reduction in food intake; our bodies can't distinguish whether a sudden change in food supply is the result of famine, forgetfulness, or the latest fad diet.

Nature also designed our sense of hunger to protect us from famine. When famine turns to feast, our bodies crave nutrition from the newly available food. As a result, we consume more than "normal" to make up for the recent deprivation. However the body's metabolism does not ramp back up as quickly as its hunger cravings do. Because feasts are often sporadic and short-lived during times of overall famine, the metabolism remains slowed. In this way, the body makes the new calorie supply last longer, just in case the feast doesn't last.

Our body's speedy and innate ability to counter starvation is quite marvelous. The female body has evolved an almost miraculous ability not only to survive famine but also to reproduce during famine, thus keeping the human species ongoing for many thousands of years.

Before puberty, a girl's body has about 12 percent body fat. During puberty, nature's hardwiring multiplies the number of fat cells until she has about 17 percent body fat—sufficient for her to safely ovulate and menstruate. If the girl's growth is natural—and uninterrupted by dieting—her mature adult body will have about 22 percent body fat.

That 22 percent supply of fat provides enough energy for an ovulating female to survive famine for nine months, the length of a full-term pregnancy. If faced with a sudden food shortage or starvation, her metabolism will slow down, and she'll gradually consume the fuel naturally provided by fat cells. Through the hardwiring of their bodies, pregnant women can survive a food shortage long enough to give birth. In this way, nature assures propagation of the human species even during famine. Nature also assures that women gain fat first in the breasts, buttocks, hips, and thighs, which helps to protect our reproductive organs and ensure lactation. It's a miracle that is all about survival.

It may seem incredibly unfair that women need a higher percentage of body fat to be healthy than men do—and that men can lose fat more easily. But that's the way it is. And, as we have seen, it is that way for a *very* good reason.

When we understand the amazing ways nature uses a woman's fat cells, our perspective about fat and weight begins to change. We recognize that the fat difference between men and women is not a weight issue; fat cell development is programmed into the female body by the internal (and eternal) wisdom of survival. Fat cells are our friends. In addition to ensuring survival, they produce estrogen, which maintains bone density and decreases the risk for osteoporosis, and help us manage symptoms of menopause, like sleep problems, hot flashes, and complexion changes.

What's more, as a result women are more likely to survive famine than men are. Only 10 percent of women die in famines, while 50 percent of men do.

Dieting and Obesity

Obesity is a major public health problem. It seems logical that dieting is the most efficient way to shed pounds, reduce obesity, and improve health. That logic doesn't hold, however, because dieting induces nutritional depletion, physical cravings, and emotional deprivation. These diet-generated hungers cause bingeing behaviors, which eventually increase weight. As illogical as it may sound, a major root of obesity is dieting, not bingeing.

Pounds on Vacation

It seems completely counterintuitive to challenge the efficacy of dieting when there appears to be an epidemic of obesity in the United States. But our evolutionary survival lesson makes it easy to understand the connections between obesity and dieting. If we go on a diet, we will lose weight. For a while. We will also see our metabolism rate drop, because that's what human bodies do to survive.

If we keep at our diet and reach our weight-loss goal, we usually then go back to a less restrictive eating pattern. However, our increased calorie intake is now entering a body with a slower metabolism that takes longer to "burn" a calorie than it did before the diet began. Remember that the body's survival mechanisms keep our metabolism from coming out of slow-down mode as quickly as it goes into it. This continued slow mode is a precaution, just in case the suddenly renewed food supply isn't permanent. (Remember, the body can't tell the difference between famine and self-induced food reduction.)

Since calories from our back-to-normal eating aren't consumed as quickly as they were before we started dieting, our bodies retain unused caloric energy in new fat cells. Plus, to one degree or another, we've been starving our body during the diet, so hunger reflexes will have us craving *more* food than the "normal" intake we had before starting the diet cycle—just as our ancestors did when feast replaced famine.

This is why nearly everyone who embarks on a food restriction diet eventually regains the lost weight and often gains additional weight. Instead of helping us lose pounds, it is more accurate to say that a diet makes the pounds go on vacation—and bring back new friends when they return.

Once we've regained the weight, most of us eventually try another diet. The same cycle repeats, with slightly greater extremes at each end. The more we yo-yo through diets over the years, the greater the extremes are, and the more out of whack our metabolism and hunger cues get. The ongoing cycle steadily ratchets up our eagerness to try another diet, shelling out time and money in search of a magic formula. Such a formula does not exist because nature—which abhors vacuums and imbalance—won't allow it.

In her book *Transforming Body Image: Love the Body You Have*, psychologist Marcia Germaine Hutchinson told how she dieted herself into being permanently overweight. Her father was a bariatrician (diet doctor) so her home life promoted thinness at any cost. Chronic dieting, alternating with chaotic overeating, totally derailed Marcia's metabolism. Today, her weight remains high, no matter how healthfully or moderately she eats.

Marcia's genetic makeup, ethnic body type, and dieting history conspired to keep her fat. But she conspired back. Through her own efforts and professional work, she not only found peace with her body (not easy in a fat-phobic culture), but she also helps other people do the same.

Researchers have known for decades that diets can't fool Mother Nature. However, the more diets we try, the more money we (and millions like us) send to the diet book publishers, pharmaceutical companies, herbal supplement manufacturers, "shaping" salons, gyms, doctors, and all the rest. The more often women believe the diet myth and go up and down the yo-yo, the more profit the diet industry makes. Many of us don't realize the incentive that diet promoters have to keep this particular body myth alive.

Diet Marketing and Health

Rates of obesity in the United States and the growth of the U.S. diet industry both ballooned in recent decades. One correlation between those two trends may be the ways that the physiology and biology of dieting ultimately stimulate weight gain and cycles of new yo-yo dieting.

New diets are very seductive to adult women, since many of us rate our worth on the bathroom scale. Marketing these new diets is also extremely lucrative for the diet industry. For example, a search for the keyword *diet* returned more than 104,000 book entries on Amazon.com and more than 35,000 on Barnesandnoble.com.

Despite the diet industry's growth, there isn't really much new about the latest diets. The basic principles are the same; all that changes are the labels:

- The Midlife Miracle Diet
- The Fight Fat after Forty Diet
- G-Index Diet: The Missing Link That Makes Permanent Weight Loss Possible
- How to Turn Off Your Body's Fat-Making Machine

The diet industry's huge profits do not diminish the danger of obesity. Obesity (for kids and adults) threatens public health because we eat too much unhealthy food and are too sedentary for our own good.

But serious problems also arise when we make weight and body shape the primary standards by which we judge a person's health. Our weight and body shape *may* signal health concerns—but being thin is no more an indicator of health than one's height or hair color.

Most people believe the body myth that there is always a direct relationship between weight and health, but no clear causal link exists. For example, the mortality risks related to obesity have been grossly oversimplified. Food intake is a major determinant of mortality risk, but the primary problem is poor nutrition, not how much someone weighs. A sedentary lifestyle also increases mortality risk, but the health culprit is exercise habits, not excess weight. Only a physician or nutritionist who has observed a woman over a period of time can determine whether the shape of her body is an indicator of her health.

Weight must be considered in context; separate it from other factors and we miss the picture entirely. For example, poverty and obesity are closely linked in the United States. But researchers find that health problems among the overweight poor may be due more to *being poor* than to *being fat*. People living in poverty have less education about nutrition, less access to healthy foods, more access to cheap and high-fat foods, and may live in unsafe neighborhoods where outdoor physical activity, like walking or playing sports, is difficult.

Myths about weight also distort perceptions about nonphysical characteristics. Superficial parameters like weight or appearance never reveal the deeper variables of character, self-discipline, or other moral qualities. Nevertheless, most of us continue to judge people (including ourselves and our kids) as good or bad by the standard of body shape, ignoring the immutable forces of genetic ancestry, internal metabolism, and body chemistry.

In fact, weight is a reliable predictor of health only at the two extremes: severe thinness and severe obesity.

Heavier people don't always eat more; they may have slower metabolisms and a genetic code that gives them a higher concentration of body fat. That genetic code may also leave them in excellent health, even though they weigh more than "average."

However, cultural prejudices about weight make it harder for heavy people to be healthy. For example, fat people often draw judgmental stares and comments on the street, at the gym, or in a yoga class. The resulting discomfort and self-consciousness may suppress their activity level, which has an adverse affect on their health.

As California psychologist and body image expert Dr. Debbie Burgard told the *New York Times*, "I don't see how we're going to stop eating disorders [and other body image problems] until we stop reading character into the size of people's bodies. It's stereotyping. We've made progress against other stereotypes, and we can make progress against this one, too."

Good Food, Bad Food

In addition to using size to prejudge a person's integrity, our culture also places a thick and distorting veneer of morality on food itself. Women of all ages frequently refer to foods as good or bad, depending on factors that have nothing to do with the quality of the foods in question.

For example, as I write this, the Atkins diet fad dominates U.S. thinking about food, so carbohydrate-rich substances like bread are considered bad, while protein-rich foods like steak are labeled good. Not many years ago, steak was considered bad because of its fat content, and carbohydrate foods like pasta were considered essential for avid exercisers. Carbs, protein, fats, and starches drift back and forth between being in the good food or bad food categories (depending on the latest sure-thing diet). Either way, our categorization of what is good and bad remains rigid.

However, our beliefs about the best diet change every few years, just like beauty ideals do. Nutritionist Francie Berg has researched diet trends for over twenty years and notes that most diet fads or beliefs last about four years before they are replaced by the next so-called solution to our weight concerns.

This rigidity in our thinking and beliefs creates what some call a "morality of orality." Everything we put in our mouths becomes weighted with meaning and value beyond what it deserves. We even invest certain foods with mythical and magical qualities, believing that as soon as we swallow them they will cure ills and solve problems.

So let's set aside the myths and look at the facts. Food is food. It doesn't have morality. It can't be good or bad. A particular food like peanuts may seem bad if we are allergic to peanuts, but *unhealthy* or *risky* are more accurate and useful adjectives for the situation. Our arteries will suffer if we eat nothing but slices of frosted cake, but that doesn't make frosted cake bad. In fact, frosted cake is perfect for celebrating a birthday or wedding.

Food interacts with our bodies. Many factors—including (but not limited to) our genetics, overall health, and level of physical activity—determine whether an individual food or type of food will be detrimental or beneficial to our body today. A food that may be detrimental to us now could be beneficial for us next year, and vice versa. To understand food's relationship with our bodies and our lives, we must discard the myth that any food has innate moral qualities, like good and magic, or bad and evil.

Glenn Gaesser's book *Big Fat Lies: The Truth about Your Weight and Your Health*, is a great resource of corrective information about the connections between the shape you're in and the true shape of your health. He summarizes complicated medical research and information in a very reader-friendly format. It is a must-read for anyone who wants to know the truth about this subject. Here are some of the truths he exposes:

- Fat in your arteries and body fat are two different things. You can have fat on your body without having fat in your arteries, and vice versa.

- The location of body fat matters. Thigh and hip fat are associated with *lower* rates of cardiovascular disease and diabetes, especially in women.

- You can be both fit and fat! Overweight or obese adults who exercise are *healthier* than thin people who do not exercise.

- Weight loss does not necessarily lead to improved health. People who are heavier than average but who do not diet have less risk of cardiovascular disease, diabetes, and other conditions usually associated with obesity than people who engage in yo-yo dieting.

- The body mass index (BMI) standards and many weight-height ratio tables are arbitrary and not based on solid research.
- The popular press gives a lot of attention to "thinner-is-better" claims but seldom reports on research showing the lack of a cause-and-effect relationship between weight and health.
- Body weights higher than those recommended by most height-weight tables are usually safe for long-term health and longevity.

We Can't Drive on Flat Spare Tires

If an adult woman gains weight as she ages, the Body Myth tells us to label her as lazy. We say: "she's let herself go" or "she really is being so bad." We've transformed eating and enjoying food into a bad or immoral state, while restricted eating and chronic caveats about food have become good and virtuous. These outrageous snap judgments grow from ignorance and denial about how nature shapes an adult woman's body before, during, and after menopause.

During our transition to menopause, our metabolism rate falls 15 to 20 percent below what it was when we were young adults. Our estrogen levels drop too, giving testosterone greater influence (yes, women have testosterone). In midlife, men's testosterone levels drop, giving estrogen greater influence (yes, men have estrogen). This shift in hormonal balance generates fat cells in the abdominal area for both women and men. Our lower metabolism rate helps keep the fat in place.

Nature designed our bodies to go through this shift because new fat cells provide the midlife woman's primary source of increasingly valuable estrogen. Normal menopausal women gain eight to twelve pounds, which usually settles around our waists (just like it does for men around the same age). Though those extra fat cells make pants and skirts fit differently, they also generate natural estrogen to reduce the severity of our menopausal symptoms.

Many doctors prescribe hormone replacement therapy (HRT) to ease our passage through menopause, but responsible physicians know that a woman is better off with the hormones her body produces naturally than she is with synthetic ones. Still, obesity concerns have many health care providers promoting midlife weight loss, without regard for the potential implications. If we diet our way through premenopause, perimenopause, and menopause, we stop reinforcing our diminishing stores of natural estrogen, potentially making our menopausal symptoms more dramatic and distressing.

When we diet during midlife, our remaining fat cells must strain harder to make up the estrogen deficit left by "lost" fat cells. Paradoxically, this makes the remaining fat cells stronger, more stubborn, and much harder to eliminate through dieting—one more example of how nature abhors an imbalance.

So, to fly in the face of another embedded Body Myth, a bit of a "spare tire" is *good for us* as we move into menopause. That's why women who gain a moderate amount of weight during menopause have fewer and less severe symptoms than underweight menopausal women. The underweight women also have a much greater risk for osteoporosis.

A most important consideration is that underweight menopausal women *die* earlier. Women who gain a moderate amount of weight at midlife have longer life expectancies. A review of multiple studies indicates that extra weight in women may actually bring them benefits by reducing the risk for illnesses such as lung cancer, premenopausal breast cancer, and osteoporosis. For example, thin women had the greatest risk for lung cancer, while obese women were much less likely to develop it. This doesn't mean that we should necessarily try to gain weight; however, if our weight is low because we are restricting our eating or overexercising, we may put our overall health at risk. Weight and health are extremely complex issues; low weight does not necessarily imply good health.

The Shape of Genetics

It is fairly common for us to read and hear—or to tell ourselves—that we should lose five or ten pounds after the holidays. Few, if any, of us ever read, hear, or tell ourselves that we should grow five or ten inches taller after the holidays, or any time of year. The notion is absurd because we know that we can't change our height.

Just like our height, and the color of our skin, eyes, and hair, our general body shape and size are genetically programmed. To a great extent, our genes determine our weight, distribution of body fat, skeletal frame, basic metabolism, and appetite. If your ancestors were short and skinny, your chances of being short and skinny are great. The same principle applies if your ancestors were tall, fat, dark skinned, pale skinned, diabetic, alcoholic, or prone to sickle-cell anemia.

Let's assume that you don't have a chronic illness, endocrine problems, or any genetic abnormalities. If you eat a balanced diet and engage in aerobic activity (not easy in a world of junk food and five-hundred-channel TV), you'll fall into the healthy weight range determined by your heritage and genetic code. Dieting throws that natural balance out of whack, which is why nearly every dieter eventually regains all her "vacationing" weight along with additional pounds.

Note that we did *not* say that you will reach your "ideal weight." Each of us has a genetically predetermined, natural weight *range* that our mature bodies seek to maintain. Because nature defaults to a balanced mode, many adults have a stable weight without really paying much attention to it, so most dieters find themselves back at their original weight.

The Body Myth that we have (and should rigidly maintain) an ideal weight ignores the flexibility that is essential to the human body and its natural developmental process. Healthy adult bodies are hardwired to burn more calories on days when we eat more and to burn fewer calories on days when we eat less. Science has repeatedly proven this phenomenon through animal research and human twin studies; twins raised apart grow up to have similar weights regardless of how much their adoptive parents weigh. There is no ideal weight, no fixed number of pounds that is right or genetically immutable.

The term Body Mass Index, or BMI, is used frequently in discussions of weight and obesity. Based on the relation between one's weight and height, BMI is calculated by multiplying weight by 703 and dividing that number by the square of the person's height (in inches). If this sounds complicated and relatively arbitrary, there's a reason. Like the weight tables developed by the insurance industry, little science underlies the connections many people make between BMI and health, even though health care professionals and researchers treat the BMI as a well-founded and critical measure of our well-being.

The National Heart, Lung, and Blood Institute recently changed the BMI at which we are deemed overweight from 26 to 25, instantly moving millions of Americans from the normal weight to the overweight classification. Many of us went to sleep in one category and then woke up in another, even though nothing about our health had actually changed.

The new agency guidelines for "normal" weight (a BMI of 18.5 to 24.9) contradicts other government studies. For example:

- A BMI of 25 (.1 above the "normal" range) is associated with the lowest death rate for white men and women.

- A BMI of 27 (2.1 above the "norm") is associated with the lowest death rate for African American men and women.

- Native Americans with a BMI between 35 and 40 (more than 10 points above "normal") do not have an increased risk of death despite being above the set standard.

- A BMI of less than 20 is associated with a higher mortality rate, although the National Heart, Lung, and Blood Institute standards say that a BMI as low as 18.5 is normal.

These confusing and contradictory uses of BMI numbers lead many women into weight reduction regimens that are far more dangerous than the pounds they carry. This issue is too complicated to be decoded by one rigid and confusing formula. It doesn't make any sense that a weight shift of one pound technically can move us from being normal to overweight, or overweight to obese. The bottom line is that as women age, there is no established relationship between moderate increases in weight and increased health risk. So we need to pay less attention to numbers and calculations and more to leading a healthy life by eating nutritious foods, exercising, and finding emotional balance.

Surviving Womanhood

An adult woman who dedicates great, or even obsessive, energy to shaping her body may get kudos from other people. But like Jennifer in chapter 1, that external praise may crash head-on with how she feels inside. Many women with eating disorders say that they were showered with compliments about their shape and their self-control on the very same days when they felt great distress, both physically and emotionally, and were afraid that they might die any minute. These "compliments" confuse, dismay, and interfere with getting help—sometimes until it is too late.

Audrey was a successful writer and activist working with a non-profit organization promoting girls' well-being. She had battled bulimia and anorexia for more than ten years, but received short-term treatment on only a few occasions, because her insurance didn't reimburse her for more than a few treatment days, and there were no inpatient treatment programs in her state.

Audrey's symptoms were intensifying again when, as part of her job, she flew across the country to attend a conference on eating disorders. On the plane, Audrey felt strong heart palpitations and feared that she might have a heart attack and die, but she said nothing to her colleagues, some of whom were in recovery from eating disorders.

By the time she returned home, Audrey was frightened because her symptoms weren't abating. Desperate for help, she finally decided to apply to the nearest eating disorders treatment program, even though she would have to drive several hours to attend it. While waiting for admission, she kept working and trying to survive, even though she continued to feel horrible. One evening, she went out with friends who lavished praise on Audrey for how thin she was and how good she looked.

Back home that night, Audrey asked her fiancé, "How could they think I look good? I feel miserable, desperate, and like I could die. I'm completely confused." She was right to wonder about her friends' perspective and to fear the intensity of her symptoms. Less than a week later, one day before she was to enter treatment, Audrey had a heart attack and died.

Audrey's friends are not to blame for her illness or death. They were not hard-hearted or mean-spirited. Like most of us, the Body Myth's distorted perspective about the importance of female appearance left them blind to the reality of their friend's life. Our culture embeds this warped value system deeply into our individual ways of seeing the people and situations around us. We believe that a woman who looks good must feel good, because she is reaching what we value as the ideal female state of beauty: thinness.

We believe the myth that a woman who looks good *is* good, because she has the moral fiber to keep herself up. We believe these things, even if they bear no relation to the particular woman's reality.

This Body Myth mind-set works with the cultural attitudes we'll discuss in chapter 7 to reinforce body image paradoxes and conflicts. Women have new authority in the world, but we still feel easily undermined by our bodies. Consider these questions:

- When was the last time we were part of an all-woman conversation where *no one* brought up the topics of weight, food, or personal appearance?

- We have more opportunities than any previous generation of women, so why is it so hard to find anything over size 12 in a dress shop?

- Women compete successfully in business, but when we enter a crowded room, why do we still scan the other women to see how we stack up in the obligatory weight-and-appearance competition?

- Liberation from old gender stereotypes brings new independence and choices, so why do we spend more time on fad diets to "get skinny with the stars" than we do figuring out how to share the struggle of balancing work and family?

- Why do we talk more about diets, exercise, and hair color than we do about our spiritual well-being?

In the last few pages, we've debunked some deeply entrenched body myths. But the facts about genetic and biological realties have a hard time sinking into our collective consciousness. We live in a culture that continually and convincingly sells the fiction that we cannot be too rich or too thin.

But even temporary alterations of the body cannot change immutable realities like a parent's death or a child's continuing march toward adulthood. As Jennifer, Audrey, and Naomi's stories illustrate, our external shape can distract us from (and mask) the actual state of our psychological, spiritual, emotional, and physical lives— and disrupt our most important human relationships. If reshaping our bodies is our first (or only) response to life's transitions, then we are living a myth that distorts our lives, not only today but also in the future.

Exercise: What Happens When
We Diet to Lose Weight?

How/Why We Diet	Results of Diet
Skip meals or decrease calories	Metabolism lowers and we store fat far more easily from fewer calories. The body's need for fuel causes rebound "munchies," usually for high fats and sugars. Hunger causes poor attention span, irritability, fatigue, muscle loss.
Cut out starches	The body loses a source of stable energy, so we're more likely to feel moody and tired. We eat higher fat and sugary foods to satisfy munchies.
Cut out meats	We may risk iron deficiency, leading to fatigue. Energy from meals does not last as long, so between meals we crave high-fat, high-sugar foods.
Preplanned meal replacement diet or liquid diet	We lose muscle mass along with fat. Metabolism slows, making it easier to store fat on liquid calories. This quick-fix doesn't teach how to eat healthy.
Fasting	The weight loss is primarily water. Muscle mass decreases; lowered metabolism results in fat gain. Prolonged fasting is physically dangerous.
To be slim	Slimness is temporary. There's a 95 percent chance that we will regain the weight we lose within two years and then diet again, with similar results. Yo-yo dieting can lead to obesity.
To be healthier	Dieting cycles increase health risks. There is no evidence that being plump is necessarily unhealthy, but there is evidence that being too slim is unhealthy.

How/Why We Diet	Results of Diet
To be healthier *(continued)*	Dieting can decrease muscle mass. Muscles are necessary for good health.
	Our body and mind don't run well when we restrict calories.
	We become moody, irritable, and obsessed with food, which is a physiological response to starvation, not the result of a lack of willpower.
To be more attractive	Genuine friends and loved ones like us for who we are, not how we look.
	Successful long-term relationships can't be built on body shape.
	Dieting makes us irritable, depressed, and less fun to be around.
	Dieting is likely to make us more self-centered rather than more attractive.

3

Women's Bodies,
Women's Lives

So what is the actual state of our psychological, spiritual, emotional, and physical lives as adult women? Does it continue to be a state of regular change, growth, loss, and transition? As we discussed in chapter 1, the development of our identity doesn't stop just because we've passed through the gates of childhood and adolescence.

We can learn important lessons about our adult development by reviewing our childhood development. As in childhood, the transitions of a woman's life bring growth, and most growth requires us to leave something behind. As we became toddlers, we left the security of being always held and coddled. But in exchange, we started experiencing the world in an independent, new, and exciting way. The first time we rode a bike without training wheels, we felt simultaneously scared of falling and liberated by our new ability to explore the neighborhood more widely and autonomously. The fear is real, but so it the reward of facing the fear and working through it.

To avoid acknowledging real (and very deep) desires and fears, contemporary women often obsess and talk continually to one another about diets, exercise, clothes, and shopping. This strategy does not get women where we need or want to go. In fact, this approach is essentially backward. The quality of a woman's life depends far more on the shape of her spirit, wisdom, emotions, and psyche than it does on the shape of her body.

This chapter explores transitions common to adult women and examines how they influence our body image, sense of self, and sense of what is possible. We will examine womanhood's complicated, ongoing development in four sections: women's bodies, women's work, women's families, and women's relationships.

Women's Bodies

Childbirth

The ability to bear children is the most concrete difference between women and men—and between the female and male bodies. It is also a concrete sign of our passage from girl to woman. Perpetuation of the species literally depends on pregnancy and childbirth. So we might expect that every aspect of our body's ability to have children would be widely and enthusiastically celebrated—including how pregnancy and childbirth change our bodies.

Instead, our appearance-obsessed Body Myth culture is far more enamored of a woman whose appearance arouses male sexual feelings (or who looks like she'd be easy for a male to have sex with) than it is with women who carry the miracle of an emerging new life. Visibly pregnant models never make a centerfold, and Madonna's revealing outfits get more mainstream press than a nation of madonnas bearing children.

Some of my eating and body image disorders clients agonize over becoming pregnant because they dread losing their shape. They contemplate having their tubes tied so that they will never gain weight by becoming pregnant. For others, pregnancy is the one time they feel free to eat, to actually enjoy a fuller, feminine shape and appetite while appreciating the wonderful things their bodies can do naturally.

Because pregnancy and childbirth radically reshape a woman's body, she is likely to feel ambivalent (at best) and distressed (at worst) about that natural reshaping. Evidence of this appears in pregnancy and mothering literature that emphasize how to restore buff, washboard abs and a tiny tush, so no one can tell you were ever pregnant. The headlines on a recent pregnancy magazine include:

- Stretch Marks: Preparing Your Skin for the Ultimate Test

- Postpartum Weight Loss: The New Exercise Machine, Part II
- "You're Beautiful!" But Does He Really Mean It?

Fertility and Infertility

Fertility problems are hard to discuss openly or socially. Women struggling with infertility may have a desperate feeling that there's something wrong with them if they can't fulfill this key part of being a woman. That's a notion often shared by people around them, making infertility a disenfranchised, hidden loss.

They may also believe that their fertility problems are disappointing the desires of others (spouse, parents, and in-laws) for a new child in their lives. Infertility, and people's reactions to it, can bring with it strong feelings of guilt, inadequacy, and depression.

Modern medicine has developed many ways to treat infertility, but the methods may traumatize a woman's relationship to her body, as she focuses intently on ovulation, temperature, and other bodily functions. Fertility work-ups are invasive, creating physical and emotional stress directly tied to a woman's body. While interacting with health care professionals, a woman may feel de-womanized and dehumanized, on top of feeling that her body is failing its womanly destiny.

Meanwhile, some fertility treatments and drugs increase weight and water retention. A woman undergoing these treatments may feel out of control and hypercritical of her highly scrutinized body, as well as deeply disappointed with its (her) performance. As she goes through the hit-and-miss fertility process, it may feel like she's on a roller coaster of high hopes followed by smashed dreams.

Intimate relationships can also swell with tension, as sexual intercourse gets analyzed and programmed in attempts to conceive—a dynamic that threatens natural spontaneity and sexual pleasure. A woman may become very critical of her sexual relationships and, therefore, of her body's role in sex and conception.

If a woman had an eating disorder earlier in life, she may also feel guilty that the disorder caused or contributed to her infertility. As you'll see in chapter 4, eating disorders do contribute to infertility by creating chaos in a woman's reproductive system, along with most other internal organs. Although there is no evidence that infertility causes eating disorders, the body-centered strain and tension of overcoming infertility might prompt women to choose (or return to) disordered eating rituals or exercise abuse to self-soothe. A number of my patients responded to their infertility treatments by developing severe eating disorders and despair about their body image, for which they needed treatment.

Postchildbirth Body

During her teens and twenties, Meredith's life was shot through with painful symptoms of anorexia. Marriage and pregnancy seemed to calm those demons somewhat. But while she was very happy as a new mom, Meredith also found herself craving that earlier era in her life when she could spend endless hours with carefree peers whose biggest concerns were shopping, dieting, and tanning. Despite the pain of those years, she longed for the camaraderie of girlfriends, the variety of male relationships, and the flirtatious energy and spontaneity of life before marriage and motherhood. Shortly after having her first child, Meredith resumed her dangerous anorexic behaviors as she tried to connect to that carefree time of life through a slimmer body that would (she hoped) betray no sign that she was now a mother.

The shape and proportions of an adult woman's body usually change after giving birth to a child; few women get their girlish bodies back. However, many women want not just a girlish body, but also what that girlish body represents: their blissful memories of happy-go-lucky youth, with its easy intimacies, assorted friends, and minimal accountability. After childbirth, many women perceive having a girlish body as their connection to that more self-centered stage of life, when there was more room for their own personal needs, pleasures, and impulses—and fewer demands about child care and family management issues that become part of a mother's responsibility.

However, nature designed women's bodies to be different after childbirth, so that we can better nurture our children (and assure the human species' survival). The shape of our bodies shifts to help us nurse, carry our kids around, and more easily give birth to subsequent children.

The change in our bodies doesn't end there. Just as a girl's body starts to prepare for puberty as early as age eight, an adult woman's body starts preparing for menopause well before its onset. We may experience our first perimenopausal symptoms as early as five to ten years before menopause itself.

Even during the years between childbirth and menopause, our bodies go through a continual process of subtle and natural change. Adult female physical development is a long-term process, not a one-time deal. Part of that process is the body gradually slowing down metabolically, making it easier to gain weight and harder to lose it. Attempts to reverse or deny that process through attempts to regain our girlish figure only dissipate our energy and open us up to dangerous physical and emotional problems.

Menopause

Ann was in her late fifties and married thirty-five years before she sought therapeutic help for a relatively recent onset of bulimia. She was a successful businesswoman with three adult children and a grandchild. Ann had navigated many twists and turns in life: raising a family, running a business, experiencing the illness and death of her parents, and maintaining her marriage. Before menopause, she felt fortunate and satisfied with her life in many ways. She was weight conscious, but not pathologically so. Looking around at her female friends, Ann observed that dieting and body discontent were the norm, but she easily controlled her weight without resorting to risky behaviors.

After menopause, however, Ann gained a few pounds that she could not seem to shed. "My old tricks didn't work anymore," she said. "I made a conscious, intellectual decision to start making myself vomit. I had seen many magazine articles about purging and watched made-for-TV movies about bulimia. I saw vomiting as an acceptable option, on the same level as Weight Watchers or the Atkins diet."

When I described the health risks of bulimia for a woman her age, Ann felt deeply affected and motivated to change her behavior. Because Ann's bulimia was not yet deeply embedded in her identity, these changes were easier for her than for many other patients. She saw bulimia as an add-on to her life, a response to her aging, and it still felt foreign to her.

Very early in treatment Ann stopped vomiting and began to address the problems that seemed to underlie her bulimia. She felt afraid of menopause, becoming a grandmother, and life in retirement without the daily feedback that her successful business career provided. She felt lingering grief over the death of her parents, the loss of her own youth, and the loss of control over her weight. Despite the many positive things in her life—a stable marriage, family, grandchildren, friends, financial resources, and a strong business reputation—Ann still encountered great difficulty navigating the important adult passage of menopause.

Why would menopause bring on a violent case of bulimia for a highly successful and well-supported woman like Ann, especially after she seemed to tolerate significant life transitions in the past? Menopause can be wrenching in a world that values women for how sexy they seem. If we are all supposed to look Barbie perfect, there is little (if any) room for hot flashes, weight gain, hormonal mood swings, and the implication that youth is over. Our bodies become the anti-Barbie, and suddenly we can't dictate the timing of hot flashes, slowing metabolism, vaginal dryness, and the other unruly physical changes. Like the adolescent body, the menopausal body runs on its own schedule, as if it has its own mind. This loss of control over her bodily changes ambushed Ann's sense of well-being and security.

The modern medical and pharmaceutical industrial complex does women a great disservice when it pathologizes the natural process of menopause. Most women do not have horrible, debilitating menopausal symptoms, but nowadays *any* symptom seems to justify medical and pharmaceutical intervention. Modern attitudes about menopause create a host of decisions on how to medicate it— something previous generations of women had little or no call to do.

This cultural shift drives us to think we need tons of information about how to medically manage menopause. We are liable to feel stupid and inadequate if we don't make what we feel must be the right choices, even if those medically marketed, endorsed, and expedient strategies trump nature's time-tested menopausal methods.

Our moms didn't pathologize menopause, or even use the term. They called it "the change." Like her peers, my mother never talked about menopause. When I asked her about what symptoms she had experienced, she responded: "I don't really remember my change; there was a lot going on in the family then." Our mothers' perspectives of "the change" are powerful symbols of how our lives are different from theirs.

On the one hand, this difference in experience may make it hard for us to relate to Mom and Grandma as we pass through menopause. On the other hand, disconnection from our ancestors' attitudes may cut *us* off from some healthy and valuable approaches.

For centuries, rich cultural rituals marked both menarche (a girl's first period) and menopause. For example, many historic cultures had something called a Red Tent, set away from the village. When passing through major life transitions, like menarche or childbirth, women left the larger community for the tent, where postmenopausal women (known as crones) provided experienced guidance and care. When a woman reached menopause, she was inducted into the corps of wise older women responsible for the tent.

In our culture, rituals to honor aging women have been swapped for rituals of hormone replacement therapy and multiple doctors' visits. Women today remember the exact timing and history of our menopause ("I was forty-nine and a half when I had my first hot flash. My periods were irregular for fourteen months, then regular again for six months, and then . . .") This transformation of perspective and attitude undermines the pride of reaching new levels of wisdom or our release from the monthly "visit" of menstruation.

Before they start menstruating, girls in our culture tend to be confident, strong, outspoken, and bold. But as they enter their teens, girls tend to lose that confidence, taking their feelings and insight underground, lest they upset someone else. The pioneering research of Dr. Carol Gilligan, Dr. Lyn Mikel Brown, and others describes this as "the silencing of girls' voices." Many of us struggle throughout adulthood to regain some of that voice and the potency we felt as sassy ten-year-olds.

I imagine menopause as a process that can free us to recapture the strength and clarity we had as girls. We can seize permission to shed the burdens of sexual expectations, reproductive pressures, and childbearing. Renowned anthropologist Margaret Mead wrote: "There is no greater power in the world today than the zest of a post-menopausal woman." Feminist author Germaine Greer saw menopause as a period of "peaceful potency," when women become less inhibited, more confident, and more action oriented. Writer Betty Friedan calls aging an opportunity for *both* sexes "to become more and more themselves," suggesting that we view this phase of life as an adventure and evolution rather than as a dead end. As one woman put it on her fortieth birthday:

> Don't get any black crepe paper for me. I am thrilled to be forty. It's like I'm walking through a door into a room where I don't have to worry anymore about whether a guy is attracted to my body or likes what I say—or don't say. Forty is my ticket to cut

loose, say what I want to say and be who I want to be. I feel like, outside my family, I don't have to give a damn what people think of me anymore.

But instead of adopting a zesty outlook, many of us see aging and menopause in a way that puts us at war with our bodies. We don't accept that this is a liminal time through which we pass for x number of months or years. Instead, this passage feels like an ordeal in which our bodies are the enemy. Rather than use older women to guide us through the change, we study (and critique) our own bodies and dwell on how they fail to measure up to the consumer image of beauty.

We turn our mental and emotional powers toward managing weight and other ways of looking younger so people don't know we're in or past menopause. We worry that our spouses may seek younger women—and we feel compelled to do anything to keep looking young, rather than confronting the uncertainty or mistrust that menopause may stir up in our relationship. We are trying to fool the world (and our intimate partners) the way we're trying to fool our bodies. Ultimately, we end up fooling ourselves.

From Intrusion to Invisibility

Our culture's obsession with looking young does not spring from a biological necessity or immutable natural force. Many other cultures respect and emulate older people more than younger ones. In these communities, crones function as fonts of wisdom and cultural continuity. Not only do people celebrate insight born of aging experience, but everyone (including older women) also wants older women to *look* their age. U.S. women traveling in Europe are often surprised that men find them attractive even if they don't look young. Our obsession with youthful appearance is not a compulsion of human nature.

Though arbitrary and culturally bound, our culture's obsession with youth and the body is still very real. It has a huge impact on us throughout youth and adulthood. From childhood onward, we have to find ways to inure and protect ourselves from intrusive and threatening comments about our bodies. When a stranger on the street or in the mall whistles and calls "Nice rack, baby!" we are more likely to feel fear and anguish about his potential advances than satisfaction about the sexuality of our body.

But when those rude remarks become less frequent (or stop altogether), we may feel ambivalent about no longer being readily objectified by men. In *The Change*, her book about menopause, Germaine Greer describes how this "loss" of random leering commentary means a loss of personal status and value: "Though [the] excessive visibility [of her youth] was anguish, her present invisibility is disorienting. She had not realized how much she depended upon her physical presence, at shop counters, at the garage, on the bus. For the first time in her life she finds she has to raise her voice or wait endlessly while other people push in front of her."

Those of us who have passed through our thirties or forties can probably remember our first "I'm invisible!" experience. Mine happened when I reached the front of the line at a local bagel shop. The thirty-something man behind the counter looked right past the forty-something me and started chatting with a twenty-something police officer standing behind me—and took his coffee order. I felt the counterman look right through and past me; because I looked "older," I was invisible.

Numerous times since, my visibly adult body has brushed up against the truism that getting older means genuine loss of status for women in the most mundane of situations. But I was truly startled at how I felt the first time. I was angry and shocked that my simple right to be served based on my place in line had suddenly disappeared, along with the assumption that my physical presence automatically mattered. My most basic prerogatives felt abruptly stripped away. I was distressed and shocked by the revulsion toward getting older that rose up in me. My long-held feelings of honor and respect for older women's wisdom crashed into my sudden, passionate resistance to being seen (or, more accurately, being ignored) as my older self. Becoming "invisible" created a head-on collision between my life philosophy and my visceral anger and fear.

In our culture, showing our age usually equals losing status. No matter how old we are, women do not want to lose status, recognition, and respect. Many of us resist invisibility by trying to prevent our body from appearing old; we color our hair, have cosmetic surgery, diet, wear youthful clothing, exercise, and stay tanned. We believe that shaping our appearance will keep us visible and noticeable—even if it means prolonging the intrusion of male leering.

Judging by the responses of other people who are also shaped by our culture, it often appears that we do retain a slightly higher status by shaping our bodies to fit the unreal beauty mold. This reinforces our belief in the cosmetic surgeon's blatantly false promise that altering our appearance can reverse the aging process. We may still feel drawn to attracting even menacing attention from men because that attention also conveys a perverse confirmation of our value.

As we traverse womanhood, we can feel as if our bodies are starting to let us down, gradually at first (I can't get into the same yoga poses as gracefully and easily as I could at twenty), and then with greater frequency (I used to run eight-minute miles easily, but now my knees prefer a slower pace). As we get older, the body is less forgiving than it used to be. It takes longer to bounce back from a broken bone or a sprained ankle. Eventually we even lose the iconic female characteristic: the ability to give birth. Our mental and emotional capacities change as we grow through and beyond menopause. In other words, our body is a concrete reminder of that essential reality: we (like everyone else) are getting older.

Death

Death and birth are the two things *all* humans have in common. As we get older, the chance that we'll experience the death of loved ones increases.

The death of a peer when we are young is tragic and seems to defy the natural order of things. But in the adult years, illness and death become part of our landscape as friends and relatives age. We start noticing the ages of people in the obituaries, even if they are strangers. Mortality looms unspoken on the horizon.

Whether death takes a spouse, parents, friend, or someone else, it will probably stir up feelings from every previous death we've experienced. That's because we always respond to death in the context of our previous losses. At the same time, each death has a unique impact and symbolism. For example my father, Ed, died in the 1970s. Many feelings about that loss resurfaced when, thirty years later, I helped my mother, Margaret, through the final months of her life. When she died, it made my good-bye to my dad more final.

Losing our parents leaves us orphaned, even if we are adults. A parent's death brings a substantial shift in our identity:

- I must act grown up now, because no one is there to rescue me anymore.
- I'm the one responsible.

- I can't maintain the illusion of being a child with a parent to back me up in a pinch.

When our parents die, we also say good-bye to a generation. We become the family vanguard, donning the role of matriarch. It is a profound, transformative, and often frightening time in our lives. Deaths can trigger the urge to look and act younger than we are, in a vain attempt to deny or defer our mortality, level of maturity, and/or need for maturity.

A mother's death brings particular challenges to our sense of identity. Mother-daughter relationships ebb and flow through a lifetime. As girls, we identify very closely with our moms and feel great intimacy with them. Then adolescence and other developmental imperatives lead many of us away from our moms emotionally; we may spend years defining ourselves by the ways we are different from Mom. Eventually, many daughters and mothers reconnect as adults, our intimacy bolstered by the shared experience of being a partner, a mother, or having other adult responsibilities. Whether we reconnect or remain separate, the intensity and meaning of this central relationship makes the loss of a mother very potent for us daughters.

For most of my life, I felt very close to my mother. But I also saw myself as very different from her. When my mother fell ill during the last few years of her life, I took over the "mothering" role to care for her. This experience brought us a level of intimacy that was both joyful and painful— a truly mixed blessing.

Like many women, I found that my need to focus on all our differences diminished during my mother's final years. Instead, I began to search for and cherish our similarities, including physical ones. In *her* forties and fifties, my mother was a natural beauty, with no frills; now I feel drawn to that same style. This process seems natural and peaceful, helping me to feel good about my mother's ongoing presence and influence in my life.

When a mother dies, her daughter may feel intense desires to find and touch the common ground she shared with her, looking to develop some of her mom's qualities in her own identity. This new concentration on connection can bring new levels of self-discovery. But this may be difficult if you haven't had the opportunity to arrive at a healthy adult relationship with your mother. It is even more problematic if your mother struggled with body image or eating problems. Every mother hands down a legacy of her relationship to food and her body, which in turn shapes the unspoken, unconscious ways you relate to food and your body. If Mom was not at peace in this area of her life, you may experience problems too.

For example, Catherine's mother died suddenly when Catherine still felt the need to be quite separate from her mom. Because the two hadn't yet moved into a more adult phase in their relationship, Catherine felt she had nothing to hang on to after Mom's death. For several years, Catherine used a chaotic relationship with food to act out her confusion about her mom, her grief, and her deep disconnection. Depressed and full of regret at unfulfilled opportunities, her discomfort about her weight and body image erupted into bulimia. When she finally entered treatment, Catherine focused on her relationship with her mom, including questions about her mother's relationship with food.

Catherine remembered her mom dieting frequently and eating in a very controlled way in front of others. However, her mother never seemed to lose weight and was very unhappy with her body. Catherine believed that her mom was a disordered eater when she was alone and depressed, using food to soothe herself. While Catherine no longer had the chance to ask her mother about these issues, she still explored this relationship in therapy. Finding ways to identify and connect spiritually to her mother, Catherine was able to give up her symptoms of restricting and purging, and find peace with her body and with food.

Many thoughts and feelings we have in reaction to a death boil down to confronting our own mortality. Reminded that our life will end, we may reexamine what we're doing with our life, taking inventory of whether we've done enough. Death makes us investigate the choices we've made. We ask ourselves questions like:

- What is the meaning of my life?
- Should I quit my job and enjoy retirement or the different challenges of a new career?
- Should I stay where I am and accomplish more here?
- Should I stay in this relationship?

Death can also make survivors start thinking seriously, or even compulsively, about the threat of illness. In an effort to prevent disease, we may develop a heightened concern about food, weight, body, and exercise—perhaps even developing a phobic obsession about eating health foods and overusing otherwise health-promoting behaviors.

Our culture's obsession with youthfulness stems in part from a deep-seated resistance to the very idea of death. Many other cultures tend to be more open about death and its impact, taking this natural phenomenon more in stride. On the other hand, our culture has a denial of death, which both reinforces and feeds on its overglorification of youth.

This pervasive denial becomes a huge barrier when one of our loved ones dies. We are allowed very little permission to mourn and openly acknowledge a death. Writer Marilyn Karr was shocked by the denial of death she felt from others after her husband died at age forty-one.

> Kevin had cancer on and off for several years before his last, terminal bout. We never hid this from anyone, and we received a lot of support from people during his prolonged illness. But after he died, some friends and acquaintances didn't seem to want to spend any time thinking about or being reminded of Kevin's actual *death*. I was stunned by the number of people who, in the days and weeks after his funeral, indicated that I should now be "over" the loss and done with my grieving. This went on for some time afterward. It was as if people put a statute of limitations on my grief and my children's grief. Granted, for a stingy few, the statute of limitations was a weekend, and for more generous others, it was a year, but all of it was about limiting the open expression of our loss and grief. It seemed to me that the motivation was "How soon can you stop reminding me that people die? When can I be done with this?"

Karr went on to become a hospice nurse, in part to support people in being able to grieve openly and healthfully for as long as they need. She adds:

> The grief experience made me long for a culture where outward expressions of loss are expected. I wanted to wear black, or give some other external sign which showed that I had stepped outside my normal life and wouldn't be back for a while. In my hospice work I've found that other people feel that same need.

The pressure to deny grief can be particularly hard on women, because we are acculturated to live up to the expectations and demands of others. Yet we are also acculturated to be closely connected to others, which makes a loved one's loss especially hard. If others are expecting us to move on after a major loss like death, it's easy to feel that our grief isn't valuable—or even that it isn't real.

Some forms of death are particularly disenfranchised losses—for example, miscarriage and infant death. People around us—including our own families—may minimize such a loss because *they* spent so little (if any) time with the baby. Since other people don't feel like they knew the baby, miscarriage and infant death often become an isolated, private grief.

This lack of support suggests to us that grieving an infant death or miscarriage isn't important or worth the effort. This creates inner conflict and turmoil, because the child is very real to the parents, whether or not the child was actually born. Every woman who has ever been pregnant knows how important that experience is.

Conflict also can spring from the different ways individuals mourn, especially men and women. Under the stress of a child's death, a mother and father may grow impatient with how each other grieves, or else they may learn new ways to support each other. Here's how a father put it a couple of years after he and his wife lost their baby: "A miscarriage will either pull you together or pull you apart."

A miscarriage or infant death also makes us feel that our body and/or our abilities are somehow inadequate. We castigate ourselves with questions like "Couldn't I have done more?" These reactions are normal and ultimately pass, if we are allowed to grieve. But they may also lead us to develop severe criticism of our bodies, opening the door to disordered eating, exercise abuse, and other forms of physical and psychological self-flagellation.

Some deaths, like those from suicide and AIDS, are especially stigmatized, with survivors getting even less support dealing with their grief than the pittance allotted for more "acceptable" deaths. Because women are socialized to take care of others, we easily take responsibility and blame ourselves for the problems of our loved ones. This adds to the grief we feel surrounding these marginalized deaths. We may find ourselves struggling with guilt-provoking questions, such as "What could I have done to prevent this?" or "Why didn't I see this coming and do something before it was too late?" The mourning process may convert into obsessive self-blame despite the many factors that combine to result in deaths from suicide, AIDS, and other less socially acceptable conditions.

Our culture's shortage of symbols, rituals, and support for mourning also makes it difficult to openly grieve losses like divorce or the death of a pet. These losses are real, even though they are usually considered as "less important."

A pet brings us pleasure, unconditional love, and acceptance. We don't feel like we should mourn its passing, although it may have functioned as an actual member of the family. Pets usually live relatively few years, and their shorter life span tends to be symbolic of important phases of our longer, human lives.

For example, a couple I know got their family dog when their daughters were in grade school. When the dog died, the children were in their mid-twenties and had moved away. The dog's death became a concrete symbol for the end of an important phase of this mother and father's life, stirring up grief over no longer being so central in their daughters' lives—itself a very real loss.

Whether or not our loved one is human, surviving her or his death is simply very stressful and sad. Our grief is complicated by how few rituals and acknowledgments of death surround us at a time when we need support for our sadness, rather than limitations on it or rejection of it. As a way to shape and soothe the sadness, some of us turn to destructive rituals involving food, eating, and exercise. Periods of bingeing and/or appetite loss are not uncommon during the early stages of mourning. However, these patterns become dangerous if they continue, which is more likely if we try to shape our grieving to the culture's expectations for the female body. The patterns are toxic for women who have struggled in the past with disordered eating, body image despair, and eating disorders.

Women's Work

The natural development and aging of our bodies are not the only challenges adult women face as we pass through adulthood. Our life situations and surroundings also evolve. Many of these situations are foreign to the generations that lived before the women's movement, with its opportunity (and expectation) to be and do everything.

That expectation is palpable for women today—as is the disappointing feeling that we haven't succeeded in doing it all or in mastering every opportunity that comes our way. That expectation is completely unrealistic; women have to make choices that fit not only us and our needs but (most of the time) also fit our family's needs.

Still, how often have we buried our many achievements under a mound of regret over one failure? What criteria do we use to review and evaluate ourselves and our accomplishments? Men struggle with these questions too, but the criteria for a man's success tend to be simpler (and more simplistic): men are supposed to focus on their careers, and success or failure is measured in terms of income and occupational opportunities.

As contemporary women, we feel like we must focus on money and career too. But we must also do child rearing, manage family logistics, and nurture the emotional life of marriage. Looking through a cascading waterfall of expectations (both internal and external), our perception of our accomplishments is blurred by what feel like endless and unquenchable demands. If our career feels under control (or, God forbid, prospers), we feel guilty about the amount of time we allow for family. If we devote some work time to family matters, we worry that it will catch up with us and affect our advancement and sense of accomplishment on the job.

Next we'll focus on how common transitions we experience as adults shape our body image in this new world for women, and how they mix with this new world's entrenched cultural myths to reinforce body image dissatisfaction.

On the Job

Women with concerns about eating and body image are likely to be talented, resourceful, and accomplished—but they seldom see themselves that way. Many women do a task not because they want the achievement, but because they depend on pleasing others to prove their self-worth. This unhealthy objective undermines any sense of real accomplishment.

If we do something for someone else rather than for ourselves, taking credit for the accomplishment feels fraudulent. Therefore, we derive little success or satisfaction from our work. We disown our own accomplishments, feel like failures, and focus on what we haven't yet done. We may feel deeply disappointed in ourselves and believe that we are not unique or special. To distract ourselves from these difficult feelings, we may pursue what we see as a successful body shape through rituals of disordered eating and body image obsessions. In the end, this obsessive pursuit undermines our most meaningful accomplishments.

Adding to this sense of failure is the fact that women still earn substantially less than men for comparable work. Our culture often fails to acknowledge and reward women fairly for their contributions. This is frustrating for any working woman, but too often we personalize this and other workplace inequities. We blame and shame ourselves rather than accepting that these problems are systemic cultural failures, not personal ones.

There are other complications for women in the workplace. If we worry that we are dedicating too much to our career, or pursuing (and succeeding at) a career path that seems too male, we may feel the need to compensate by looking more feminine physically. We may develop appearance, weight, or eating problems in order to balance what's seen as overly masculine behavior. We may be tempted to act girlish and flirty to offset assertive or aggressive work behaviors that might be seen as too masculine and, therefore, offensive.

In addition, there are certain professions where a highly attractive appearance is considered essential for success. A ballerina knows pretty clearly what shape and appearance her body is required to have. But heavy emphasis on appearance shapes women's success even in the most conventional professions. Listen to the murky path one female Realtor must constantly tread:

> My clothes, my makeup, my weight—they are all an ordeal every day. If I look "too good," people either don't take me seriously, or accuse me of being seductive and manipulative to make a sale. That attitude is especially strong among many of my male colleagues. On the other hand, looking "too plain" projects an unprofessional image. How can I make it to "in between" every day? I can't even tell for sure what "in-between" is! An outfit that seems to work well most days will unexpectedly strike a colleague or customer as too sexy or too frumpy on other days. I feel like my body and clothes are on display as much as they are for any supermodel. But if I was a model, at least I'd know what I was supposed to look like. When it comes to my "professional look," most days I feel like I don't know and I can't win.

This Realtor's story is one small example of how the cultural transition from "women expected to stay home" to "women expected to work" is not over, despite the apparent advances made by women on the job.

Work-Family Balance

The world of work and career brings our generation of women much greater opportunity than what previous generations had. It also brings increased demands on (and ambiguity about) our place as women in the world. For starters, we may feel some guilt, or even disloyalty, for surpassing Mom and other family matriarchs on the career track.

If our mother and/or grandmother didn't have a paying career, we may feel they (and other family members, like Dad) give us failing grades on our work and family choices. If they don't understand our experience of work and our standards for career success, we may feel that they don't understand us. Narrow, superficial activities like shopping or dieting may seem like the only ways to share and connect with Mom.

When we focus on career, we may feel that we are not doing enough for our family. When giving attention to our family, we may feel that we are not maximizing our career potential. We may feel that we must be on the go ceaselessly in order to manage the conflicts. The Superwoman response to uncertainty and guilt brings high levels of stress that intrude on our life and well-being. A 2000 AFL-CIO survey finds that more than half of mothers with children under six find the work-family balance more difficult than it was only four years earlier, with 30 percent saying it was "much harder."

These work-family balancing acts tend to be more difficult for women than for men because women, men, and the larger culture expect us to be more responsible for family life—especially child rearing. Women and men both tend to think of fathers as second-class parents, giving fathers a pass on child-rearing responsibilities—and child-rearing joys too. That means couples who choose an "alternative" way of balancing their respective family and work responsibilities are often ridiculed, or at least lack support.

Many people still see working as merely an option for women. For example, a 2003 *New York Times Magazine* cover story profiled affluent women who are opting out of the career track. Left unmentioned were the vast majority of working women who are not affluent. For them, opting out is not an option. Most of us have a job to support our families, whether in tandem with a partner or alone as a single parent. But high-profile stories about women abandoning the career track make it hard not to feel guilty or ask, "Why can't I do what my kids need me to do, and give all my time to them?"

Being on the career-and-family seesaw, we may long for role models that can show us how to manage our many life demands. However, such role models may simply not exist, or may be very hard to find, because our lives are so different from the lives of our mothers and other women of past generations. Meanwhile, our friends and peers are immigrants like us, making up solutions as they go along. Self-help and self-improvement literature, reflecting our youth-focused culture, seldom discuss adult development or how to age well. For adult women, there isn't much beyond "When I grow old, I shall wear purple" (a good idea, but an insufficient road map).

Decisions about balancing family and work are seldom easy or simple. This ambiguity sometimes reinforces our desire to seek more measurable answers by working to have control over at least our body, the one element we've been told (mistakenly) that we can control and measure.

Competing with Younger Women

Women are more visible than ever in the workplace and other social realms. While these new opportunities are often positive, they also present more opportunities for competition over appearance with other women, many of them younger. There are more opportunities for a woman's body to be judged, which leads to more opportunities for us to feel unhappy, uneasy, or fearful about our body.

Previous generations of women worried about competing with younger women for husbands. But today we feel the need to compete for men's attention in the career world too, often with good reason: men still hold the majority of management positions. We're not psychotic or crazy if we think that more attractive colleagues get more promotions, status, and pay. They do. Appearance discrimination is an embedded concrete reality: older and/or fatter women are systematically paid less and passed over for promotion.

We may strive for a slender, androgynous look, hoping to be taken seriously, rather than be judged by our bodies' sexual and reproductive qualities. Instead of celebrating how younger women reap the rewards of our pioneering in the workplace, we resent it—especially when they take weaker stances on women's issues or discount our contribution to their opportunity.

Dealing with the sexual energy in a workplace is a challenge for women of all ages. We often struggle to find the authority and balance needed to avoid being burned by the mixing and manipulation of sex and power at work. Jealousy makes it hard for us to mentor younger women, who need our insight as they begin their careers.

In addition, we haven't talked enough with one another and our male colleagues about successfully (and fairly) negotiating issues of sex, power, collegiality, and communication on the job. Men often interpret a woman's energy, attention, or interactions as sexual or potentially sexual. Simultaneously, we tend to hold women more accountable than men for sexual transgressions, both in and outside of the workplace. This imbalance in implied responsibility is reflected in what a man recently told me: "You feminists need to understand men's hormones." For many women these hotly charged attitudes and tensions infuse the workplace with self-doubt and confusion.

Knowing how male colleagues often respond to our energy, we are understandably hesitant to initiate powerful, energized interactions with them—and thus we undercut the authority we may need to succeed in business. Collegiality, friendship, and even intimacy are the goals for some male coworkers, but for others, the motivation for interaction with female colleagues is primarily sexual.

These loaded topics are difficult to discuss openly in the workplace. Too often, we try to paper over complex office tensions by shaping our appearance and behavior into a form that is pleasing to the men we work with and for. That unhealthy diversion of our energies does nothing to confront the very real challenges that both men and women face at work.

Retirement

Retirement looks a lot different than it did a generation ago. More women than ever have careers lasting long enough to end with formal retirement. Fewer people retire to sitting on the beach or playing golf all day, every day. Instead, many of today's retirees keep working and/or volunteering.

This is another area of life where women don't have many role models. To a certain extent, we have to make up retirement as we go along (whatever form it takes). If we pour so much into work, what else is there when work is over? What value do we now have to those colleagues who provided our validation and approval and with whom we've spent so much time?

Retirement brings important logistical questions about the future. If we interrupted a career for child rearing and were paid historically lower wages because we were women, do we have enough money to retire well? Do we sell the house? Start another career? We may feel skilled in the math of fat grams and calories, but do we feel inept and inadequate at managing money and IRAs?

Some retirement questions are downright scary. What do we want to do now? How far can we go to explore the dreams, goals, and interests that our career diverted us from? Will that exploration disrupt other aspects of our life and relationships? How will we know if we're doing well at something without a boss or coworker to tell us? Can we do something new without following someone else's direction and lead? As a "retired" woman what value do we have to our profession, community, and the culture at large?

If work life has centered on proving one's self over and over (as it tends to be for women), retirement takes away a central arena for basing our worth on proven performance. In retirement, we may feel that the only way left to prove our worth is by being attractive. Once again, however, intense attention on appearance obscures the more important (and more ephemeral) challenges like: "After decades of doing for others, do I have the right to have a want or desire of my own?"

Women's Families

Child Rearing

Within moments of giving birth, a child-rearing mother is responsible for feeding her child. This responsibility usually extends into preparing food for the entire family. For years and years, most women are always within a few feet and a few hours of providing meals. That can make life very hard if we have conflicted or negative feelings and behaviors surrounding food. (More on this in chapter 6.)

If we already struggle with body image issues, we may become overly focused on our children's appearance, clothes, and shape as early as the toddler years. This can lead to a competitive relationship between the generations that saps energy from us *and* our children.

Some of us are actually jealous of our children's youth, slender frame, and lack of concern about weight!

We may also envy our children's emerging, vibrant sexuality as they grow into adolescence. We are suddenly surrounded by young people experimenting with and oozing sensuality. It's not unusual to feel a subtle or overt need to compete with our daughters, their friends, or our son's girlfriends as we strive to show them (and us) that we are still sexually attractive.

For some of us, lingering feelings from our own adolescence may trigger renewed desires to have the best body possible. Instead of "acting our age," we may dress like kids, sculpt our bodies down to more willowy figures, and exercise more just to prove our youthfulness and vitality. This behavior can confuse and annoy our kids.

When a mother tries to compete with her daughter, it can foster reciprocal competition from her daughter—whose adolescence already supplies enough insecurity about her appearance and social standing. When young people speak about body image, they often bring up concerns about their mother's eating, exercise, and body issues, saying: "The last person I should have to compete with right now is my mom."

During a time when it can be very difficult for mothers and daughters to stay emotionally connected, our daughters' attention to dieting, clothing, cosmetics, and so forth can also become a major form of bonding between them and us. That can add further twists to an already knotty relationship. A daughter's preoccupation with her body may also trigger latent or fresh obsessions in her mother.

If our daughter develops eating disorders, we may have intense trouble managing our own relationship to food and our body. Some of us develop significant personal problems as we anguish about our daughters' struggles. Many young clients with eating disorders are followed into treatment by their mothers, who had suffered in silence for years. The adult women are unsure if they really deserve help, struggling with guilt for having any needs of their own.

Parenting itself provides stressors and disappointments for which we may not be prepared. Every minute of mothering isn't exciting or rewarding, so it may feel like it doesn't "measure up" in our instant-gratification world. Our children's needs can be draining, monotonous, painful, and not at all like our romantic notions of what mothering would be like.

It gets old to give so much of our lives to the family, and to children who are not yet developmentally able to appreciate our sacrifices. Resultant feelings of resentment, depression, or emptiness may lead us to use food to dull the pain, or just to feel that some part of our life is still ours alone, we may focus on our bodies as a means of having a sense of control or accomplishment.

Since we rarely talk about our true hungers and needs as women, our complex emotions about our roles as mothers and family members get shoved under the carpet. If we felt free to honestly air these feelings, we might not be as apt to convert them into eating problems or body image despair.

Deciding Not to Have Children

There have always been women who choose to forgo motherhood. Some contemporary women make the decision out of fear for how pregnancy and childbirth might make them lose control of their weight and shape and threaten their status of being young and attractive. Other women today (and throughout history) make the childless choice for more altruistic and thoughtful reasons, like the generations of nuns who have dedicated their lives to spiritual growth and serving the community. Freedom from the responsibility of child rearing can help a woman make many contributions to the world. Nevertheless, in this new women's world, women who choose not to be mothers endure far more scrutiny, distrust, and suspicion than adult men without children.

With far greater encouragement to pursue careers and opportunities that were off limits to our foremothers, many of us feel it may be impossible to successfully meld the new tradition of having a career with the old tradition of mothering. As we consider how to balance our interests, opportunities, and commitments with the time and energy that children require, some of us opt out of the child-rearing choice. Others make this decision based purely on philosophical or political beliefs about issues like overpopulation. Regardless of our motivations, the childless choice is foreign and threatening to many people.

Friends and relatives may actually ask, "What's wrong with you that you don't want kids?" We may feel like round pegs being forced into square holes, struggling to feel okay about taking a path that is different from the mainstream mothering journey expected of women. To soothe feelings of inadequacy, loneliness, or depression, we may resort to eating behaviors that can endanger our health.

Going against cultural expectations is challenging, especially for women socialized to care about others' expectations and feelings. Having such a deeply personal decision scrutinized by others can make any woman feel uncertain or uncomfortable. Even if we remain confident in our choice, we may not feel confident that others will accept and respect it as they should.

One way of fighting back may be to use our bodies as a way of saying that we are still young and free. We may flaunt our abs to show how much sexier we look than friends with their childbirth stretch marks. Making our bodies impervious to criticism by dieting, exercising, and meeting the ultimate standards for beauty may seem an attractive solution. We may believe that measuring up to the traditional standard of beauty will relieve those complicated feelings of guilt and anxiety over how we may have disappointed others.

Empty Nest

When our children leave home to launch their own adulthoods, we end a crucial phase of our lives. We derive much of our identity from parenting because the mother role is so deeply imbedded in our nature, our expectations for ourselves, and the world's expectations for us. Since our culture still treats fathers as second-class parents, empty-nest time is sometimes a greater challenge for Mom than it is for Dad.

Life without daily responsibility for our children means developing a new relationship with ourselves and our future. It also means rethinking and readjusting our relationships with our children, our partner, and our community. What is our role now that a central part of our womanly identity feels like it is over? We may wonder:

- What will happen to my marriage now that the kids aren't here to fill up all that space and use up all of our attention?
- The kids added so much life to our home; will I be interesting enough to my partner now?
- Will he or she be interesting enough to me?
- Do we stay in this house or move?
- Is it now time for me to explore my dreams, goals, and interests that family responsibilities took me away from?

- Can I handle quitting my job or moving?
- What do I stand to lose if I do make major changes?
- Will that exploration or any other reexamination of life's priorities threaten my marriage or otherwise make me examine something I'm afraid of?

Because transitioning to become an empty nester is such a major life change, it comes with a fair share of insecurity. Even if we couldn't wait to be released from being so needed by our kids, we may have forgotten how to have a relationship without being needed in that same intense way.

Directing time and energy toward making our outsides look better may seem safer than asking essential questions about our inner selves and our future. In addition, we can't help but think about aging, mortality, and the loss of attractiveness when watching our little babies morph into full-grown adults. Body obsessions may seem like a way to avoid looking older and resist the passages of time and life.

Marriage of Children

The marriage of our children is an explicit example of how joy and sorrow weave together into life's important transitions. Witnessing a child choose a life partner is a loss with a reward at its heart. It is a beginning that marks an end, and an end that marks a beginning. Our family gets smaller as our child moves away from us and into her new family. At the same time, our family expands with the addition of that child's spouse, the spouse's family, and, possibly grandchildren.

Unfortunately, those historic truths about marriage often get lost in preparations for the modern wedding. Alongside timetables for printing invitations and buying flowers, modern wedding planning books and Web sites now include dieting schedules for the mothers, bride, and bridesmaids. Proud as we are to be mothers of brides and grooms, we don't want anyone to see us as being "that old." A child's marriage feels as if it strips away our status of being young.

This may trigger obsessions about looking young, fit, and stylish. It may even spark competition with our daughter or daughter-in-law over weight and shape at a stage in life when there is much to celebrate—including the natural beauty of aging, a child's life partnership, and grandchildren. We may eagerly anticipate and intensely cherish the experience of having grandchildren, but few of us want to look like grandmothers.

Aging Parents

As with other family demands, the needs of aging parents are often considered an optional responsibility for men but are required for women. The demands of caring for aging or ailing parents are added to our other life duties—with none of those other demands taken away.

If we are mothers, we feel caught between fulfilling our children's needs and our parents' needs—which is why we're sometimes called the sandwich generation. It has become normal to feel that we're not sufficiently fulfilling our roles as spouse, child, parent, worker, and community member—or securing enough time to recharge ourselves and grow. This addition without subtraction leaves us counting the ways we don't measure up or don't do things well enough, no matter how highly functioning and efficient we are.

Caring for an older parent can bring up unresolved issues from our childhood, reawakening the pain of our old unmet needs as we try to meet our older parents' current needs. Grief, loss, and anger can result, as can that hopeless feeling that we don't have the time and ability to address these lifelong conflicts in a productive way. On the other hand, renewed daughter-parent contact can provide the chance to work through the past, say and listen to things that need to be said, and ultimately make peace with our parents and our childhood.

Often, our "sandwich" role requires caring for our parents' bodies. We experience a vast array of powerful and painful emotions as we become very familiar with the ways our parents' bodies break down. Furthermore, we begin to confront the reality that our own bodies are aging and naturally losing their former capabilities. Obsessions about eating and body image can easily emerge at these times.

Our desire to be forever young and healthy is easily stimulated as we cope with the demise of our parents' bodies. Vowing not to age as our parents did or suffer the same illnesses, we may jump into obsessive (and even pathological) rituals of exercise, eating, and attention to our bodies. These rituals appear to promise a predictable structure for the liminal time between being children with parents and being orphans. But if this new attention to eating and the body goes too far, it distracts us from acknowledging the emotions stirred up as we care for, and then lose, our parents. Goals for weight loss, hours at the gym, and slimming down a size or two may feel much more manageable than the huge life transition of seeing our parents age and die.

Women's Relationships

Infidelity and Desire

Sally was a good girl her entire life, always living for others—and she especially wanted to please her father. Even though she was now in her late thirties, few achievements of Sally's dutiful life were aimed at pleasing herself. Dieting and her appearance had always been important to her but had never gotten out of control before. Sally looked like she had it all—a great education, exciting career, two children, and marriage to a well-respected, equally accomplished guy named George. But her perfect persona was in fact disconnected from any real desire, happiness, and self-satisfaction.

Never permitting herself to acknowledge, let alone act on, any impulses, Sally was not prepared for the strong attraction she developed for Jeff, a colleague at work. Their high-powered, fast-moving business demanded endless hours and energy. In this environment, it was easy to get close to Jeff and allow a distance to grow between her and George. All of a sudden, Sally plunged deeply into an extramarital affair and felt guilty and overwhelmed at her transgressions. She cared deeply about both men but was ashamed and afraid of being discovered. So she stopped eating to numb these feelings.

A close friend who recognized Sally's weight loss and anxious mood convinced her to seek therapy. Gradually Sally began coming to terms with the multiple reasons for her affair, dealing more directly with these emotions, and making decisions about herself and her marriage. A pivotal moment in therapy occurred when Sally heard me mention that the late thirties are usually the peak of a woman's sexual desire and satisfaction. This normalized and legitimized her feelings, while helping her make sense of her affair.

While she hasn't resolved everything yet, Sally is much more aware of her own needs and feelings, allowing more room in her life and psyche for recognizing her true hungers. She and I labeled her weight loss as ultimately a positive event—not because it made Sally look better, but because it led her into therapy, which eventually gave her permission to appreciate her deepest appetites. Sally is still unsure what her ultimate decisions will be. But for the first time, she is allowing herself to live without an external "script" for her future.

Both women and men can be unfaithful in their primary intimate relationships. But women are often judged more harshly than men on infidelity or being outside the box sexually. A woman who is unfaithful is called (and may think of herself as) a slut, even if hers is a one-time infidelity.

This double standard reflects how little we respect or discuss women's sexual appetites, or even acknowledge that they exist. Clichés like "boys will be boys" and "guys just have to sow their wild oats" demonstrate our culture's willingness to openly grant men their sexual desires. Even though we think grown men shouldn't act on such adolescent urges, we tend to resign ourselves to the fact that they will anyway.

There is a much different standard for women. From the earliest days of puberty, we expect that a girl's response to sexual desire should be to just say no. Boys who sleep around are studs, while girls who go to third base are whores. Since we learn that sexual appetites are never okay for a female, we seldom develop the power to freely say yes as girls. Many of us still don't know how to give a healthy yes as we reach our sexual peak in our thirties and forties. Women young and old have many desires and needs, but we lack positive ways to openly express them.

These same conflicted dynamics of desire occur in lesbian relationships and are reinforced by a cultural environment that is intolerant of lesbians and gays. Homophobia can complicate our experience of trust and tension in an intimate same-sex relationship. Lesbians are not immune from falling back on the language of fat and body image distortion as a way to avoid dealing directly with relationship difficulties. There is scant research on eating and body image obsessions among lesbians, but clinical experience indicates that lesbians who have to hide their true nature, identity, and appetites are at great risk for developing these problems.

It is virtually impossible to separate how we feel about our body from how we experience an intimate relationship, whether it lasts a week or a lifetime. It is also virtually impossible to separate how we feel about our body from a sexual affair, no matter what its motivation.

In an affair, women are often striving to keep alive an important piece of themselves that they feel is otherwise dying. We may feel disappointed about not achieving—or even knowing how to ask for and get—the intimacy we want in our primary relationship. An affair may be our attempt to prove that we are still attractive and desirable because we fear we are losing our looks, or fear that our partner is losing interest in us. We may seek recognition from someone else because we feel smothered, not alive, and not appreciated in our family and marriage. Lingering, unresolved issues with our parents may influence our relationships with our partners and the individuals we have affairs with. We may be trying to reclaim or find important parts of ourself. Or we may simply want to experience more sexually.

It is very difficult to openly explore these questions through a hidden affair, or while being condemned if the affair is revealed. The infidelity double standard increases our shame while reinforcing disrespect toward women's sexuality, our sexual desires, and even the notion that women have appetites of any kind.

These distorted beliefs about our sexual appetites provoke resentment against any urges and hungers—whether sexual, physical, or emotional—and encourage us to turn that anger against our body, the source of those unruly desires.

A Partner's Infidelity

When a woman's partner has an affair, it can be an incredible blow to our body image—"He's out there because I'm not attractive or sexually enticing to him anymore"; "She cheated on me because I'm inadequate." We may resort to "winning him or her back" by trying to reshape our bodies to prove that we are not inadequate, unattractive, and unsexy. This reaction can quickly kick into a pattern of exercise abuse, extreme dieting, cosmetic surgery, and other behaviors that threaten our health. Cosmetic makeovers aimed at making over relationships are misdirected and ultimately futile. Changing our appearance does nothing to address infidelity's violation of trust (the core of any intimate relationship), nor does it nurture the trust we need in any attempt to heal the relationship.

If a big part of our partner's crisis originates in his feeling that he is getting old or looking old, we may react by trying to appear young ourselves. If our partner is acting strangely or playing around, we may try to increase our feminine charms, resorting to a "sexy" facade rather than directly addressing how the crisis is affecting our partner, us, and our relationship. In turn, we may respond to her or his crisis with stress, anxiety, and depression—problems that we may attempt to self-soothe through disordered eating or other body image obsessions.

Women are acculturated to take responsibility for other people's feelings. Therefore, if a partner goes through a difficult emotional stretch—like a midlife crisis or an affair—we may feel responsible, overdo our help, and discount our own needs, wants, and desires.

Many women feel great ambivalence about whether they can be angry about a partner's infidelity. "If I want to make it better, how can I be angry? That might drive my partner away." In addition, most people don't like angry women, so we may stay stuck in sadness to cover over our anger. As a friend once quipped, "Depression is anger without enthusiasm." If we don't feel entitled to express our natural anger, it has to go somewhere—eating behaviors that affect our body are visible and handy receptacles for it.

After our partner has an affair, we naturally (and reasonably) have a large load of distrust. But the crisis of trust triggered (or brought to the surface) by the affair *does* have the potential to ultimately strengthen our intimate bond. Repairing a postaffair relationship takes a great deal of effort and usually professional help. It requires paying attention and being courageous, committed and willing to take risks. While looking better may be an attractive strategy, it isn't a solution.

Divorce

Like terrorism, the possibility of divorce can feel like a chronic, disconcerting threat to any intimate relationship. When we enter long-term relationships, we know that a staggering number of them end in divorce (my shorthand for the breakup of a long-term intimate partnership, whether or not it includes a state-sanctioned marriage).

Women are more likely to blame ourselves for this devastating loss, since we tend to take on more emotional responsibility and emotional work than men in an intimate relationship. So on top of the loneliness, sadness, and anger over the end of this important relationship, we are also likely to go through a period of serious self-criticism.

After divorce or separation, we feel inadequate and that we've profoundly failed at something women are supposed to know instinctively how to do: maintain an intimate partnership. Here are some common responses to divorce that women have told me in therapy:

- It was such a surprise. I always felt sure we would be together forever—everyone thought we were perfect together. What did I do to mess this up?

- I'm the first one in my family to get divorced, and now I've let down and disappointed my parents, my in-laws, and all the rest of my family.

- Is there something wrong with me? Were the unmet needs in our marriage my fault? Was I expecting too much?

- I initiated the breakup; he didn't want it. I'm probably being way too selfish.

Women sometimes show anger about the breakup but are more likely to express sadness and grief. When we see other angry women labeled as bitches, we may not feel entitled to be angry. We may tamp it down or turn it against ourselves through depression, substance abuse, disordered eating, or other self-destructive avenues.

It's normal for individuals going through a divorce to feel traumatized and depressed by their situation. For many women, this means a case of the Separation Skinnies. At first, the stress and shock may cause us to lose weight unintentionally. Soon we may start to feel good about this "accomplishment" (and the compliments we get) and begin more conscious efforts to lose more weight. Or we may start overeating and bingeing in response to the strain and sadness.

Many of us put at least some blame for a divorce on our bodies. "If only I'd been more attractive, or stayed sexier, he or she would still be with me." But partners who seek sexy trophy brides are often acting out anxieties they can't seem to address directly. For example, they may fear getting old and dying.

We still teach young boys more about how to maintain what men's activist Jackson Katz calls a "tough guise" than we teach them about emotional literacy. Boys often carry this handicap into adulthood and their intimate relationships. Shaping our bodies into something "too good for him to leave" does nothing to address that underlying problem. My coauthor, Joe Kelly, has written that a man who claims to bolt a marriage because of his partner's body shape is lying to himself:

When I met my wife nearly thirty years ago, I was very attracted to her body. It will come as no shock that neither one of us look exactly like we did in the 1970s. No creature, human or otherwise, looks the same after decades of life. But even in our earliest years together, I was attracted to her, not just her body. Her body no longer fits the mold of what TV tells us is attractive, but I am still attracted to who she is.

A few months before our wedding, my late mother-in-law (who was divorced) expressed her fear that I'd leave Nancy once I got tired of the sex or her body. I replied: "I don't have that much imagination or need for continually changing sexual thrills. If your fears were justified, I would have taken off by now, since we've already been living together for more than a year." I guess my answer would be the same today as it was then. It's nice that we still find each other physically attractive much of the time. But that's hardly the central element of our relationship. No man or woman can build a successful marriage first and foremost on body parts.

Divorce is difficult at any age, but it may be an especially profound loss to a woman who invested many years in a marriage, is older, feels less attractive, and does not want to be alone—or dating. The older we get, especially in our youth- and appearance-focused world, the tougher it is to tolerate not attaining the physical shape that attracts potential mates. This can trigger a cycle of being obsessed about the shape of our bodies.

The rituals of excessive exercise, restricted eating, or bingeing can supply structure to what seems like a chaotic time, although they don't provide the cohesion and schedule of an intimate human relationship. "I don't have to go home, so I go to the gym" may seem like a good solution (and moderate exercise certainly helps with depression), but that approach quickly becomes hollow if it is the primary or only approach we take to addressing the end of what we thought was a lifelong relationship.

Postdivorce Parenting

After divorce, we often continue to feel responsible for the relationships between our children and the other parent(s)—maintaining a cycle common during marriage. As veteran divorced mother Sarah puts it:

Of course I wanted my kids to keep having a relationship with their dad, and wanted it to be at least tolerable, if not actually pretty good. I wanted all that despite being really pissed off at Tim for how he behaved before the divorce, and how he seemed to be acting after it. But I felt I had to control all those feelings and definitely hide them from the kids. Meanwhile, it seemed like he was acting out his anger toward me through the kids, spoiling them and not seeming to give them any limits. I felt in a totally impossible position. I wasn't allowed to show any anger toward him, but he could sabotage me through the kids on the weekend, and I was responsible for picking up all the pieces during the week.

Even if relations with an ex are fairly good, we often oversee his parenting, his difficulties, and perhaps even his emotional life. We remain the family switchboard, managing the schedule and mediating between kids and Dad. This may be a matter of habit or the result of guilt about the fallout from our breakup and/or the conflicted and complex feelings we still have about our exes.

Meanwhile, we are living in a culture where one doesn't seem to be a whole number, so we may feel compelled to secure another mate immediately. Our culture intensely romanticizes (and overromanticizes) relationships, and we can feel wrong or out of place if we're alone. Pressure to be part of a pair can also come from parents and family members. Plus, there is the natural desire for humans to partner with one another, a sense that may be especially heightened after a previous partnering has ended.

Naturally when we think about trying to find a partner, we start worrying about how we look. Our awareness of our appearance and body image is heightened, and not always in a good way.

But it is important to remember that one is a whole number. We are valuable living outside a couple, and we can make valuable contributions to our families, friends, and the world.

The Common Thread

Any adult transition, change, or challenge can bring loss, pain, and uncertainty. It can bring great excitement, vision, freedom, and opportunity too. And it can also trigger serious problems involving body loathing, food obsessions, yo-yo dieting, life-threatening eating disorders, depression, addiction, and more.

For women, the thread of body image weaves through every one of these problems. Most of the time, we either don't see that thread or else look at it through lenses that magnify the Body Myth rather than reflect reality.

That's why it is so hard for us to keep sight of the truth about weight and survival as we traverse the rough roads of adulthood. It is as if we immigrants are slogging our way across the frontier through a tenacious fog. With our vision distorted and blocked, we fall into deep crevasses or smack headfirst into insurmountable cliffs. The results can be horrible to contemplate, as we're about to see.

Loss Inventory

Think about one particular loss you experienced, such as a death, health problem, or change of status for you or your family. The loss might be very obvious to others, like the death of a close family member, or it could be more symbolic to you personally, such as your parents selling the home in which you were raised.

As you remember that loss, jot down your answers to these questions:

- Have you talked about this loss with others?
- If not, what has stopped you from sharing it?
- If you have talked to others, how did you feel about their response?
- Have you received the support you need from others?
- How did this loss affect you? Has it changed your relationships?
- Do you feel different as a person as a result of this loss?
- Has this loss brought anything new into your life?
- Has it brought you closer to anyone?
- How has it affected your sense of self and identity as an adult female?

- How has it affected your attitude toward life?
- Has it changed your attitude toward your body?
- Do you pay more, less, or different attention to your health and self care as a result of this loss?
- When you initially experienced the loss, did you change your eating, exercise, or other body-related attitudes and behaviors?
- What is your body's typical reaction to stress and loss?
- Are there ways you could take better care of yourself during periods of loss and grief?
- How did you feel about answering these questions?

We each respond to loss in an individual way. There is no singular path toward healing and resolution. However, it is normal for the intense stress of loss to affect our physical functioning, including eating. We may eat more than usual, or temporarily lose our appetite. The disruption of severe loss upsets the routine of our daily lives. During these times of loss and transition, the best course is to maintain a physically healthy routine, especially when it comes to maintaining good nutrition, sleep, and exercise.

The Change Balance Sheet: What Are My Adult Transition Gains and Losses?

Do this exercise by yourself, with a trusted friend or in a small group. Write your answers down so you can reflect on them over time.

- What were the five most important things you gained during your twenties?
- What were the five hardest things to lose in that decade?
- Which two of these ten things were the most important to your personal growth and development, shaping who you are today? Do they come from the gain or the loss column?
- What kind of shape were you in emotionally and spiritually during this phase of life?

- How important was your physical shape during that period; did it overshadow other things happening in your life? Did it overshadow the kind of shape you were in emotionally and spiritually?

Repeat this exercise for each decade you've lived through.

What do your written answers reveal? Is there a pattern here? Was one decade more challenging to your personal growth than another? What do your answers teach you about your adult development?

4

The Shape of
Eating Disorders

In the months following Anna Westin's death from anorexia, her parents became outspoken advocates for access to eating disorders treatment and for education to prevent them. One evening Anna's mother, Kitty Westin, attended the premier screening and reception for a PBS documentary about eating disorders treatment. After the screening, one of the anorexic patients profiled in the film took questions from the audience, alongside her physician. The crowd was overwhelmingly female, and nearly all the questions asked the woman for very specific details about her dieting patterns and obsessive exercise. Kitty recalls:

> It was bizarre and disturbing. You figure these women have some awareness and concern about the plague of eating disorders; otherwise they wouldn't be at a screening for this film. But here they were asking things like, "How far did you run every day? I know that got to be a problem for you, but how far do you think it would have been OK for you to run? By the way, you know, I think you look great!" Most of the questions amounted to asking "How far can I go with your techniques so I can be sure to lose weight, but not slip over the edge into anorexia?" They were belittling the disease that was consuming this brave woman onstage and that killed my daughter. Even after seeing a

documentary on the horrors of eating disorders, they seemed blind to how obsession with weight was already eating up their own lives, and blind to how their eagerness to uncover the "techniques" of bulimia and anorexia might endanger them—and the young woman onstage. How could this be when the damage was staring right at them in the person of this young woman trying to answer their sick questions? She was clearly struggling with her own pain and the horrific stories in the film—while simultaneously hurt and confused by how eagerly the audience sought to learn the "tricks" of her pathology. I was furious.

Seduced by the Shape

I tell Kitty's story for a very pointed reason. This chapter describes what eating disorders look like. Because the Body Myth exerts so much personal and cultural pressure on women to focus on their appearance, we may have deeply mixed feelings about these symptoms, even if we don't currently engage in disordered eating or other symptoms. We may feel drawn to use some of these strategies to shape our own bodies. We may think thoughts like these:

- I can figure out a way to work just a few anorexic tactics into my life, because it clearly helped anorexics lose weight; those women just went too far.

- I'd only do a few of those things, and only to get myself to a healthy weight.

- It really would make me feel better, and I wouldn't go far enough to get into trouble.

- After all, we can shape our bodies at will. The only thing keeping me from the perfect body is effort, the right formula, and willpower.

- I'd only vomit up meals occasionally, especially when I eat a "forbidden" food.

- That time I went a few days without eating, I lost more weight than ever, and people really noticed. They kept complimenting me on how good I looked.

- I think one of my colleagues at work is probably bulimic. Maybe I can ask her how she stays so thin, and then copy her just a little bit. It seems to work for her, and I'm sure I can control it.

These thoughts and feelings are normal for women in our culture. We are seduced by the seemingly positive results of anorexic behavior and feel tempted to pump a bulimic for information about how she does it. The positive outcomes look so good—surely there couldn't be any harm in trying just a little bit of restricted eating, overexercising, or purging, right?

Wrong.

Those seductive thoughts are dangerous, even if they seem (or actually are) normal to us. Acting on these thoughts is not normal, healthy, or safe—no matter how often our culture seems to endorse them, and no matter how many women around us seem to share them. Even the thoughts themselves, without any action, are dangerous. They sap our energy, distract us from more important things in life, affect our mental health, and can make it easier to subconsciously slip into patterns of behavior that can directly endanger our physical health.

Women with eating disorders and body image obsessions never anticipate how much suffering will eventually result from starting down their destructive path. They don't set out to cause themselves and their loved ones pain. They start down this road because they are trying to deal with their emotions and meet life's challenges by changing their body's shape—they don't go down it looking for a dead end. But a dead end is figuratively—and sometimes literally—what they find.

Disordered eating may work in the short run, giving us a sense of power and control or helping us feel more attractive to others, but it doesn't solve the underlying problems. Our body is not the journey or the destination. It cannot ultimately determine the shape of our life and happiness.

When people learn that I specialize in eating disorders, they often tell me, "I'd like to have anorexia for just a week or two, so I could lose some weight," or "I just want to be bulimic when I eat too much and feel stuffed." Sometimes I'll reply:

Well, cancer and chemotherapy also make people lose weight. Even if it were possible, would you like to have cancer for just a week or two? Eating disorders and body image obsessions are no different from other serious illnesses. It isn't wise to joke about them or pretend that they can disappear on command or be easily cured. Nor should we wish them on ourselves or others.

Even when they don't end a woman's life, eating disorders steal years of it. What follows is the only demand I will make of you while reading this book: as we go through the rest of this chapter, I want you to reject the belief that you (or anyone else, including me) are above or immune from eating disorders. We can't dabble in pathological behavior and expect to keep it under control. If we play with this fire, we *will* get burned. If this chapter upsets, frightens, or distresses you, consider seeking help, even if you don't think you have a text-book eating disorder.

What Are Eating Disorders?

Eating disorders are detectable illnesses that affect the sufferer's physical, psychological, spiritual, emotional, and relationship life. They are not a passing fad or the fashionable illness *de jour* of the rich and famous. Modern medicine has recognized eating disorders for many years as diagnosable, life-threatening conditions suffered by people (primarily women) of all socioeconomic classes. This isn't a new phenomenon either; in centuries-old documents, medical historians find regular mention of symptoms that are recognized today as eating disorders.

Calling this type of illness "eating" disorders can easily misdirect us from some important truths. Anorexia, bulimia, and other eating disorders *involve* food and eating (or not eating), but they are not really *about* eating. It may help us think more clearly about eating disorders if we imagine the illness having a different name, something like: body image addiction, mirror obsession, mirror distortion syndrome, perfection disorder, or bad body talk. The central issue for a woman with eating disorders is how she feels about her life, the pressures she feels to prove her self-worth, and the destructive behaviors and attitudes she employs to try to feel (and be seen as) valuable.

For women in our Body Myth culture, proving our worth gets tangled together with the fear of being fat, or not thin enough. Self-image entangles with cultural attitudes to foster fat phobia, weightism, and

"thin-itis," thereby normalizing and validating unhealthy and haz-
ardous practices. Because our culture fosters these dangerous behaviors, we have difficulty knowing the difference between what is
healthy and what is pathological.

The shape and progression of eating disorders change as women
age. Some women recover from severe eating disorders in their youth
but still have subclinical obsessions (which means having some, but
not all, of the symptoms that indicate a full-blown eating disorder)
with their eating or appearance. Their symptoms may change over
time, morphing into exercise abuse, overcontrol of their or their family's food intake, constant anxiety and rumination about their body
and appearance, obsessive shopping, or repeated cosmetic surgeries.
Because these habits seem normal in our culture, they are harder to
recognize than, say, severe anorexia. Therefore the problems go
unidentified by us, our health care providers, or our loved ones.
Meanwhile many adult sufferers wonder if they need or deserve help
because they no longer fit the clinical, teenage stereotype of someone
who has an eating disorder.

Like alcoholism, an eating disorder is not caused by a moral failure or lack of willpower. It is a real, treatable medical illness in which
certain maladaptive eating patterns take on a life of their own. These
serious disturbances in eating behavior include extreme reduction of
food intake, severe overeating, and distress or extreme concern about
body shape or weight. Researchers have yet to nail down exactly how
and why initially voluntary behaviors, like dieting, develop into an
eating disorder for some people but not for others.

Types of Eating Disorders

Anorexia Nervosa

People with anorexia nervosa can look in a mirror and perceive themselves as fat even when they are dangerously thin. Eating becomes an
obsession involving abnormal habits, like weighing food and keeping
a strict account of caloric intake. A woman with anorexia may skip
meals entirely, eat only certain foods (and those only in small por-
tions), weigh her body obsessively, exercise compulsively, vomit, and
use stimulants, laxatives, enemas, and diuretics in misguided
attempts to lose weight.

A woman struggling with anorexia denies that she has a problem and may develop elaborate excuses, rationalizations, and behaviors to convince herself and others that nothing is wrong. Her sense of worth and sense of self are determined primarily, if not exclusively, by her body shape. She has an intense fear of becoming fat and will resist eating normally or maintaining an average weight for her age and height. Her ovulation and menstruation are disrupted and may cease altogether.

Some people fully recover after a single episode of anorexia. Some go through fluctuating patterns of weight gain and relapse. Others slide steadily down a chronically deteriorating course of illness over many years. The National Institute of Mental Health estimates anorexia's mortality rate at about twelve times higher than any other cause of death among females ages fifteen to twenty-four in the general population. Among all mental illnesses, anorexia has the highest mortality rate. The most common causes of death are cardiac arrest, electrolyte imbalance, and suicide.

The picture doesn't get prettier after age twenty-four. The longer a woman suffers from an eating disorder, the more likely she will have severe medical problems—or die. For example, 5 percent of women with anorexia are likely to die after enduring five years of the illness; after twenty years with anorexia, the mortality rate increases to between 15 and 20 percent. (Alcohol abuse among women with eating disorders increases mortality risk and is associated with deaths related to both medical deterioration and to suicide.) While the threshold for serious medical problems and death is different for each person, our bodies can only take so much abuse. Also, since our bodies are less resilient as they age, we play a dangerous game if we abuse them with eating disorders, addiction, or other unhealthy behaviors.

In chapter 2's discussion of metabolism, we saw how the body slows down and uses fat stores when facing a restriction of food intake. Faced with the chronic food restriction of anorexia, the body eventually starts consuming the fat and then breaks down the muscle in vital organs like the heart, causing irreversible damage and, sometimes, organ failure. The disease also consumes self-worth and breaks down the vital psychological will to live, which is why many women with anorexia commit suicide.

Here are some common health risks associated with anorexia nervosa:

- Abnormally low blood pressure, which means that the heart muscle is weakening. The risk for heart failure rises as heart rate and blood pressure levels sink.

- Muscle loss and weakness.

- Severe dehydration.

- Kidney failure

- Reduction of bone density (osteoporosis), which results in dry, brittle bones that are more likely to fracture, causing other health problems.

- Irregular and/or absent menstrual periods.

- Infertility

- Fainting, fatigue, and overall weakness.

- Dry hair, dry skin, and hair loss.

- Growth of a downy layer of hair called lanugo all over the body, including the face, in an effort to keep the body warm. (Lanugo is the hair a newborn has for warmth but quickly loses.)

- Increased anxiety, depression, and irritability.

- Poor concentration and obsessive thoughts about food, weight, and appearance.

- Increased self-doubt and sensitivity to rejection.

- Premature death.

Anorexia nervosa is a frightening and stubborn illness. Researchers are still examining the numerous contributing factors and searching for more effective ways to treat and prevent it. There is no quick-fix for anorexia, but most sufferers will recover with proper care. However, in the more serious cases, recovery can take an average of five to seven years.

Bulimia Nervosa

A woman with bulimia engages in a cycle euphemistically called bingeing and purging. As with anorexia, bulimia's symptoms include being in strong denial, having a distorted perception of body image, and the sufferer deeply believing that her body shape and weight determine her worth.

A woman with bulimia will compulsively and repeatedly eat excessive amounts of food over a short time. She feels out of control during these binges. After a binge, she will take extreme steps to keep from gaining any additional weight from consuming all that food.

These steps include self-induced vomiting, obsessive exercise, extreme fasting, and abuse of laxatives, enemas, diuretics, and other drugs. Bulimic bingeing and purging are almost always done in secret, and sufferers usually go to great lengths to hide their behavior. They are ashamed and disgusted with themselves while bingeing and purging, although the behaviors may bring temporary emotional release, relief, and/or a numbing of feelings.

Researchers estimate that between 1 and 4 percent of women develop bulimia during their lifetime. A woman with bulimia may be harder to recognize than one with anorexia. Since people with bulimia continue to eat (with overeating compensated for by purging), they often fall within the normal weight range for their age and height. However, they share the anorexic's fear of gaining pounds, obsessive desire to lose weight, and deep dissatisfaction with their bodies.

The health consequences of bulimia are all negative:

- Electrolyte imbalances that can lead to irregular heartbeats, cardiac or respiratory arrest, and premature death. This is due to the loss of potassium and other nutrients from the body as a result of purging behaviors.

- Inflammation, tearing, and possible rupture of the esophagus from frequent vomiting.

- Tooth decay and staining from stomach acids released during frequent vomiting.

- Chronic irregular bowel movements and constipation as a result of laxative abuse.

- Muscle aches, fatigue, dizziness, and a general sense of malaise.

- Increased self-consciousness, self-doubt, depression, isolation, and shame.

- Loss of concentration.

- Increased emotional volatility.

- Irregular or absent menstrual periods.

Clinicians officially diagnose bulimia when the patient is bingeing and purging an average of twice a week over a three-month period. A significant number of women have symptoms of both anorexia and bulimia, or may alternate between bulimic and anorexic periods during the course of their illness.

Some women attempting to recover from anorexia have difficulty controlling or accepting new, healthy eating patterns, so they resort to purging, especially if they are not receiving adequate professional help. Similarly, some women with bulimia use anorexic behavior to cut their caloric intake severely as they try to avoid purging. There is more commonality than differences between bulimia and anorexia, especially in how they keep sufferers from dealing with shared fundamental issues.

Clinical experience shows that many underlying issues are common across ethnic lines, as well as between sufferers of one type of eating disorder and another. However, the ways particular eating disorders are expressed may differ among various ethnic groups. For example, African American women may be more likely to purge with laxatives than with vomiting; West Indian women may use Epsom salts or other purgatives; Native American or Latino women may be more likely to overeat and then severely restrict, and so on.

Eating Disorder Not Otherwise Specified

Therapists use eating disorder not otherwise specified (EDNOS) to describe serious eating disorders that are related, but not necessarily identical, to anorexia or bulimia. The line between EDNOS and other eating disorders is not black and white. The term itself is less than exact and sometimes interferes with acknowledging the real phenomenon that falls under the EDNOS label.

Many women display some signs of anorexia, or bulimia, or both, but they do not meet all the diagnostic criteria for either one. Still, they are suffering severe physical and psychological problems and face serious health risks. For example, they may have lost a significant number of pounds but still be in the normal weight range. They may miss some menstrual periods but not enough to cross the threshold for a medical diagnosis of anorexia.

Women with EDNOS may purge without bingeing, or they may purge less often than the frequency required to diagnose bulimia. Others may chew food and spit it out; they don't vomit, but they don't swallow what they eat either. Although discussed less frequently, these atypical eating disorders wreak just as much havoc in the lives of the women who suffer from them and bring many of the same physical and psychological dangers.

Binge Eating Disorder (BED)

People with binge eating disorder have frequent episodes of compulsive, out-of-control eating, similar to the bingeing seen with bulimia. The difference is that people with binge eating disorder (BED) do not usually purge after a binge. Because they don't purge excess calories, many people with BED are overweight for their age and height. The disease and cultural prejudice against fat people combine to produce feelings of self-disgust and shame in BED sufferers. This often leads to renewed cycles of binge eating.

A woman with binge eating disorder eats large quantities even when she doesn't feel hungry, eats more rapidly than normal, and/or eats until she is painfully full or falls asleep. An official diagnosis of BED requires bingeing twice a week for six months or longer.

The health risks of BED are closely associated with the risks of clinical obesity. They include:

- high blood pressure
- high cholesterol levels
- heart disease
- diabetes
- gallbladder disease
- depression

More men have BED than any other eating disorder, which makes sense, when we consider common male and female attitudes and fears. When it comes to body image, men are more afraid of being small and women are more afraid of being big. Hence the male drive to bulk up and the female drive to diet.

Compulsive Eating

While binge eaters consume a large amount of food quickly, in a very driven manner, compulsive eaters may instead constantly graze throughout the day, eating unconsciously and without regard to hunger. These behaviors evolve into the compulsive eater having a negative body image and feeling shame and embarrassment, which further isolates the individual from social supports, making food more important than ever.

Compulsive eaters can be any shape and size. This eating pattern usually causes weight gain, but some sufferers also abuse exercise or diet often enough that their weight stays within the normal range or yo-yos up and down in a predictable range. Still, the distress they have regarding their bodies overwhelms their self-image, eroding their quality of life.

Compulsive eating can pose the same physical threats as BED, as well as intense negative emotions in feeling that one's eating habits are out of control. A compulsive eater feels deep distress about her eating, self-image, and self-esteem and may try to compensate with numerous diets or fasts.

Many women with BED or compulsive eating are often simply seen as having weight problems and are referred to diet programs, which seldom work. Recovery and alternative coping mechanisms depend upon understanding the underlying emotional issues of self-worth and identity that build up and manifest themselves in food obsessions.

Orthorexia

Clinicians see an increasing number of patients who compulsively use and abuse health food or compulsively consume alternative foods. Although it is not yet recognized as a medical diagnosis, this behavior is known as orthorexia, which means "fixation on righteous eating." If a woman with orthorexia doesn't have access to her specific foods, she becomes extremely anxious and feels out of control. For her, health food takes on a much greater meaning.

"It's great to eat healthy food, and most of us could benefit by paying a little more attention to what we eat," according to Steven Bratman, M.D., the doctor credited with coining the term orthorexia. "However, some people have the opposite problem: they take the concept of healthy eating to such an extreme that it becomes an obsession."

We are bombarded with contradictory media reports about the healthy and unhealthy qualities of certain foods. Indeed, highly processed foods do contribute to a number of health problems. All this information sometimes feels overwhelming as we try to feed ourselves and our families. But concern about food can mushroom into something greater, especially as we get older and worry more about our health, youth, and beauty.

Orthorexics are health food junkies who actually become emaciated as fewer and fewer foods seem acceptable to them—or when they can't easily obtain health food, especially when traveling away from home. The so-called raw food movement often fosters orthorexia, and its practitioners can become deficient in protein, fat, and other essential nutrients. Some orthorexia patients have orange-tinted skin when they start treatment; by eating too many fruits and vegetables, they get too much of a good thing, like carotene.

Initially a lifestyle choice, an obsession about health foods can become an eating disorder as serious as anorexia or bulimia. Orthorexia interferes with the quality of life, contributes to depressed moods and anxiety, causes social isolation, and even shortens life expectancy. Despite the similarities between orthorexia and other eating disorders, the motivation for orthorexia is different.

The strongest desire for someone with anorexia, bulimia, and related disorders is to lose weight and change her appearance. In orthorexia, the first desire is to be pure, healthy, and natural. (The desire for purity can also affect people with other eating disorders.) As we'll see in chapter 8, recovery depends on understanding the multiple motivations underlying eating disorders.

Subclinical Eating Disorders

Psychologists and physicians have devised specific guidelines for diagnosing anorexia, bulimia, or binge eating disorder. If a woman's symptoms have less frequency and/or severity than a clinical eating disorder, she doesn't cross the "brink" of being diagnosed with one.

However, physicians and psychologists recognize that eating disorders occur along a continuum. Some women develop symptoms that harm the quality of their life but do not necessarily indicate a full-blown eating disorder.

For example, as mentioned earlier, the psychiatric indicators for a diagnosis of bulimia include purging at least twice a week for a period of at least three months. If a woman purges less frequently than that (say once a week or sporadically over the years), then she may not be diagnosed with bulimia, because her behavior doesn't meet the clinical criteria for that diagnosis. Similarly, a woman who severely restricts her food intake but hasn't crossed the severe weight-loss threshold indicated for an anorexia diagnosis, won't be diagnosed with it.

Of course, purging and severe food restriction are not natural or healthy, even if they don't rise to the clinical definition of bulimia or anorexia. Therefore, such a condition is known as a subclinical eating disorder. Even though the behaviors are subclinical, they still cause anxiety, sadness, and negative feelings as well as physical problems, including gastrointestinal disruption, impaired immune system, osteoporosis, and generally poor health. As of yet, we do not have scientifically reliable estimates of how many people have subclinical eating disorders, but most professionals in the field are concerned that it is a growing problem and see many cases that eventually develop into full-blown eating disorders.

Symptoms of subclinical eating disorders are similar to those for diagnosed eating disorders, but they occur with less frequency or intensity. A sufferer may switch among symptoms and go through stretches of eating normally. With that distinction in mind, the signs of subclinical eating disorders include:

- counting calories, fat grams, or carbohydrates every time she eats
- chronic restrictive dieting
- exercising obsessively in order to burn up calories consumed
- skipping meals as often as possible
- trying to go days without eating
- repeated weighings
- using laxatives, diuretics, diet pills, or other over-the-counter medications to lose weight
- wishing she was anorexic or bulimic
- engaging in some anorexic or bulimic behaviors, although inconsistently
- feeling guilty if she allows herself to enjoy food
- alternating between periods of excessive control and excessive indulgence with food
- cooking for others but not eating
- maintaining many rules about good versus bad food
- feelings of sinning, being immoral, or being bad when eating a forbidden food

- smoking cigarettes, chewing gum, or drinking coffee, soda, or water to avoid eating
- obsessively anticipating what food will not be eaten or how calories eaten will be burned up.

We could argue that these behaviors are normal for Western women. Unfortunately, we'd be correct, which is a frightening reflection on our culture (more on this in chapter 7). The biggest health concerns arise from repetition of these behaviors, and the level of emotional investment we make in them. If we determine our self-esteem and self-worth are based on what we've eaten and what we weigh—and we engage in these behaviors normally or frequently—we may have a subclinical eating disorder. When women with subclinical eating disorders feel overwhelmed by adult stressors, some will slip down into the pit of fully diagnosable eating disorders.

The Shape of Our Relationship to Food and Our Bodies

In her thought-provoking book, *Like Mother, Like Daughter: How Women Are Influenced by Their Mothers' Relationship with Food—and How to Break the Pattern*, Debra Waterhouse reports the following statistics about adult women:

- 96 percent worry about their weight.
- 60 percent have engaged in pathogenic weight control (repeated dieting, skipping meals, fasting, laxatives, diuretics, vomiting, excessive exercise).
- Only 6 percent say they like their bodies.
- The most disliked body part is the thigh (where fat is actually associated with a *decreased* risk for cardiovascular disease) followed by stomach, hips, and buttocks.
- The average woman has dieted away 100 pounds over her lifetime but regained 125.
- 60 percent can be described as disordered eaters (80 percent of teen girls can be).
- 90 percent have a poor body image.
- 40 percent are restrained eaters, denying themselves pleasure with food.
- 40 percent are overeaters who indulge and then feel guilty.

- Only 20 percent are instinctive eaters who eat moderately, what they want, without guilt.

- 60 percent believe they should only eat low-fat foods.

- 50 percent say their eating is devoid of pleasure and causes them to feel guilty.

- The average U.S. woman eats fewer than 1,500 calories a day (about what a toddler needs) and doesn't lose weight.

So is dieting *always* an early warning sign of a potential eating disorder? One quick test is whether we stop dieting once we reach our goal. Diets are unpleasant because success depends on constantly depriving ourselves. Therefore, on many levels, the desired conclusion of a diet is to end it as soon as possible and not subject ourselves to another one. But if we never stop these dieting cycles, or if we equate dieting with self-control and moral strength, our diets may warn of something more serious. Our food deprivation may be masking other issues.

Remember that undereating actually lowers metabolism, so dieting usually ends up adding weight. The average woman today eats two hundred calories less than she did thirty years ago but weighs eight pounds more! Between the slower metabolism and the rebound eating that follow most diets, it is very easy to gain weight, continuing the cycle of body image despair, poor nutrition, and shame.

Self Assessment Tool

Do this exercise alone, at a time when you won't be interrupted. Read each statement, and fill in the response that best reflects how you feel and think right now. Be honest with your responses; no one will judge you on your answers. For each statement, choose from these five possible answers: **A**ll the Time, **F**requently, **S**ometimes, **R**arely, or **N**ever.

	A	F	S	R	N
I read about dieting or weight loss obsessively.	☐	☐	☐	☐	☐
I make excuses for not eating.	☐	☐	☐	☐	☐

	A	F	S	R	N
I skip meals intentionally.	☐	☐	☐	☐	☐
I try to go as long as possible without eating.	☐	☐	☐	☐	☐
I diet or restrict my food intake.	☐	☐	☐	☐	☐
I avoid social situations that involve food.	☐	☐	☐	☐	☐
I eat secretly.	☐	☐	☐	☐	☐
I have strict rules about food.	☐	☐	☐	☐	☐
I believe that some foods are good and some are bad.	☐	☐	☐	☐	☐
I only feel safe eating certain foods.	☐	☐	☐	☐	☐
I obsess about food.	☐	☐	☐	☐	☐
I feel guilty if I break my rules about food or eat something I didn't plan.	☐	☐	☐	☐	☐
I worry about my weight.	☐	☐	☐	☐	☐
I watch what others eat and compare my intake with theirs.	☐	☐	☐	☐	☐
I chew gum or suck on hard candy to avoid eating.	☐	☐	☐	☐	☐
I smoke cigarettes to curb my appetite, avoid eating, and maintain my weight.	☐	☐	☐	☐	☐
I drink diet soda, coffee, tea, or water to avoid eating and feel full.	☐	☐	☐	☐	☐
I cook for others but refuse to eat those foods.	☐	☐	☐	☐	☐
I count calories, fat grams, protein grams, or carbohydrates.	☐	☐	☐	☐	☐
I use food to reward or punish myself.	☐	☐	☐	☐	☐
I feel out of control about my eating.	☐	☐	☐	☐	☐
I take laxatives, diet pills, diuretics, metabolism boosters, or other supplements to control my weight.	☐	☐	☐	☐	☐
I have had irregular menstrual periods or infertility problems.	☐	☐	☐	☐	☐

Before tallying your responses, acknowledge how you felt while taking this assessment and how you feel afterward.

Look at the pattern of your responses. If most are in the Never or Rarely category, your eating concerns are probably manageable and do not interfere with the quality of your life. The more you checked Sometimes, Frequently, or All the Time, the greater the probability that you have an eating problem. Talk this over with a trusted friend and consider making an appointment with a therapist who specializes in this area. Your feelings alone may indicate whether you are suffering unduly and would benefit from some form of therapy.

Beyond Eating Disorders: Body Image Distress

Despair, dissatisfaction, and shame about the body are not the exclusive domain of women with diagnosable eating disorders. Many readers who do not yet see themselves described in this chapter may still battle body hatred on a regular (if not constant) basis.

This section is for those women, because it explains how the struggle with body image may manifest itself in serious problems beyond eating disorders. In fact, some problems related to body image are so severe that they reach the level of diagnosable disorders themselves.

This may be hard for most women to believe. After all, many of the symptoms we will discuss seem like a routine part of our everyday lives. However, they only seem typical because the Body Myth and our culture's impossible standards for women *normalize* body image despair. Sadly, this normalcy doesn't diminish the harm. In fact, body image struggles can infect our lives and become so incapacitating that they require intense psychological intervention.

Body Dysmorphic Disorder

This psychiatric term describes preoccupation with an imagined defect in our appearance or an exaggerated reaction to a slight defect. Someone with body dysmorphic disorder (BDD) overreacts or reacts uncontrollably (that is, pathologically) to moles, freckles, acne, minor scars or skin discoloration, hair on her face, body, or head, and the shape and size of breasts, muscles, and genitalia. One or more of these supposed defects can trigger significant emotional distress and erode our overall ability to function normally. People with BDD avoid social situations and often develop other problems like depression, anxiety, and phobias.

Some actresses and models admit to having BDD, despite how perfect their bodies may look to the rest of us, because body image is not a rational thing. Instead, our body image is usually constructed on the insecurity and self-doubt endemic to a culture that constantly assaults women with unattainable images of beauty and achievement. The irony is that even the rare women who meet today's narrow definition of beauty often don't feel beautiful!

BDD includes the following behaviors:

- often gazing into mirrors or avoiding them
- obsessively grooming
- obsessively using clothes or makeup to conceal real or imagined flaws
- making repeated medical visits to dermatologists or plastic surgeons to treat the perceived problem
- constantly comparing your appearance to others' appearance
- constantly fishing for compliments or reassurance about appearance

These symptoms look like pretty normal behaviors for most women in a culture where entire industries like cosmetics, fashion, magazines, beauty, fitness, and even areas of medicine are built on the premise that something is wrong with us that we must change immediately.

So if these behaviors are normal, how can they constitute a disorder? Doesn't "disorder" suggest *ab*normal? In a sense, it does. But medicine and psychiatry refer to a disorder as being a sickness, disturbance, or disease. The level of discord seen in body dysmorphic disorder is unnatural; it disturbs the norms of nature. Unfortunately, the same discord is often the norm for women in our culture. The logical conclusion is this: our cultural norms are themselves disturbed and disordered.

Chapter 7 will explore this cultural contradiction in more depth, but meanwhile let's take a simple example. Many cultural norms apply more often to women than they do to men, and vice versa. Therefore a simple way to examine the underpinnings of a cultural norm is to imagine applying it to the opposite gender.

Let's try it. Imagine a *man* who engages in:

- repetitive mirror gazing or avoidance of mirrors
- obsessive grooming
- obsessively using clothes or makeup to conceal real or imagined flaws
- repeated medical visits to dermatologists or plastic surgeons to treat the perceived problem

We don't have to imagine a man like that; we find a real example in Michael Jackson, the celebrity singer who has undergone repeated plastic surgeries and is said to wear makeup twenty-four hours a day. Most people consider Jackson's appearance-related behavior abnormal, obsessive, inexplicable, and a sign of mental and emotional disturbance. Perhaps he has body dysmorphic disorder.

With women, however, not only do we let the same behaviors pass without comment, but we also usually expect them. For example, many of us don't even let our lovers see us unprotected by a 24/7 armor of makeup and coiffed hair. Many of us will only be intimate in the dark, because we are afraid or ashamed of being seen naked, even by our own closest partners.

Perhaps this is why some women feel relief at being diagnosed with BDD; it helps make sense of their obsessions, releasing them from feeling isolated and freakish. These women are not alone, despite how isolated they feel. Self-consciousness, self-scrutiny, and self-doubt are part of the body image norm that envelops nearly all women in Western culture.

Exercise Abuse

Exercise can be an effective and enjoyable stress reliever and a source of solace, achievement, and strength. It can also become a way that women punish themselves for feelings of inadequacy. Many of us exercise primarily to change our bodies, not to enjoy them.

Adult female celebrities like Oprah Winfrey, Demi Moore, and Cher dedicate a large portion of their waking hours to rigid exercise regimens that are overseen by personal trainers. Younger generations of stars also live as though success and riches require exercise frenzy in pursuit of the perfect body. If we believe magazines and talk shows, these are the women we should emulate, making fitness one more area where we may fall short of the female ideal.

Exercise abuse is exactly what it sounds like: mistreatment of our bodies through physical exertion. Too much exercise combined with too little nutritional intake can push the body into a dangerous slowing of metabolism that lowers all of our body's basic functions, like pulse, blood pressure, and temperature. This state, called hypometabolism, disrupts the body's enzymatic reactions and immune system, making us more vulnerable to bacterial, fungal, and viral infections. It produces symptoms like anxiety, depression, intolerance for heat and cold, hives, dry skin, hair loss, unhealthy nails, insomnia, fluid retention, asthma, fatigue, headaches, irritability—and reduction in ambition, motivation, sex drive, concentration, and memory. As we learned in chapter 2, a slowed metabolism also makes it harder to lose those hated pounds, so we have to exercise more to reach our goal, continuing the downward spiral.

Exercise abuse also leads to overtraining syndrome, which brings physical exhaustion, diminished performance, fatigue, stiffness, aches and pains, and a general lack of strength. It can also result in chronic injuries such as torn muscles, ligaments, or tendons, stress fractures, and even osteoarthritis. If we are not eating well, recovery from these injuries takes much longer. As fat stores become depleted, muscle tissues are also laid waste. In extreme cases, or when we put additional stress on the body (for example, from using laxatives, diet pills, or purging), exercise abuse can bring on cardiac problems and sudden death.

Here is a list I created to help my patients tell the difference between healthy exercise and excess exercise:

- I judge a day as good or bad based on how much I exercised.
- I base my self-worth on how much I exercise.
- I never take a break from exercise, no matter how I feel or how inconvenient it is.
- I exercise even though I am injured.
- I arrange work and social obligations around exercise.
- I cancel family or social engagements to exercise.
- I become angry, anxious, or agitated when something interferes with my exercise.

- I know others are worried about how much I exercise, but I don't listen to them.
- I always have to do more (laps, miles, weights) and rarely feel satisfied with what I have done.
- I count how many calories I burn while exercising.
- I exercise to compensate for eating too much.

A Warning to Athletes:
Not Eating Can't Help You Win

Poor nutrition and low caloric intake undermine the purpose of exercise, even for athletes. It wastes training time, depresses metabolic rate, and can lead to serious eating disorders.

When food and fluid intake are too low, athletes experience:

Poor Training Benefit

- Energy intake is too low to meet training demands.
- Carbohydrate intake is too low for optimal recovery from training.
- Fluid intake is too low to rehydrate optimally after training.
- Performance shows minimal or no improvement.

Early Fatigue

- Low levels of muscle glycogen limit capacity for high-intensity exercise.
- Dehydration limits exercise and impairs body temperature regulation.
- Low iron stores increase risk of anemia and compromise work capacity.

Reduced Muscle Strength, Muscle Endurance, Speed, and Coordination

- Weight loss reduces muscle mass.
- Muscle is broken down to provide fuel for movement.
- Less able to meet training demands.

Low Blood Sugar

- Less able to concentrate.
- Poor judgment and decision-making ability.
- Feelings of hunger, fatigue, light-headedness.
- May precipitate overeating, followed by guilt and sometimes by purging.

Increased Risk of Injury and Illness

- Stress fractures.
- Respiratory illness.

Extended Recovery Time after Injury or Illness

Feelings of Inadequacy, Anxiety, Anger, Irritability, Depression, and Loneliness

While exercise can be a very positive way to diffuse difficult feelings, our hours at the gym or track can become addictive distractions, preventing us from addressing our emotional, relational, and spiritual shape. If exercise is our only coping mechanism, we open the door to abusive excess exercise, sliding from self-discipline into self-destruction. Our bottom-line question about fitness should be: "Is my fitness goal to *be* strong and healthy or to *look* good?"

The Shape of Substances

Women spend billions each year on pills, supplements, and other products in hopes we will magically eliminate weight and reshape our bodies. Some widely used supplements turn out to be quite dangerous, even though they are benignly packaged and sold as health products in drug stores, nutrition centers, and health food catalogs. Others are totally ineffectual and harmless, except to our pocketbooks and psyches, since we want so badly to lose weight. These drugs are seductively marketed to seem like the answer when nothing else seems to help.

Most over-the-counter diet drugs and appetite suppressants contain caffeine and/or amphetamines (central nervous system stimulants). Both substances can generate jitters, anxiety, headaches, and sleeplessness. Depending on the drug's potency and the body's reactions, our hearts can race too fast, causing cardiac problems and even heart attacks.

The *New England Journal of Medicine* and the National Task Force on Prevention and Treatment of Obesity recommend that diet drugs be used *only* in extreme cases and when *closely monitored* by a physician. However, many of us take these heavy drugs lightly—and repeatedly. Research regularly exposes serious health risks stemming from some commonly used drugs, forcing a few off the market. But that doesn't seem to stop our search for a pill-shaped weight-loss chimera.

By the late 1990s, more than nine million adults (mostly women) were taking over-the-counter diet pills with phenylpropanolamine, a central nervous system stimulant found in appetite suppressants (and cold medicines). After over twenty years on the market, research found that people taking phenylpropanolamine (PPA) have a 1,558 percent higher risk of strokes! That isn't a typo: the stroke risk is one thousand, five hundred fifty-eight percent higher. The Food and Drug Administration warned the public about phenylpropanolamine and asked pharmaceutical companies to stop selling products containing it. Yet PPA remains in many diet and nondiet products.

Similarly, the FDA banned continued U.S. sale of fen-phen, the diet drug combination of fenfluramine and phentermine. Responding to an FDA request, manufacturers pulled fenfluramine and another diet drug dexfenfluramine (trade name Redux) after studies showed as many as 30 percent of users developed significant medical problems resulting in heart valve defects or primary pulmonary hypertension (usually a fatal condition). Even short-term use was found dangerous—one otherwise healthy young woman, trying to lose weight for her wedding, died after taking fen-phen for only three weeks. Although fenfluramine and dexfenfluramine have been banned, women who took them may have side effects requiring expensive and intense medical follow-up for the rest of their lives.

Until recently, ephedra (or ephedrine or pseudoephedrine; also available as the herb ma huang) was a very popular weight-loss drug and metabolism booster. Ephedra increases heart rate and blood pressure, and it *sometimes* causes weight loss, but with a very high risk. When combined with caffeine and other ingredients, it is associated with heart attacks, strokes, seizures, tremors, anxiety, insomnia, and even death. After numerous studies, the Food and Drug Administration banned ephedra at the end of 2003. However, there is concern that it may reappear in some other form or become easily available on the street (or in the gym).

Women often use products designed for another purpose (like laxatives) in an attempt to shed pounds. Over-the-counter cathartic laxatives like Dulcolax can be very dangerous when used in excess, depending on the ingredients and how our bodies react to taking them. (Cathartic laxatives use a different means of relieving constipation than bulk laxatives like Metamucil.) However, cathartic laxatives actually produce little real weight loss, because our bodies absorb most nutrients and calories at higher levels of the gastrointestinal system. Instead, laxative abuse can (and does) cause dehydration followed by rebound water retention.

Abusive cycles of laxative-induced dehydration and rebound water retention cause weight shifts that can be very distressing and keep the cycles going. Bloating leads to feeling fat; this leads to more laxative use, which leads to dehydration, and then more rebound water-retention bloating, and so on. This dehydration–water retention cycle creates chemical changes that can lead to electrolyte imbalances, cardiac arrhythmias, heart attacks, and even death. Additional ingredients in laxatives may irritate the stomach and bowel, causing cramping and gastric distress.

Furthermore, cathartic laxatives allow the colon to get lazy; if we stop taking them, we end up constipated. Therefore, laxatives set up addictionlike patterns; once we depend on them, our bodies need them to function normally. As with addictive drugs, the only safe way to stop laxative abuse is to taper off under close medical supervision.

Unfortunately, medical professionals often miss the signs of laxative abuse. A woman with gastric distress or dehydration may get an extensive gastrointestinal work-up from her physician, rather than being asked to answer simple questions to uncover her pattern of laxative use. To be more effective helping female patients, health care professionals must routinely ask questions about weight management and the use of supplements or over-the-counter medicines (more on effective medical intervention in chapter 5).

Some women respond to body image distress with near-religious pursuit of extreme measures like colonics and fasting, pursuing them with near-religious passion. At colonics retreat spas we can pay $3,500 a week to not eat and empty out our systems. Highly profitable businesses like this laugh all the way to the bank as they manipulate and feed off our culturally crippled body image.

This section has barely scratched the surface of dangerous substances that risk our health while failing to deliver what they promise. Given their profitability, popular diet products and services change each season, with something new always being offered as *the* magic weight-loss formula. But we stubbornly refuse to learn our lesson.

That brings to mind the old folk definition of insanity: doing the same thing over and over again, but expecting different results. When it comes to diet products, caveat emptor! (buyer beware.) Or, better yet, let's keep our own money or give it to worthwhile causes and charities.

Cosmetic Plastic Surgery

Attitudes about plastic surgery have changed dramatically. Thirty years ago, the stereotypical plastic surgery patient was a vain, self-centered, and wealthy older woman with too much time and money on her hands.

Nowadays, elective cosmetic surgery is considered almost as normal as visiting the beauty parlor. In 2003, 45 percent of cosmetic surgery was performed on people age thirty-five to fifty, 23 percent on people ages fifty-one to sixty-four, and only 5 percent on those over age sixty-five. (To round out the data, 3 percent was done on people younger than eighteen and 24 percent on nineteen- to thirty-four-year-olds.) It almost goes without saying that the vast majority of elective plastic surgery is done on women (82 percent in 2003).

Let's be clear: what we're discussing here is *aesthetic*, cosmetic, plastic surgery, not reconstructive plastic surgery that repairs *medical* problems like cleft palate or a radical mastectomy. The American Society of Plastic Surgeons (ASPS) calls this elective surgery, which it defines as "action to proactively manage signs of aging or [to] enhance appearance." If that sounds like marketing language, it is. Plastic surgeons make their biggest profits when people elect to have surgery; without aesthetic surgeries, the pool of patients stays limited to people needing medically necessary reconstructive procedures.

Plastic surgery marketing reached new heights with ABC's highly rated reality show *Extreme Makeover*. More than ten thousand people attended casting calls or sent written applications in the show's first season, vying to get what producers call "a truly Cinderella-like experience: a real-life fairy tale in which their wishes come true, not just to change their looks, but their lives and destinies."

Plastic surgeons, eye surgeons, cosmetic dentists, hair stylists, and makeup artists put participants through various operations and other procedures, culminating in what the producers call "a climactic unveiling—'the after'—when the candidates reveal their new selves to their families and friends." Among *Extreme Makeover*'s many ironies is how the reality show is literally based on making people less real than when they started.

A Fox TV series, *The Swan*, takes normal women, also known as "ugly ducklings," and uses plastic surgery and makeovers to ready them for competition in the official Swan Pageant. Each week, contestants go through a boot camp regimen of exercise, dieting, and "therapy" to reach their goals. They are assigned a team of specialists: a trainer, life coach, therapist, plastic surgeon, and dentist. Each week, two transformed women are featured, and one wins the opportunity to participate in the annual Swan Pageant and become The Ultimate Swan.

The success of shows like *The Swan* and *Extreme Makeover* reflects the explosion in elective cosmetic surgery. According to ASPS, the 2002 ratio of elective to reconstructive surgery was 51 to 49. In 2003, it leapt to 59 to 41, a huge jump that owes a lot to intense marketing. (ASPS inexplicably lists breast reduction and breast implant *removal* as reconstructive procedures; the elective surgery statistics soar even higher when those numbers are moved into the elective column.)

According to ASPS statistics, more than 8.7 million elective cosmetic surgeries were performed in the United States during 2003—up 32 percent from 2002 (and up 2,175 percent from 1992). The top five cosmetic surgeries in 2003 were nose reshaping (356,554), liposuction (320,022), breast augmentation (254,140), eyelid surgery (246,633), and face-lift (128,667). These staggering numbers are actually *low* estimates because they do not include procedures done by medical aestheticians, or by physicians who don't submit data to ASPS.

Plastic surgeons are opening clinics in shopping centers and other locations that convey the notion that cosmetic surgery should be as ordinary and frequent as getting our hair done at the beauty parlor next door. In this environment, some of us offhandedly decide to get a quick nip or tuck, without much thought or planning. After Sarah finished a therapy session with me, she impulsively stopped at a plastic surgeon's office in the same office building and had Botox injections, without any advance scheduling or consultation. After

developing an allergic reaction and infection, Sarah blamed herself
for wasting her money, saying, "This was one more stupid mistake; I
do these things all the time, when it's really about how I feel about
myself and my life. When I do this impulsive stuff, I keep on screw-
ing things up more. And I end up feeling worse about myself."

Ashamed that she had once more succumbed to a quick fix for her
deeper problems, Sarah was angry with herself. She felt like a failure,
and even told me that she saw the infection as a justified punishment.
The ease and convenience of Sarah's Botox treatment masked its real
meaning and impact.

Techniques like Botox injections, chemical peels, microdermabra-
sion, permanent makeup, and laser hair removal don't require major
surgery, so they appear less threatening or extreme. Yet all of these
procedures can have complications, and the idea of being injected
with synthetic botulism still seems like something that should give us
pause.

Since the effects of most so-called nonsurgical procedures don't
endure, the process needs to be repeated in order to achieve the same
effect. As a result, having such procedures can become somewhat
addictive. Botox and collagen injections last only a few months at
best. Surgical techniques like eye lifts or face-lifts need to be repeated
in most cases. The optimal scenario for breast implants is surgical
repair or replacement every ten to fifteen years—much sooner if the
implant leaks or ruptures. Some cosmetic surgeries improve one feature but leave the rest of the face or body looking out of sync, so it's
back to the drawing board. Once we get on that merry-go-round of
surgical self-improvement, it's hard to get off.

During her first therapy session, an intelligent, attractive adult
woman named Elaine reported that she finally got motivated to stop
vomiting after deciding to have her "face done." Elaine explained
that she did not want to waste the money she'd spent on the face-lift,
and she knew that if she continued to vomit, the results wouldn't last.
Unfortunately, instead of vomiting, Elaine started restricting her food
intake and abusing laxatives. Despite being an interesting and
resourceful woman, Elaine never sought help for these problems
until it was almost too late; she nearly died after over thirty years of
self-inflicted body abuse. Clearly, neither surgery nor disordered eating behaviors helped Elaine confront and resolve her core problems.

Does cosmetic plastic surgery ever help women struggling with
issues about body image? Not if they have eating or body dysmor-

phic disorders In one study, 83 percent of women with BDD had either no improvement or an increase in their distress after electing to have cosmetic surgery. In another more recent study, the number was 93 percent. Women with eating disorders often have *increased* body image disturbance after cosmetic plastic surgery, because the core issues that resulted in the condition are still present.

The Smoking Gun

What's the number one reason girls start smoking tobacco? They think it will help them stay thin. Concerns about body image and weight also increase adult women's cigarette use, along with adverse emotional states like depression or anxiety. Although the number of U.S. women who smoke declined between the 1960s and the late 1990s, recent data shows another increase in our tobacco use; about 20 percent of us now smoke. Adult women addicted to tobacco each spend thousands of dollars a year for cigarettes while increasing their risks for serious health problems.

Few of us would consciously choose to manage our weight with heroin or cocaine, and yet nicotine is just as addictive. Cigarettes contain four thousand chemicals, forty of which are known to cause cancer. Women who smoke are twelve times more likely to develop lung cancer and twice as likely to have a heart attack. Women smokers have higher risk for strokes, circulatory problems, and lung disease (like chronic bronchitis and emphysema). The good news is that our bodies begin to heal within twelve hours of our last cigarette. Within twenty-four hours, our risk of heart attack starts dropping; within one year, the risk is half that for an active smoker.

But let's examine two basic assumptions women have about tobacco: (1) Smoking helps us lose weight, and (2) Quitting smoking makes us gain weight.

Women who smoke weigh an average of four pounds less than their peers who don't smoke. That's a plus, right? Well, only if we ignore the fact that women smokers die younger than nonsmokers, and tobacco-related illnesses such as lung and mouth cancer are not very attractive or fun. Neither are smelly clothes, stained teeth, and tobacco breath.

Many of us say we can't surrender our cigarette packs because quitting is sure to pack on the pounds. The National Institutes of Health reports that not everyone gains weight when they stop smoking. Some quitters have a short-term weight gain of three to five pounds (mostly due to water retention) and then return to the weight their bodies were meant to be. Most others gain an average of ten pounds. The highest weight gains are associated with decades of smoking more than a pack a day. The bottom line is: the health risks of smoking far outweigh the five or ten pounds we might gain. In fact, we would have to gain between *one hundred and five hundred* pounds to equal the health risk of continuing to smoke.

If you start smoking (or keep smoking) out of fear about your weight, now is the time to reconsider. The improvement in your health will be huge when you stop, even if you gain a few pounds. The people who love you will be really relieved—and also will have a radically reduced risk of lung and heart disease from secondhand smoke. Plus, you'll eventually enjoy life more than ever and have quite a bit more money in your pockets.

Extinguishing the Smoke

The first six months are the hardest after quitting smoking. It does get easier. Most women have several relapses before being able to quit completely—expect that to be part of the process. Here are some helpful thoughts.

- Your teeth and breath will be cleaner.
- Your appearance will actually improve!
- The stains on your fingers and nails will fade.
- Your skin will be less wrinkled.
- Your lung capacity will improve, so exercise and endurance will also improve. Some women don't have any problem with weight gain because they actually feel so much better and can do more physically!
- You don't have to do this alone; local hospitals, HMOs, or American Lung Association chapters have smoking cessation programs in your area.
- Talk to your doctor about medical interventions, like nicotine replacement (the patch, spray, or inhaler) or prescription medication.

- Ask friends to help you by encouraging your abstinence, providing moral support, and not smoking around you.

- Plan concrete changes in your lifestyle, even if they seem small. If you always smoked after dinner, plan a phone date with your best friend, go for a walk, or arrange another distraction instead. Change daily routines to help break the natural impulse to light up.

- Decide what to do with the money you are saving; plan a vacation or a special purchase that will give you enjoyment.

- Visit www.4Woman.gov for helpful hints and links to other Web sites.

- Don't expect yourself to be perfect—even reducing your smoking will help!

Compulsive Shopping

Shopping seems normal, innocuous, and even necessary. Often it is. But shopping can also be a compulsive way to avoid feelings of emptiness, insecurity, loneliness, and inadequacy, especially for women with eating disorders and body image problems.

In our culture, being an intense consumer often feels as normal as hating our body image. We are socialized to believe that wanting and obtaining an inanimate product will satisfy deep, living longings in our souls. Women suffering from eating and body image disorders frequently shop compulsively for cosmetics, clothes, home furnishings, cars, jewelry, or other expensive items that falsely promise the solace these women desperately seek.

For example, many of us obsess about beauty products. Women in the United States spend tens of millions of dollars every week to temporarily change the hue of our hair, skin, and eyes. We spend endless hours applying these products and maintaining a look, believing that cosmetics will make a substantial difference in our lives. But cosmetics can never deliver on that promise.

Our consumer culture provides constant sources of distraction from our deeper needs and makes handsome profits in the process. The energy absorbed by shopping helps keep women occupied in a futile cycle of trying to make their bodies meet others' expectations.

I thought I should know, intuitively, how to be that [ideal] woman, how to combine sexuality and ambition, how to navigate all those fuzzy lines between femininity and authority, relationships and autonomy. And not knowing these things intuitively, I thought I was missing something . . . or . . . might acquire something only if I looked in the right places . . . if only, if only. This is what's insidious about consumerism: It's not that it encourages us to shop but that it encourages us to forget, not that it sparks need but that it dilutes it, shrink-wraps it and flings it into the handiest and most tangible containers.

—Caroline Knapp

But love and fulfillment can't be bought (or even found) at the mall. The more we shop for self-worth, the fewer our chances of satisfying our profound longings—and the more money retailers make off us.

Just as an active anorexic will never be a weight that's good enough for her, a compulsive shopper can search and spend forever without ever finding what she really seeks. Instead of dealing directly with the inner emptiness, she tries to squeeze into smaller sizes, obsessively comparing the size 2s at one store with the size 2s at another store, desperate to fit into the smallest size possible.

Of course, this doesn't mean we can never spend another dime at the mall. A little shopping can be a satisfying bit of retail therapy. A fun outfit, new haircut, or sun-drenched skin can feel great, and rightly so. Shopping can be a way to express our own sense of style, show ourselves kindness, reward ourselves when there isn't time to do more, or to connect with a friend by spending some time together. In fact, healthy shopping can be the modern equivalent of what gathering was/is for women in hunting and gathering societies: a chance to be together, roam around, look at what we and our families need, and bring it back home.

Not every dollar or minute spent shopping is wasted. But we must recognize whether our shopping has gone over the edge into an addictionlike avoidance. If shopping feels like the only safe way for us to spend time together, then we must examine the shape of our relationships with friends and relatives (particularly Mom). Finally, we must investigate how much of our time and energy is misplaced—

and can never be retrieved—as we vainly (in both senses of the word) try to use products to change our natural state.

Now that we've described the havoc and damage that can result from eating and body image disorders, it's time we asked who is at risk, why those women start down this dangerous road, and why it is so difficult for them to change direction.

Check Out Your Shopping

On her Web site, www.stoppingovershopping.com, April Lane Benson, Ph.D., offers these signs of compulsive buying or a shopping disorder:

- frequent buying binges
- spending inordinate amounts of time shopping on the Internet, shopping channels, and through toll-free phone numbers, and catalogs
- using shopping to avoid other things
- feeling high when shopping, but low or guilty afterward
- buying impulsively
- feeling out of control of your spending habits
- getting into debt, especially credit card debt
- hiding your purchases or bills from your partner
- believing that you will feel better if you buy something.

If these behaviors or feelings describe you, you may be using consumerism to cope with the shape of your life. Commit to change and work to understand how shopping relates to the shape you're in. A visit to this Web site could be the first stop.

The Shape of Your Body Image

Is body image distorting the shape of your life? Do this exercise alone, at a time when you won't be interrupted. Read each statement, and fill in the response that best reflects how you feel and think right now. Be honest with your responses;

no one will judge you on your answers. For each statement, choose from these five possible answers: **Never**, **Rarely**, **Sometimes**, **Often**, or **Usually**.

	N	R	S	O	U
I am ashamed of how I look.	☐	☐	☐	☐	☐
I compare my looks to other people's.	☐	☐	☐	☐	☐
I dissect my body into its parts instead of feeling at one with my whole body.	☐	☐	☐	☐	☐
I associate thinness or physical perfection with happiness, success, and self-control.	☐	☐	☐	☐	☐
I call myself fat, ugly, or gross aloud or in my thoughts.	☐	☐	☐	☐	☐
I am certain that others see me as fat or unattractive.	☐	☐	☐	☐	☐
I believe that life will be better if I lose weight, fit into a smaller size, or correct my body's defects.	☐	☐	☐	☐	☐
I dismiss, disregard, or disparage compliments from others.	☐	☐	☐	☐	☐
I feel unable to enjoy life because of my body shape or appearance.	☐	☐	☐	☐	☐
I feel dependent on what others say about my appearance, but still feel unable to believe anything positive they say.	☐	☐	☐	☐	☐
I am preoccupied with my weight.	☐	☐	☐	☐	☐
I hate my body.	☐	☐	☐	☐	☐
I dress in styles to hide my body.	☐	☐	☐	☐	☐
I am never satisfied with my appearance.	☐	☐	☐	☐	☐
I avoid social situations because of how I feel about my body.	☐	☐	☐	☐	☐

	N	R	S	O	U
I will not wear a bathing suit or other revealing clothes in warm weather.	☐	☐	☐	☐	☐
I hate certain parts of my body.	☐	☐	☐	☐	☐
I consider having cosmetic plastic surgery.	☐	☐	☐	☐	☐
I want to be thinner than my friends.	☐	☐	☐	☐	☐
I hate the mirror.	☐	☐	☐	☐	☐
I repeatedly check myself in the mirror.	☐	☐	☐	☐	☐
I exercise only to lose weight.	☐	☐	☐	☐	☐
I get irritated if others say I exercise too much.	☐	☐	☐	☐	☐
I cancel social plans to exercise.	☐	☐	☐	☐	☐
I panic if unable to exercise.	☐	☐	☐	☐	☐
I base my self-esteem and mood on my appearance.	☐	☐	☐	☐	☐

Before tallying your responses, acknowledge how you felt while taking this quiz and how you feel afterward.

Look at the pattern of your responses. If most of your answers are in the Never or Rarely category, your concerns about body image are probably manageable and do not interfere with the quality of your life. If most of your answers are in the Sometimes, Often, or Usually categories, that may be a warning sign that body image constitutes more than its share of your self-image. Talk this over with a trusted friend and consider making an appointment with a therapist who specializes in this area. Your feelings alone may indicate whether you are suffering unduly and would benefit from some form of therapy.

Take inventory of how deeply these thoughts and beliefs intrude into your psyche. Consider ways to rework those thoughts and beliefs so you can free up energy for you and the things that will truly bring you happiness (more on this in chapter 10).

5

So Why Do People Do It?

The symptoms of eating disorders are painful to contemplate. Just picture your child or best friend sneaking off to the bathroom after every meal, sticking her fingers down her throat, and forcing herself to vomit. Or imagine that feeling empty feels good, and emptier even better.

Imagine your child or best friend obsessively looking in every mirror she passes, compulsively changing clothes and leaving piles of discarded outfits behind, loading her suitcase with free weights when taking a weekend away, or running ten miles even though she has the flu. Imagine that the only time she feels good is in the fleeting seconds after someone compliments her appearance.

Eating and body image obsessions isolate the woman sufferer behind a thick wall of denial where she spends her energy looking inward, feeling frightened, despairing, and alone. Sadly, the emptiness from starvation, excess exercise, or purging feels safer than the satisfaction the rest of us get from eating.

In this chapter, we'll learn that disordered eating and obsessions about body image are not actually about eating, food, or weight. They are about the meanings that food, eating, and body image assume when life seems frightening, empty, and spinning out of control.

Who Has Them

For a long time, it appeared that only white, upper-middle-class, smart, driven teenaged girls developed eating disorders and body image despair. That's not how reality looks today. Perhaps the problem wasn't as prevalent among other groups of women and girls in the past, or perhaps the prevalence went unnoticed.

Either way, eating disorders and body image despair are now homogenized throughout all classes, races, and ethnicities in our culture. Clinical eating disorders show up in girls as young as eight, geriatric patients, and women of every age in between. Women from many backgrounds translate deep concerns about their lives into the language of fat and body image disgust.

Thirty years ago, African American women seemed less likely to develop body image and eating problems. Many lived in a matrilineal culture that resisted the Body Myth, respected and honored women, and viewed larger female bodies as strong and attractive. Self-worth grew primarily from spiritual strength, exemplified by and in big black women.

But waves of multiculturalism (particularly multicultural marketing) brought widespread images of black women with thin bodies and light skin—with the unintended consequence of perceiving black women as most attractive when they move closest to the white ideal of beauty. Meanwhile, assimilation pressure loosened African American women's ties to the protection of a strong, matrilineal heritage. Combine these trends over a few decades, and it helps explain the concurrent increase in eating and body image problems among African American women.

However, research indicates that black women and girls who remain closely tied to family and community are more likely to reject media beauty ideals as unattainable—and not important in the opinions of family, friends—and even partners. Instead, community-connected black women and girls compare themselves to women they know and judge beauty more as movement, character, and style than as weight and appearance.

The risk remains high for other women, however, including immigrants from other countries trying to assimilate into the dominant Body Myth definition of a successful woman: thin, perfectly groomed, well sculpted, and (usually) white. This exacerbates obsession about weight, food, and appearance, which are already intense questions of identity for women trying to fit into our culture.

Even though women from many backgrounds are just as likely to develop eating and body image problems, women of color and from less affluent social classes are less likely to be referred to a physician or clinician to get help. Because outdated biases about who is at risk remain entrenched, health care professionals may overlook important signs of trouble and not even ask these women about concerns over body image and eating.

As I mentioned earlier, we don't yet have solid research on the number of adult women with body and eating disorders; nor do we have solid numbers on subsets, like women from specific ethnic groups. However, Centers for Disease Control statistics on high-risk dieting practices among adolescents are compelling and conclusively show the problem to be cross-cultural.

Where They Are

For many years, eating and body image concerns were found only in highly industrialized nations in North America and Western Europe. Globalization has changed this equation dramatically. Nearly forty countries now report that eating disorders are prevalent, including Nigeria, India, China, South Korea, South Africa, the former Soviet Republics, and Mexico.

As Western media saturates countries worldwide, attitudes and behaviors about food and women's bodies shift markedly. A dramatic example is what happened on the Pacific island of Fiji after U.S. television programming arrived in 1995.

Long-held Fijian traditions valued large female bodies for their strength and contribution to family and community, while food was celebrated and enjoyed with deep ritual meaning. Similar traditions are common in less developed countries because eating is revered and celebrated in cultures where food tends to be scarce. A large body signifies that a woman has access to a most precious commodity: food. Big is her shape of success, a sign of true well-being.

But globalized media can change this with blinding speed. After less than three years of limited exposure to mainstream U.S. television fare (including reruns of *Beverly Hills, 90210*), dieting and eating disorders—all but nonexistent before 1995—were rampant in Fiji. By

1998, 11 percent of Fijian women and girls engaged in self-induced vomiting, 29 percent were at risk for clinical eating disorders, 69 percent had dieted, and 74 percent felt "too fat."

Those three years brought no radical change in the Fijian diet or behavior (like an explosion in morbid obesity), other than an increase in hours spent watching TV. The popular female images on TV created a desire for Hollywood's superthin shape of success, quickly overturning centuries of strong Fijian traditions and values.

With greater access to education and the paid workplace, an unsettling process of transformation infuses women's personal lives—as well as the life of local cultures now faced with new questions about gender roles and gender justice. Like us, women in developing countries are becoming immigrants in their own land as a new culture enters, making familiar surroundings suddenly seem foreign.

Globalization increases the number of cultures that idealize thin women's bodies—and have clinical eating disorders. Rapidly growing economies, technologies, and markets spread the powerful Western consumer culture wider and wider. This process intensifies narrow expectations about female appearance and beauty while dramatically revising the cultural role of women.

Global consumer culture also introduces the sedentary Western lifestyle and craftily marketed prepared foods, which are high in calories and fat. The resulting increase in obesity sparks self-defeating weight-loss cycles—which creates demand for heavily marketed (no pun intended) diet products and services. Along with swift shifts in cultural roles, global women and girls feel, in unfamiliar and dangerous ways, the conflict between the reality of what their bodies are versus the unrealistic ideal of the consumer culture.

Why They Are

Knowing the who and where of eating and body image obsessions doesn't tell us why some women start down such a destructive path, while others do not. The answer to that mystery remains hidden. Although some risk factors for these multidimensional illnesses have emerged, there is still no sure way to predict who will and who will not develop the problem.

Women who grew up with an eating disorder sufferer in the family are more likely to fall victim themselves. Research with such women suggests that both genetics and environment may play a role. Women seem to have less chance of developing an eating disorder if they are resilient, manage stress well, use healthy emotional coping skills, and have a good body image, as well as positive role models and support systems.

If we do fall victim, the rituals associated with eating and body image obsessions initially soothe us when dealing with life's transitions and stress. The rituals allow us to feel in control as they gradually become very normal and feel like second nature. Fixated on the shape we're in physically, the rest of our lives start unraveling. The rituals are seductive, but they risk our well-being and our very lives.

Self-Soothing

Women with eating disorders and body image despair use their compulsive eating, exercise, or appearance behaviors to soothe their discomfort, stress, uncertainty, pain, sadness, desire, and (eventually) all feelings. No matter where these women live, what color their skin, or how much money they have, these self-soothing rituals are central to their lives and identity.

So how can anyone come to experience vomiting and starvation as self-soothing?

For women with bulimia, vomiting provides physical (if temporary and dangerous) relief from pent-up emotional tension and stress, as well as a euphoric feeling due to brain chemistry changes following their purging. Women with anorexia also get a short "high" (dizziness due to chemical and nutritional imbalance) from denying themselves food. Exercise abusers may feel invincible, at least until injuries and fatigue overpower the body's inherent limitations. Even when sufferers understand the huge risks, most cannot stop on their own. They believe that these temporary sensations soothe their souls in ways that nothing else can.

Many women who recovered from eating disorders report that their illness functioned as a comrade, in a bizarre and destructive way. The rituals associated with anorexia or bulimia offered qualities we seek in friends: a feeling of stability, reliability, predictability. The illusory sense of being in control felt irreplaceable while passing through times of intense emotion and substantial life changes. As one woman told me, "When everything else was changing, the anorexia felt reliable, at least at first. It felt like it grounded me and was always there for me. But then it spun out of control too."

Eating disorders often serve as an unconscious response to physical and/or sexual abuse in our present or past. Starving, bingeing, and other ritualistic eating disordered behaviors can symbolize limits we need in order to protect against further hurt or intrusion by others. Purging can feel like a cathartic revulsion of the shameful, painful invasion inherent in sexual trauma. Other times, the rituals manifest our (mistaken) belief that we don't deserve nourishment because we are dirty, worthless people who invited or deserved the abuse we endured.

Soon the dangerous rituals numb and isolate us from any anger, anxiety, and angst we feel about the abuse. People around us see these behaviors as self-punitive, continuing the pattern of pain. But the eating disordered survivor of abuse perceives them as the only way to care for herself. Her self-abuse feels more soothing than her experiences with others. It calms her, the way a sedative might.

In a sea of unresolved pain, the eating disorder feels like a life preserver we squeeze for dear life because we know no other way to swim to safety. Without alternate, healthy ways to cope with life's waves, letting go of an eating disorder looks like a fatal mistake. In that way, an eating disorder can seem like the most reliable coping mechanism during periods of emergency, stress, or crisis.

But like life preservers, eating disorders offer only temporary relief. If a life preserver is our lone way to traverse the sea, we will surely drown. And since it keeps only one person afloat, we will surely drown alone.

Eating disorders and body image obsessions start out as self-soothing coping strategies that look like they'll help us through a difficult time or stage. But reducing life to a scorecard of calories, pounds, and clothing sizes reduces us to bouncing between brief spurts of feeling soothed and persistent periods of painful upheaval.

It is good to feel soothed and to try to soothe ourselves. We deserve comfort when times are difficult. However, eating disorders and body image obsessions blind us to two crucial realities about soothing: (1) no problem can be solved with soothing alone. If we don't address, work through, and make peace with our problems, they keep resurfacing and we can't grow. As is true for everything else in nature, if we are not changing and growing, we are shrinking and dying; and (2) we can be soothed in ways that don't destroy us, so we should learn healthy ways to self-soothe.

Control

Closely related to our desire to soothe life's discomforts is our desire to control them. Every one of the life transitions we discussed in chapter 3 is disruptive. Nearly every one of us will go through several of those stages—while seeing the media lionize the successful, they-can-do-it-all Superwomen standard we simply can't meet. These model Superwomen seem immune from disruption, change, and uncertainty.

Facing the prospect of unattainable perfection, micromanaging the shape of our bodies seems like a good substitute for setting our own standards and taking charge of our lives.

Our image may become as important as it was when we were sixteen, creating significant anxiety and uncertainty. We fret over how other people see us as we pass through pregnancy, perimenopause, menopause, and beyond—just like we did when we sprouted breasts, grew pubic hair, and started menstruating. Rituals of not eating, overeating, purging, and excess exercise look like ways to appear in control when our inner lives feel the exact opposite.

Some sufferers say that their illness acted like a shield against cultural pressures. As Mary put it, "Once my body was small, bony, frail, unattractive, and androgynous-looking, then my body and I were much less likely to be sexually objectified by men and the culture. I really believed that my body shape was a radical political challenge to the objectification of women."

Unfortunately, this fear of intrusion by objectification quickly slips into a compulsion to be untouchable. The wall of untouchability erases the hope of achieving connection, intimacy, and even friendship. An initial attempt to make a powerful political statement ends up creating a place of empty powerlessness.

Many times we feel much like we did at puberty. Internal and external changes come too fast and furiously for us to handle them comfortably, and we want no part of them! It seems far easier to change the shape of our rebelliously aging bodies than to contemplate the changes that aging itself brings into our lives.

Rachel, a thirty-eight-year-old married mother of three, was never encouraged to be an athlete as a girl. But after having children, she was drawn to jogging as a way to manage her weight. She soon evolved from a recreational runner into a marathoner who trained obsessively. In addition to reducing her weight, Rachel received kudos for running winning races, which boosted her self-esteem while giving her a new identity and focus in her life. For a while, Rachel achieved racing goals that few other women her age could achieve.

Rachel used food and exercise rituals to gain a false sense of control over herself, how others saw her, and the many changes in her life. At least her weight was under control, even if everything else was changing: kids growing up and her body starting to look and be older.

But Rachel's running remained compulsive, and her weight dropped dangerously low. Soon she developed knee problems and other injuries, because her undernourished body could no longer take the excessive exercise regimen. But Rachel wasn't listening to her body anymore, and she kept on running despite the physical damage.

What brought Rachel into therapy, however, was her worry over the negative comments that her teenage daughter was constantly making about her own body. In short order, Rachel and I were exploring her anorexic behaviors. After resisting it for a long time, she gradually had to give up running because of her injuries.

However, she continued cutting her food intake more and more because, without the compulsive exercise, her body was taking longer to burn calories. Rachel developed elaborate and rigid rules about food, eating minimal amounts of low-fat food herself while still cooking for her family and trying to help her kids deal with their own adolescent self-consciousness about their bodies. After a year of therapy, Rachel still hadn't made peace with her changing body, her anorexia, or her sense of self-loathing. She stopped coming to see me and went back to struggling alone.

Identity

Women obsessed with body image and eating use their disorders to foster an identity that seems unique, memorable, and worthwhile. On the surface, this seems to work. Cultural standards would have us believe that a woman who looks good *is* good—good at everything, mastering all challenges that come her way. The better-looking our persona is, the better a person we are.

Starting at birth, external appearance and beauty are emphasized for girls, creating a lifelong link between our identity and what we look like. The link doesn't magically break as we age. Womanhood is complex and ambiguous. Parameters for female achievement become more fluid in some areas of our culture, but female identity still rests on the foundation of looks and sexual attractiveness.

Using our bodies to define our identity seems to have internal and external advantages. Calories and pounds are concrete. They appear personally manageable (although that appearance is an illusion, as we saw in chapter 2). Meanwhile, the media glorify thin women, even those believed to be ill, urging us to emulate them. Body image and eating obsessions provide a script for crafting an "acceptable" image, which in turn defines our identity—even if the script is made entirely of endless, rigid, perverse, and destructive rules for living.

Gradually a totally false self emerges—one that *looks* happy, confident, and able to handle anything—based entirely on what the sufferer weighs, what size she wears, or how she looks. But this exterior is flimsy, and the interior feels worse and worse. As the outer public shell grows less real or genuine, we become afraid to let the facade fall and admit reality.

We believe others only like us for our physical attributes, so we shrink in dread at being exposed as an imposter, losing the positive identity we are sacrificing so much to get. We believe that working harder to shore up the facade will keep us safe by maintaining this one good thing about us.

Soon, not eating, exercising compulsively, purging, and shaping our look become the core of our identity—an identity that feels insane to abandon, even when we know it is false. Many sufferers panic when challenged to give up their rituals. They believe they will become invisible to themselves and others. Here are some thoughts that women regularly tell me in therapy:

- But who will I be if I stop this?
- I am known as the one who doesn't eat. I have nothing else special about me.
- But I'm the skinny one; I'll disappear if I gain weight.
- This is my role in the family—the only thing anyone seems to notice. If I give it up, I give up my whole identity. I'll be nothing again.

For many women in our culture—and, often, for the culture itself—body shape becomes indistinguishable from identity. We seem to live by the motto that Bodies "R" Us.

Beguiled by the "Benefits"

Like a very addictive drug, eating and body disorders are effective in the very short term. They briefly distract us from all kinds of pain.

After months of drug use, an addict's haggard appearance seldom draws applause. But a body image addict's exterior gets plenty of praise in our appearance-obsessed culture. Many sufferers' find their outsides showered with compliments while their insides are doubled over in pain. The praise is seductive, yet the dissonance between body and spirit sends them reeling.

Another person's envy and adulation of us are like narcotics: difficult to give up, even if we know we obtain and use them for all the wrong reasons. The physical and emotional hooks come from pleasure and fear, just as they do for an alcoholic.

The ill-gotten praise reassures us when we're uncertain how to measure up in the complicated roles women play. We are beguiled by the attention we get for dangerous weight loss: "You have such self-control! You look great!" In our culture, thin and sexy equal triumph for women. Medical providers echo the praise, making it even harder to let go of the behaviors.

Rigid adherence to our obsession also provides seductive feelings of being special and superior. But ultimately, our powerlessness and self-doubt aren't mollified by this false and fleeting sense of power. Others may perceive an external image of power in a sufferer's polished look and sculpted body, but they don't have a clue about what we really feel or how we really perceive ourselves. As the gap between self-perception and other-perception widens, rituals of food, exercise, and appearance become more central and, therefore, more frightening to abandon.

If we give up our obsessive rituals, we sacrifice the addictive praise they generate. If we stop, everyone will know the real truth: we are imposters, not the beautiful image we have portrayed. If we feel we haven't measured up in life, we want to hang on tight to our precarious special status.

It is appealing to judge ourselves and our world with the clarity of dichotomous standards: fat means failure and thin means success. Having achieved what our culture defines as success, who in their right mind would want to let it go? Only someone who understands that this dichotomous standard of success is arbitrary, flies in the face of nature, eats away at our true identity, and—worst of all—can never truly be attained.

The Physical Process

Eating disorders are not only emotionally but also physically alluring and addicting. At first, most sufferers feel more energy, as they focus everything on their goal and get some positive feedback. If we haven't been mindful of nutrition before, we may actually eat more balanced meals at first, before gradually eliminating more and more nourishment. The purging of excess exercise and vomiting may temporarily produce a so-called runner's high from the release of endorphins. If we lack other life experiences that make us happy, disordered eating behaviors may provide a few blissful sensations—but only temporarily.

Less pleasant secondary physical symptoms also contribute to the addictive hook of eating and body image disorders. For example, the body easily becomes dependent on laxatives. Laxative withdrawal usually results in painful constipation and weight gain due to fluid shifts, unless the detoxification process incorporates medical and nutritional supervision. Similarly, withdrawal from diuretics may generate unpleasant bloating or "water weight" because the body instinctively holds on to extra fluid after being so dehydrated. Bloated with the sensations of being full and fat, we are easily seduced by how quickly eating disorder behaviors make these negative feelings go away, leaving us feeling empty and in control again. Also, diet pills or other stimulants may seem necessary to keep us awake and functioning, as we fail to fuel our bodies with food and fatigue takes over.

If we restrict food intake for substantial lengths of time, simply beginning to eat more food is literally a physical challenge. Responding to starvation cues from our restriction, gastric secretions in the gut slow down. This keeps food in the stomach longer when we resume eating, making us feel full and uncomfortable—and providing increased awareness of that unwanted stomach. Melanie, an adult anorexic in recovery, describes the sensation: "When I started eating again, every meal left me feeling like I did after a full Thanksgiving dinner in my childhood. I was absolutely stuffed even after eating very small amounts of food." Hannah, another patient, compares the physical effects of bulimia to those of starvation:

> I'm in recovery from my bulimia for about as long as my husband has been sober from his alcoholism. There are many similarities between our situations, because my bulimia is very much like an addiction. But there's a very, very big difference too.
>
> I know it's not always easy, but my husband can "put the plug in the jug" today without anywhere near the complications I face. Booze was a tiger that ripped apart his life, just like food and purging ripped apart my life. Thank God, we both learned ways to stay "sober" and lock each tiger up in a cage.
>
> But he won't starve if he never goes back to booze. I will starve if I never go back to food. I think of it like this: he can keep his tiger locked up, and choose not to think about it today. I, on the other hand, have to take my tiger out of the cage for a walk three times a day.

The physical changes of the illness and the discomfort of recovery make it difficult to give up an eating disorder. Our health looks less important than feeling empty, with a flat stomach and no bloating. The disorder's destructive behaviors seem like foolproof methods for getting the ideal look, which seems like the foolproof method for being valued and admired by others—a truly seductive process.

Of course, many things are seductive. The seductions of romance or the first days of spring can lead to lasting and satisfying experiences—as long as we don't stay stuck in the seduction phase. Other seductions, like the first days of cocaine use or of self-induced vomiting, are purely addictive and incapable of leading us to any lasting self-satisfaction, health, or happiness.

The Voice

What keeps women on the deadly path of body and eating disorders? Many women say the most powerful motivator is what they call The Voice. As Meredith explains:

> I knew it was crazy to keep contributing to the physical problems that my anorexia brought down on me, or even to keep living with them. But that knowledge got drowned out by The Voice. It

felt like there was a mean little guy in my brain telling me that wrong was right, up was down, and that no matter what I did, I was fat, ugly and worthless and people didn't like me. Of course, people *did* like me—some even loved me—even when I was in the worst shape and having my worst days. But I never heard that. I felt like The Voice was leading me through a carnival fun house; all around me were mirrors that distorted every aspect of my life and who I am. Every day, I felt The Voice shouting lies in my ear, and I believed it.

The language of fat and body image despair is very potent, even if we don't have an eating disorder. Most women hear some version of The Voice trying to keep us in our place and distorting our ability to see and act on our strengths.

The Voice feels deeply imbedded in eating disorders sufferers, even though it is not really a part of them. It is part of the *illness* and separate from the person's identity. To help distinguish the voice from the self, and to externalize it, I sometimes encourage patients to call it ED (short for Eating Disorder) as a reminder that The Voice is not their own voice.

The Voice, ED, or whatever we call it, keeps sufferers on a short leash, always pulling at them, yanking their chain, leaving them uncertain of their own convictions. In fact, The Voice gains power by making them feel like they can't survive or succeed without it.

The Voice doesn't have an on-off switch. Most of us hear it a little bit and face the challenge of turning down its volume and developing

---

[E]ven now, years past anorexia, that sense of an independent force persists, as though some judgmental entity—me, but not quite me—lives on in a corner of my mind where it stands watch, always aware of the body, attuned to every nuance of shape and heft and contour, always anticipating the worst, always poised to deliver a slap at any hint of laziness or sloth or relaxed control. Sometimes the voice is proactive: Don't eat that brownie, don't take seconds; you'll feel pious, you'll feel resolute and thin. More often, it's punitive, a voice of sneering disdain: Look at that stomach. Look at those thighs. You're turning into a cow.

—Caroline Knapp

a more positive, alternative voice to counteract it. The Voice seldom disappears entirely, but eating and body disorder recovery starts when a sufferer decides to quiet and manage the voice, and listen to it less.

A thought process of The Voice capitalizes on the seduction of the positives, reinforcing the illusion of control. Psychologists call this dichotomous reasoning: a tendency to see things only in the extremes, such as saintliness versus evil or success versus failure. We come to see ourselves as all one or all the other—moral or worthless, thin or fat—and are not able to see any nuance in between.

This is an unforgiving way to live. This rigid system of impossible expectation and self-perception magnifies The Voice and sets up endless self-defeating messages of failure and inadequacy which, in turn, continue fueling the obsessions with weight, food, and body image.

Gradual Adaptation

Over time, persistent habits begin to feel normal, whether or not they are good for us. We just get used to doing what we do and feeling what we feel, even if those actions and emotions are deadly. With eating disorders, sensations as essential and basic as hunger and fullness become so completely masked that sufferers have no idea whether they are hungry, full, or somewhere in between.

Anything in the stomach feels uncomfortable, and yet the stomach growls and gurgles. Do those sensations mean the body wants more, or is it complaining of too much? Women with eating disorders have lost their capacity to know the answer, as if the body speaks a code they can no longer decipher.

That's why it is useless to tell a sufferer "just eat till you feel full" or "listen to your hunger." It takes a long time to reclaim knowledge of these very basic states. Experienced dietitians and therapists often prescribe a meal plan that doesn't focus on hunger but rather on fueling the body at regular intervals with sufficient nutrients. It takes time, patience, and guts to recover this basic body knowledge and relearn how to decode body cues. (More on the recovery process in chapters 8, 9, and 10.)

Surprisingly, it is easy to get used to feeling physically lousy. We can adapt to virtually anything if it creeps up on us slowly, as eating disorders do. Vitality, concentration, and mood gradually deteriorate during the illness. Incrementally, we feel less energetic, less in tune with what is happening around us, and less able to focus and think things through. The slow pace of change can blind families and friends to the problem; they have trouble perceiving the incremental change in their loved one and may not pick up signs that an outsider might. Meanwhile, the sufferer completely loses track of how she used to feel.

Soon it is normal to fall asleep in the middle of the day at work, or even while driving. But even those incidents may not be visible to others because a woman with an eating disorder dedicates great energy to covering up her fatigue, malaise, and muddled thinking. She works harder and harder at keeping up appearances, and this increased effort eventually feels normal as well. The demand of this effort, combined with the volume of The Voice, make it impossible to tune in to her inner state, difficult to hear the concern of loved ones, and so she is unaware that she's running on empty.

Specific eating disorder behaviors also appear normal after a while. Vomiting, taking laxatives and/or diet pills, starving, bingeing, or exercising excessively are all unusual, unpleasant things to do. But as The Voice brainwashes, the rules of fat and body image despair take over. Strange and destructive habits soon become solutions to what we feel and believe about ourselves, temporarily taming those relentless negative self-perceptions and emotions.

The eating disorder gradually becomes a precious cloak we wrap ourselves up in. Even as it morphs into a steadily tightening strait-jacket, the cloak of disease feels so comfortable, so safe, something no one can take away. What began as a relief from life's problems takes on a life of its own. The destructive habits and negative self-talk are so ingrained that we use them even when we don't really feel so bad. Vomiting may start out as a way to deal with negative feelings left over from family conflict or a bad day at the office. But eventually it is just what we do every time we're alone in the house or when everyone is asleep. It is just an automatic, mindless behavior.

Denial

A cornerstone of any eating disorder is a sufferer's denial of its seriousness and implications. As with addiction to alcohol or heroin, denial is the most stubborn barrier between illness and recovery.

Gradual adaptation helps denial to blossom: once we've gotten used to purging or starving for months and years, we believe that there is nothing wrong or abnormal about these behaviors as we completely lose touch with the body's cues. Like an alcoholic who spends hours in bars, we may surround ourselves with people who also starve themselves, purge, and exercise too much, building up denial's ability to normalize sick conduct. Or like the alcoholic who drinks alone at home, we may just keep our symptoms so secret that we do not admit or see them.

But denial has even more cunning, baffling, and powerful qualities.

When confronted by unavoidable facts, many adult women with eating disorders refuse to believe the impact that eating disorders have on the body. Even when the body provides tangible, visible consequences—heart abnormalities, osteoporosis, bloody stools and vomit—denial can refuse to budge.

These women revisit the adolescent state of omnipotence, convinced that they are somehow immune from the devastating results of an eating disorder. In therapy, they tell me:

- That won't happen to me; I'm different.
- Those rules apply to everyone else; I'm okay doing this.
- This damage isn't because of my eating.
- Don't worry; I'm in control. I know just what I can do and get away with.
- I'm not really sick; I don't weigh seventy-five pounds and I've never had to be force-fed through a tube.

Steeped in denial, women with eating disorders stubbornly ignore the signals and second chances their bodies provide. If the denial doesn't break down, then their bodies eventually will. Permanent, irreversible damage happens. Second chances expire, and suicide, choking, bleeding of the esophagus, cardiac arrest, or other organ failures eventually can (and do) kill.

Frequently, the physical damage that accompanies eating disorders isn't visible until a medical crisis mushrooms. Laboratory tests and blood work can be normal one hour and deadly the next. The physical day of reckoning too often comes too late. That is why it is so important to demolish denial before the eating disorder demolishes life itself.

The Doctor's Perspective

Health care professionals continue to overlook how frequently eating disorders and despair about body image affect adult women. Much of the medical community still believes these are adolescent issues, making it hard for adult women to get appropriate help.

Furthermore, health care biases sometimes foster the problem instead of confronting it. Remember the story of Jennifer from chapter 1. Desperate for help, she finally felt ready to confide in her physician, only to hear him and his staff praise her weight loss. They never even asked how she achieved it or how she felt about it. Demoralized and discouraged by the doctor's remarks, Jennifer left his office more disoriented and alone than when she entered. Fortunately, she did not give up and eventually found recovery resources. Wisely, she also found a new physician.

In recent years, major advances, many of them beneficial to women, have been made in medicine and health care. But there remain cultural and financial forces in medicine that still wage war on our bodies. For example, standardized tables designed to determine healthy or ideal weights rely on narrow, simplistic formulas developed more than eighty years ago by life insurance companies seeking ways to screen customers. Since weight is easy and cheap to track, companies began correlating weight with mortality, even though there is seldom a direct connection between the two.

The most influential tables, originally published by New York Metropolitan Life Insurance Company in the 1940s (revised several times since), equated *average* weight with *ideal* weight. They also allowed no adjustment for age (even though men and women gain natural and healthy weight at different ages), increased insurance premiums for people who added pounds during adulthood, and fostered the false impression that weight was the country's primary health problem.

The influence of Met Life's tables and the slightly more complicated formula of the body mass index (BMI) linger today. Health care professionals continue to misperceive the connection between weight and health. Capitalizing on these flaws, the diet industry is a capitalist dream come true, with a self-generating market renewed by the industry's own inherent failure rate. Even children feel the effects:

- Forty-two percent of girls in grades one through three want to lose weight.

- Forty-five percent of children in grades three through six want to be thinner; 37 percent have already been on a diet.
- Half of nine- and ten-year-old girls feel better about themselves when dieting.
- Nine percent of nine-year-old girls say they have vomited to lose weight.
- By high school, 70 percent of girls who have normal weight feel fat and go on diets.

Since most medical personnel are indoctrinated in the war against obesity, they idealize all forms of weight loss instead of examining the reasons and methods behind them. In weight management, how we lose weight is usually more important than how much we lose. When medical providers encourage overly restrictive eating or overemphasize weight as the prime indicator of health, they can trigger bingeing, exercise abuse, anorexic behavior, body dysmorphic disorder, and purging—even in women who never before obsessed about food and body image. When physicians focus merely on weight without asking other relevant questions, they ignore essential clues to the nature of women's relationship to food, body, and health.

The Physicians' Role in the Prevention of Eating Disorders

Primary prevention. Reducing or eliminating the problem by understanding and addressing causes and risk factors. Physicians are doing primary prevention whether they know it or not when they:

- educate patients about nutrition
- play the role of health educator
- encourage healthy physical activity
- promote positive body image
- help families to communicate effectively and have healthy relationships and help everyone build self-esteem
- guide parents and children through the challenges of growth and individuation.

Secondary prevention. Identifying the problem early, before it becomes severe. Physicians play an important role by:

- noticing changes in physical parameters such as growth, weight, and vital signs
- sharing concerns and providing initial counseling
- educating patients about the importance of adequate nutrition and health habits
- consulting with schools, athletic organizations, and other influential groups.

Tertiary prevention. Developing strategies to keep the problem from getting worse. Physicians are unique in their ability to:

- refer for appropriate therapy by knowing the resources in their area
- break the denial by giving an historic perspective of their observations of the patient's condition and potential consequences of the eating disorders
- educate patients about the positive benefits of treatment
- monitor the medical status of patients and keep them stable while treatment proceeds
- set a positive example of needing others by collaborating and communicating with mental health professionals
- advocate for appropriate care when third-party payers (like HMOs) deny it.

--------------------------------- ✿ ---------------------------------

The brief, time-pressured consultations when we are face-to-face with our doctor, which is part of our managed care medical system, raise additional barriers. When women already sensitive to being judged or misunderstood receive rushed exams and curt comments, they come away feeling that their concerns and symptoms don't really merit attention or treatment. Excruciating embarrassment and shame stem from being weighed in an open area (as many clinics do) or hearing insensitive comments or jokes around the scale. When starting treatment, some of my adult patients admit that they haven't seen a doctor in years, because such experiences were so painful.

Not enough traditional health care professionals serve as resources to adult women struggling with despair about body image and eating disorders. I spend many hours preparing clients for their medical visits and decoding the mixed messages doctors and nurses give. I also train medical professionals on the impact of insensitive comments and how to assess and intervene with those suffering from eating disorders and body image despair. But many more initiatives must come from within the medical establishment. It is truly heartbreaking when medical treatment is part of the problem rather than the solution.

To be fair, the medical profession is merely reflecting the biases of the larger culture in which they and we live. In chapter 7, we'll look more closely at the influences of this larger culture, which is taking over the role of extended family in our lives.

But first, chapter 6 looks to the sufferer's more immediate family to see the many ways that our childhood and adult families feed our struggles with body image, food, and weight. Both chapters 6 and 7 provide some wider answers to the question: Why do people do it?

Detecting The Voice

The Voice is part of a woman's experience if she struggles with eating disorders and body image despair. It becomes so normal that many of us no longer notice it. How many of the following statements do you hear in your head? How often? Be honest with your responses; no one will judge you on your answers. For each statement, choose from these four possible answers: Rarely, Weekly, Daily, or Multiple Times a Day.

	R	W	D	M
You are a failure.	☐	☐	☐	☐
You are ugly and eating makes you uglier.	☐	☐	☐	☐
You are fat and disgusting.	☐	☐	☐	☐
Food is evil and will make you fat.	☐	☐	☐	☐
You don't deserve anything.	☐	☐	☐	☐
No one really cares about you.	☐	☐	☐	☐
If you eat, you'll get fat and people will like you even less.	☐	☐	☐	☐

	R	W	D	M
Only weak people eat.	☐	☐	☐	☐
You are a big disappointment.	☐	☐	☐	☐
You are worthless.	☐	☐	☐	☐
You deserve to feel lousy.	☐	☐	☐	☐
Your body is repulsive.	☐	☐	☐	☐
You are strong only when you don't eat/ when you purge/when you exercise.	☐	☐	☐	☐
No one is ever going to want to be with you if they find out who you really are.	☐	☐	☐	☐

These thoughts control us by attacking our self-esteem, degrading us, and convincing us to continue these behaviors by ignoring the damage they cause. Keep track of the intrusion of these thoughts; make them more conscious and share them in therapy. They gradually will become less powerful and convincing, but this will take time. The Voice is stubborn and doesn't give up easily.

6

How Family Shapes Us

At thirty-eight years old, Joan sought me for therapy because she worried about her own reactions to her children's eating. She sometimes pushed food on the kids but then was afraid that they were eating too much. To counter the fear, Joan would restrict their snacks, making sure that only so-called good food was in the house. She was terrified that her children, especially her six-year-old daughter, might end up fat.

Joan soon acknowledged her own bulimia, while insisting that her children not learn about it. She felt like a defective out-of-control freak. She described her bulimia as a personal moral failure. Joan acted as her own prosecutor, judge, and jury—indicting, blaming, and shaming herself for the bulimia. Joan saw herself as hopeless but wanted to be sure her children didn't end up with painful eating disorders.

When she was a girl, Joan's father was dedicated more to work than to his family. He wasn't around much, and when he did appear, he tended to be critical and harsh. Joan's mother and other family members rarely stood up to her father because he was easily angered and not so easily calmed. Joan felt guilty whenever she felt she caused his anger and disrupted the family peace. While her father routinely pressured Joan to eat large quantities of food, she also knew that he valued thinness, especially in women. She worried that her eating might please him in the short term, but that a fat body would anger him in the long term. Joan found a secret way to avoid this dilemma by beginning to vomit in her early teens.

Initially, Joan resisted talking about her parents during therapy, defensively asking why her family history mattered. Grudgingly, she traced the lasting impacts of her father's intrusive demands about food and appearance, and she understood how bulimia helped her cope with the stress and contradictions. Bulimia made Joan feel like she exerted control over her weight by vomiting, but she could still please her father by eating.

For years Joan believed she had no choice over either what she could eat or the expectation that she should be thin. She *had* to eat what people offered, just as she had to eat for her father. She *had* to be thin and look good for others, including her father. During therapy, however, Joan recognized that her father felt the need to control and choreograph everything around him; his controlling was not a personal indictment of Joan. This helped her see that her childhood impulses were not bad. Appreciating the link between her decades of bulimia and the excessive power her father exerted, she discovered a larger family context in which her bulimia made sense.

Joan didn't talk to her father about her new insights because she didn't think he would understand, and she wanted to avoid being disappointed by his response. Nevertheless, she also began to connect the dots between *his* childhood and his attitude about food during *her* childhood. As a boy, Joan's father had to help raise his siblings after his own father died. Money and food were scarce, and he began working when he was a child to help put food on the table. Because of these experiences, food was never a neutral substance to Joan's father. While necessary for survival, food's symbolism in his life made eating both a privilege and a duty in his eyes.

As her treatment progressed, Joan admitted how angry she was at her mother for not asserting more strength in her marriage and for allowing Joan's father to rule the roost. Joan felt conflicted about this anger because she also knew that her mom sacrificed much of her own life for the family. Joan began to grasp that her mother never openly endorsed female appetites or ambitions (including her own or Joan's). With this insight, Joan discovered how unprepared she was for the complexities of being a woman today.

In learning about the dynamics between Dad, Mom, siblings, and herself, Joan became more aware and comfortable handling food and dealing with interactions surrounding eating with her own children and husband. Understanding the family context of her bulimia helped her find ways to avoid duplicating that same context with her kids. Joan still struggled to trust her children's appetites, but with help, she began to separate her food issues from theirs. Like many mothers with eating disorders, Joan needed a great deal of support on this because she was still primarily responsible for feeding the family. And since the children were her initial motivation for seeking treatment, she didn't want to disappoint them.

Joan's husband, Steve, was a warm, loving man but had little understanding of Joan's illness or the stress she felt as a daughter and a parent. He wasn't particularly intuitive or inquisitive and sometimes thought that problems were best handled by being left alone. Compared to his contemporaries, Steve was an involved dad, but he duplicated his own parent's example and left most family and parenting decisions up to Joan.

Joan's increasing ability to assert herself in her marriage was an important step in her treatment. Eventually she involved Steve in some therapy sessions to help address their partnership and communication issues. Steve responded with the willingness to change and he became a more active and supportive husband and father. This strengthened their marriage and took some pressure off Joan. It also made both of them freer to develop personal parenting styles more independent of the previous generation's dynamics. Joan was especially happy with that change.

Despite all of her progress, Joan still resisted giving up her destructive coping behaviors. After decades of inconsistent eating and vomiting, it was hard to stop defining her feelings through her body and judging her self-worth by bulimia's distorted standard. Even though it was very hard, Joan tolerated her discomfort with new questions like: How will normal eating affect my weight and shape? In fact, Joan did gain weight, but therapy helped her to see the many other, more important things she gained as well—things that bulimia always denied her.

Still, after twenty-five years with an eating disorder, Joan's first impulse when angry, upset, or anxious is to vomit or restrict her eating. Like many women in recovery, she occasionally has a slip with her symptoms, but she works on understanding the contributing stressors and no longer indicts herself when this occurs. She is steadily developing other coping mechanisms to replace her bulimia.

Joan feels like she can be more herself and feels her self-worth grow-ing. She now believes that her wants, needs, and hungers are accept-able and should be met. Just as she has come to understand the multiple reasons for her father's behavior, she is also learning to con-nect the dots about the effects of her own behavior. And she can for-give both her family and herself.

The Family Table

Joan's story is one example of how our families live on in our adult lives and identities, decades beyond our childhood. Until Joan gained perspective on her past and how it affected her present, she was not able to gain control of her eating disorder or of her life. That under-standing did not make recovery come easy, but it came.

While we can never fully decipher the mystery that is family, our best classroom may be the dining table. Food is never just a neutral tool of nutrition; all families and cultures fill food with symbolism, meaning, and emotion. In fact, among the first things anthropologists study about a culture are the customs and rituals surrounding food. While eating is certainly functional, it also serves as an emotional cop-ing mechanism, celebratory ritual, communication method, and many other roles. The ways we use food shed light on central cultural and family mores about power, gender, roles, class, social order, and belief systems.

Women have an added risk for developing eating disorders because our cultural role is so closely tied to providing and preparing food for others, especially our families. Usually, we begin doing food-related chores as girls—setting the table, cleaning up, serving oth-ers—before taking on primary responsibility as adults for shopping and cooking. Thus for most women, food is an inescapable part of our social role and identity, often in positive ways. Yet at the same time, food is a potential enemy, threatening to make us feel fat and imper-fect if we dare to indulge our appetites. Our food-related roles teach us to nurture others but not ourselves. Food is always around us, and it influences our body's shape. Therefore, it can become an occasion for problems in a culture where we are so unrealistically judged by our appearance.

Ethnicity and heritage also influence our relationships to food. For example, immigrant families retain their traditional food choices, preparation, and customs to feel a sense of continuity during their transition to a new culture. Food-related rituals also live generations beyond the apparent completion of acculturation. Even if our clan has lived here for centuries, we use ethnic foods to celebrate family occasions: corned beef and cabbage, grits and fatback, pasta and meatballs, bratwurst and kraut, kung pao chicken. Despite this rich and lasting heritage, we seldom (if ever) talk about the multiple meanings food has in our families and lives. Few of us conceptualize how much our relationship to food is our own, and how much is dictated by family, history, ancestors, and culture.

Anthropologists and social historians find that no matter where or when people live, food preparation and meals seem to be women's work. So when mothers hand down recipes to their daughters, they also hand down deep (and mostly unspoken) attitudes, beliefs, and emotions about food—and a woman's relationship with it. A mother's meal legacy may convey celebration, creativity, joy, and a peaceful relationship with food. Or it may convey disturbance, resentment, dissatisfaction with playing cook, ambivalence about feeding one's own hungers, or anxiety about body image. If we look with an anthropologist's eyes, we also see how families use food as a form of social control. We use food to reward, punish, soothe, and socialize, especially with young children.

Understanding how our families of origin affect our relationships with our bodies and food helps us to identify how these patterns and dynamics live on in our adult relationships with our own partners and children. This does not mean that our families, past or current, are to blame for our problems. We simultaneously shape and are shaped by our family experience. Making the family into either the villain or victim doesn't help us—such easy explanations just don't exist when it comes to eating problems and body image despair.

The Clean Plate Club

If we look at our family of origin as an anthropologist would, we learn interesting things about ourselves. We observed and absorbed the family and cultural experience our parents and grandparents brought from their childhood to our first dining table. For one example, look at the authoritarian clean plate club that some parents impose on their children. Relatives who grew up in traumatic historical times like the Great Depression of the 1930s may have visceral reactions to "wasting" food. When my coauthor was a child, his parents and grandparents (vividly recalling the Depression) often said, "Think of the starving Armenians" or "What about the children in China?" when he didn't eat everything on his plate.

Clearly, someone who lived through a trauma like the Depression or the Nazi Holocaust doesn't make her children eat simply to teach an abstract moral lesson or because their eating will do anything to help starving Armenians or erase the Holocaust's evil. She does it because of what food symbolizes for her. For example, Nazi concentration camps wreaked death, deprivation, disease—and starvation—on innocent bystanders. But even in the camps, people gathered for meals. One or two generations later, meals and food serve as concrete, daily reminders to the survivor of this trauma and loss (perhaps including the loss of her own parents) that Nazism inflicted on her life. Small wonder if she invests food with meaning and passion.

I often see patients who grew up in families where food was very tightly controlled or scarce. As girls, these women naturally wondered if they would get enough to eat. Their feelings of uncertainty and deprivation last into adulthood, when they continue to feel anxious and unsatiated, even if food is readily available. Guilt for wanting more can trigger restricting, and fear of deprivation can spark compulsive eating, bingeing and sometimes purging. Women often tell me that no matter what they feel, they eat. In a very real sense, they cannot feel without eating.

Although frequently joked about, the clean plate club may profoundly hamper our ability to tune in to and satisfy our personal hungers. It can set up battles for control between parents and children so that saying no to food becomes a major power struggle.

The clean plate club is only one example of how families may unconsciously force children to sublimate their appetites and body awareness to the needs of their families. In some families, every single emotion and event is associated with food. Some parents insist that children eat certain foods (whether they like them or not), eat according to a very rigid schedule, or eat constantly, regardless of hunger. One study shows that anorexic mothers were particularly upset by and compulsive about the mess their toddlers make when eating. Since messy food play is a developmental necessity for toddlers, a no-mess policy cannot succeed and clearly represents unresolved issues for the mother. Because these strictures are unrelated to the child's desires and needs, they interfere with recognizing her body's natural cues, putting her at risk for disordered and emotion-driven eating.

Of course, parents rarely adopt a clean plate club attitude with malicious intent. They are simply living out the influences of their own families and experience. Nevertheless, pressure on a child to please parents by eating can easily confuse her ability to assess and respond to her basic hunger and satiety. Some children eventually resort to food restriction as a coping mechanism. Others purge to take some control over how the clean plate ethic affects their lives. Some will binge on large amounts of food because they lose touch with internal cues about hunger and many other feelings. Still others will respond with balanced, healthy attitudes and behaviors about eating, emotion, and food.

Why do some of us grow up with disturbed notions about food and eating while others of us grow up with devil-may-care attitudes? There is no easy answer or predictable, hard-and-fast rule. The emotional health and socioeconomic status of our family are factors. Genetics play a role, although we still know precious little about their influence. But if we ask, Why her and not me?, no one can say for sure, at least not based on the scientific and psychosocial knowledge anyone has today.

Still there is a lot we can learn by looking at the family factors that seem most common among adult women with body and eating disorders.

Daddy's Little Girl

As Joan learned, even when Mom runs the kitchen, Dad plays a crucial role in our relationships to food and body. Fathers often leave all food responsibility to mothers but undermine it by criticizing them, without appreciating the huge task of managing a family's food intake, health, and well-being. Dad may have different expectations than Mom about food, be more insistent or authoritarian about eating, or be indulgent with treats. Kids are sensitive to such mixed messages and may play one parent against the other, but simultaneously feel guilty and blame themselves for the parental conflict. Sometimes, marital tensions having nothing to do with food are deflected onto the children's eating and played out around the kitchen table.

For example, some of my patients remember childhood meals as being chaotic, emotionally negative, and even violent events that created painful associations between unwanted emotions and food. Such women frequently recall starving themselves to numb the pain and create an invisible barrier from their family, or else purging to rid themselves of the unwanted emotions they were forced to experience.

Other patients from abusive or conflict-ridden homes tell me that the only freely given nurturance came in the form of food. While everything else felt threatening or out of control, Mom or Grandma cooked and served wonderful meals. Food was a refuge and the only positive expression of love. Years later, these women maintain a love-hate relationship with food, often punishing themselves by eating too much or too little.

Momma's Little Girl

As a therapist, I see many women who have meals only in the morning and evening. They don't find it strange to never, ever have lunch. That's because they never saw or heard of their mothers eating lunch. While these mothers may not have had eating disorders, and probably seemed normal to their acquaintances, their avoidance of lunch shows how they quietly battled their bodies. As they literally denied their midday hunger, they unconsciously set an example that, years later, keeps their daughters conflicted about meeting their basic needs. Our family's important women role models can normalize generational patterns of abnormal eating. Even in recovery, many adult women don't feel they can incorporate daily lunch because the idea is simply so foreign to their experience and family history.

We may take on Mom's body attitude and style, a move than can be beneficial or dangerous, depending on her own body image. For some of us, the relationship with Mom was (or still is) dominated by conversations and concerns about appearance, weight, dieting, shopping, and managing one's body. Our most frequent shared activity may be dieting or going to the gym together. Social historian Joan Jacobs Brumberg notes that shopping is a common bond between mother and daughters today. Connection by consumerism and body dissatisfaction can never satisfy the deep hunger daughters and mothers have for intimacy. But it can feed a shallow, ultimately dangerous fixation on form over substance, under which we work to reshape our bodies together rather than striving to connect our spirits.

If important women in our lives seem to deny their physical and spiritual hungers, it is difficult to believe we should eat. It is even more difficult to imagine eating regularly with freedom and enjoyment or gaining healthy control of our body image in adulthood.

Eating Lessons

Take some time to think about the lessons your families taught about eating.

- What were my family's unspoken rules about food and eating?
- What happened if I challenged or broke these rules?
- How was food tied into other family dynamics, like rewarding and punishing behavior (mine or someone else's)?
- Who was in charge of my eating?
- How important were my own cues or desires? Were they respected?
- How did my family's eating patterns relate to our ethnic or cultural background?
- What was my mother's relationship to food? My father's? My siblings'? My grandmother's? My grandfather's? Other important people in my family?
- How has my eating been affected by theirs?
- What were the lessons I learned about food? Was it something to be enjoyed, feared, cherished, or hated?
- What emotions were tied to food and eating?
- Have I passed on some of these lessons and feelings to others?
- Is there anything I need or want to change about myself in light of these patterns?

Answering these questions will help us to understand our present situations, and if we are a parent, to avoid repeating negative patterns.

The Family-Built Body Image

While our body images are deeply personal and idiosyncratic, they are also shaped by both our family's response to cultural body ideals and its level of emotional openness. Body image development begins well before adolescence. Even before birth, expectant parents and grandparents imagine how their babies will look and anticipate their body characteristics or abilities ("He'll have the build for football" or "I want her to be a ballerina, tall and thin"). When we see a newborn in her crib, we form body associations—"She looks just like Aunt Susie"—that also have emotional associations, depending on how we feel about Aunt Susie.

In many ways, our personal body image is a shared body image, crafted in part by both family and culture. It is natural for parents and family members to be pleased by certain characteristics of our bodies and appearance, and when these family desires are affirming, this can be a good thing. I know a woman who, when changing her grandchildren's diapers, always grabbed their ankles and said, "You have such good, strong, chubby legs!" Because children respond to what pleases their parents and grandparents, these comments equate strength with size, give *chubby* a positive connotation, and focus attention on what the child's body can do, rather than on how it looks.

During our own childhood, we may have gravitated toward lace and frills if the family valued a traditional feminine image, or gravitated toward rough-and-tumble dungarees and sweatshirts if the family seemed to prefer girls who were tomboys. As girls, we may also feel a conflict between the two extremes, sensing that a boyish, athletic body may satisfy Dad, while more feminine characteristics may please Mom, or vice versa.

Much of our response is unconscious, layering our family's perceptions of our body atop our own developing sense of body. If we live in a family with body insecurity or loathing, we tend to internalize the negative, critical attitudes early and unconsciously, making it hard to escape with good body esteem. If a family places a high value on external beauty, we may gain some degree of acceptance and approval by living up to the standard, but we may have to sacrifice our ability to know and love our natural bodies in order to pull it off. Or we may rebel against the look that we know will please our families, just to assert some authority in our lives. Either way, our bodies take on importance; they are statements about who we are, who our families are, and the fit between us and our families.

As our bodies change during adolescence, the family investment in our body image changes. Our emerging sexuality may disturb or frighten our fathers, who may withdraw or push us away. Our mothers may compete with us and our peers over who has the best body. Both parents may put pressure on us to look a certain way, watch our weight, and invest heavily in appearance—perhaps in an attempt to prepare us for survival and success in an appearance-first culture, or because they were teased or otherwise pained by their adolescent bodies.

As girls, many of us saw our maturing, growing, and bigger bodies as problems for our families, displeasing our parents, and causing unwanted tensions or creating distance with them. Perhaps we tried to keep our bodies small, young, and less mature in an attempt to avoid the challenges of growing up, delay the loss of childhood security, and hang on to (or regain) closeness with a parent. Rita experienced this:

> My father and I were very close and affectionate. But as soon as I started developing breasts, he stopped hugging me. I instinctively knew that that was why. I decided that if my breasts were going to get in the way, I'd try to make them stop—and try to make myself stop growing up—because I didn't want to lose him. So I stopped eating. And I ended up in the hospital with anorexia.

Some families actively promote the culture's ideals for beauty and weight because they haven't learned to understand and decode a lifetime of unnatural beauty myths. In many families, self-improvement means doing just about anything to change our bodies—from dieting to having radical cosmetic surgery. Some of my adult patients struggle to accept themselves as is, because well into adulthood, their families retain a deep and ongoing stake in their physical appearance and weight.

As we go through our adult years, we may not identify with how our mothers, aunts, and grandmothers "did" aging, even if their responses were positive. Womanhood is evolving so quickly that we may not have confidence that the lessons of Mom's life apply to ours or that the ways her spouse and family reacted to her life changes will bear any relation to how our spouse and family are responding to us.

That can leave us feeling out of sync with our nearest role models, uncertain of what will happen next, ambivalent about our bodies, and willing to abuse them.

Step Back Exercise II

Do this alone, with a friend, or in a small group of women you trust, building in time to talk about your feelings and insights afterward.

- Stand comfortably, preferably without shoes, so you can feel the ground or floor. Keep enough space around you to be able to move back and forward several feet.

- Close your eyes and relax.

- Take a step backward and imagine that you are stepping into your body of ten years ago. Take a few minutes to get used to being in this body and mind-set. Remember how your body felt and what it meant to you.

- Take another step backward and step into your body of twenty years ago. Take a few minutes to reacquaint yourself with how it feels to be in this body and mind-set.

- Continue this routine, one decade at a time, until you reach your early twenties. With each step back, take time to get used to being in that life and body.

- Next, step back to your high school body. Again soak up what this body feels and means to you.

- Continue to roll back the clock by stepping into your body in elementary school, then as a preschooler, and then your body in your earliest memories.

- Finally, step back a bit further and imagine what your infant and toddler body felt like.

- Stay in that baby body and imagine how your family responded to your shape, your weight, your appearance, and your appetite.

  - Did they like how you looked as a baby?

  - Did you feel criticized or accepted; what was your body esteem?

- Did your family think you were eating too much or not enough?
- Now step forward to being a toddler and ask those same questions.
- Step forward to preschool and then elementary school, asking the same questions.
- Now step forward to your adolescent body and remember how your family responded to you.
- Step forward to your late teens and early twenties, asking again what messages your family was giving you about your body, weight, appetites.
- Step forward a decade at a time to the present, considering what messages you received from your family. Are they different now than they were then?

Reflecting on this exercise, can you identify family messages that were harmful to your body image and sense of self? Can you identify family messages that were positive? Were there any particular turning points in your body image and feelings about your needs and appetites?

Take a few minutes to absorb these insights. How did body or beauty concerns evolve throughout these years? In what ways do you feel connected to your family's messages? In what ways do you feel alone or disconnected from your family or from your past? What surprised you as you traversed these bodies and eras in your life? How do you feel about this experience?

Write these perceptions down in a journal so you can reflect on them over time. If you do the exercise in a group, make time to share your experiences and insights with one another.

Family Dynamics

In Louise's family, everyone had to be happy and nice to everyone else. Conflict, anger, anxiety, and tension weren't allowed out in the open, even after Louise's grandmother moved in and strained everyone's established routine. Because the emotional electricity was never discharged, Louise developed no skills or experience in expressing difficult emotions.

Nevertheless, Louise did sense that she *had* lots of those feelings. However, since there were no signs that anyone else in the family shared them, Louise felt different and alone. She felt sure that the others must be right and she was wrong.

As a teen, Louise felt lucky that her body included features fitting the culture's beauty standard. Her family gave her positive attention for this, so she came to feel that her appearance was her most important attribute. Her body became and remained the means through which she expressed her emotional life—and her very identity—even after she married and had children. As she passed through natural phases of adulthood, she began feeling that her naturally aging body was no longer adequate. Meanwhile, all of her emotional stress continued to settle in and on her body. Purging seemed like the solution: a single method to maintain her looks, relieve her emotional tension, and self-soothe. Soon she had full-blown bulimia and needed multiple rounds of treatment before reaching recovery.

Louise says her recovery depended (and still depends) on finding ways to deal more directly with emotions, feel justified about having them, and express herself in constructive ways—instead of through her bulimia. The result is a deeper intimacy in her relationships with her husband, her sons, and even her parents. After years of work, her growth revealed a new understanding about her family dynamics, which in turn facilitated her further emotional growth and insight. "For example, I used to think only negative feelings were taboo in my family," Louise says. "But now I realize that I really didn't know how to express positive ones either. At least for me, my family's happy-and-nice routine was a facade that wasn't really happy *or* nice."

Our families have the overwhelming and endless job of teaching us many incredibly complicated things about ourselves and life. Remember that all families have strengths and weaknesses, so we gain little by blaming them for our current situation. Instead, it is much more productive to understand how our family shaped (and still shapes) us. These insights make it considerably easier to address adult challenges and avoid replicating negative family dynamics in other relationships (especially if we are parents ourselves), and actively replicate the family's *positive* dynamics in our lives and relationships.

As Louise's story illustrates, the family's toughest task is teaching us to understand and manage our emotional experience. In the families of eating-disordered women, this process is often blunted as parents model how to suppress emotion rather than how to express it. When individual feelings are not easily tolerated, anger, grief, anxiety, sadness, loss, and other emotions just go underground.

But they can't stay there. When powerful emotions are not identified or articulated, they need an outlet. In a culture that pressures women to eat and look a certain way, it is easy for those emotions to be expressed through, or become intertwined with, how we manage food or our bodies. That's why identifying family patterns and dynamics is so crucial when treating an eating disorder. What follows is a very brief summary of family dynamics common in the histories of women with body image and eating disorders.

The Center of Emotion

Some families expect that every member share the same feelings; this dynamic is sometimes manifested in the expectation that everyone eat the same foods. The pressure to feel and act like other family members separates us from our own feelings. We lose touch with our core, become fake, and act as if we were like the others. Expressing ourselves and our feelings becomes dangerous because we may be rejected or criticized.

In many instances, one person's feelings dominate the entire family. Many of my patients describe families organized primarily by Mom's or Dad's needs and emotions. Everyone else must tiptoe around to avoid upsetting this parent, no matter what they sacrifice to do it. In other cases, no one in the family has permission to express any emotional affect. In each of these situations, the most important things in life are hidden, nothing is shared openly and honestly, and people suffer in silence. The concept of saying "I need something" is very foreign. Our needs, desires, and longings become confused or even invisible to ourselves.

Self-Regulation

Despite countless accomplishments in life, many of my adult patients lack basic skills in emotional and psychological self-regulation, which is the ability to turn down our emotional volume and cope with feelings effectively. They don't know what to do when they are angry, sad, lonely, tired, anxious, hungry, or anything else. Since these women weren't taught to identify and respond to these internal cues, they are easily overwhelmed. Going way past being hungry, they starve themselves into numbness or impulsively binge. Going way past being tired, they push themselves relentlessly until they crash and burn. Going way past being angry, they completely deny that they ever feel anger and/or feel that they will self-destruct in an explosion of rage.

When we don't learn how to articulate and pay attention to feelings, they become more powerful, disorganized, and frightening. If the important people in our young lives did not teach us self-regulation, we are likely to be inept when it comes to saying no to others, setting limits, or knowing when to stop, no matter what the activity. Among other things, self-regulation allows us to recognize and manage our hungers and feelings. It helps us know when we have had enough food, stress, work, emotion, or anything else. Without these skills, it can be nearly impossible to understand and take care of ourselves as adults (or teach self-regulation to our own children).

Perfectionism

Many families substitute perfectionism for self-regulation. Because they have little practice at moderation, perfectionistic families tend to live by all-or-nothing, dichotomous thinking. In this environment, it is easy to feel like a total failure if we are not outstanding at everything. Many of my patients struggle mightily to get beyond their families' perfectionist black-and-white extremes and start to see the gray areas of life and of their identity.

Family perfectionism constantly raises the bar on expectations regarding our performance on matters large and small, from our career success to our shoeshine. No one in these families truly feels good enough. Losing weight, sculpting our bodies, or dieting to the extreme can all become ways to manage this impossible quest for perfection.

Addictive behaviors (such as alcoholism, workaholism, eating disorders) are common in families that go to extremes and demand that everyone meet impossible standards. The inability to self-regulate, know when to stop, and interpret internal cues creates fertile soil for addictions. In many families the problem of perfectionism and limit setting are distinctly female, handed down from one generation of women to the next, with reinforcement from cultural expectations.

A Woman's Place

Our families influence our sense of what are and are not acceptable appetites for women, particularly through the gender roles our mothers and other female relatives played. If women were second-class citizens, seen but not heard, and expected to slavishly serve the family, then we may feel guilt if we ever act on our own desires. Or we may feel alone, detached from our origins, with a sense of emptiness no matter how full our lives look to outsiders.

Many adult women grew up in traditional homes that had strict gender roles and a black-and-white clarity about a woman's place. But our culture's norms have dramatically evolved, and our lives are very different than our mother's. So is the definition of a woman's *place*. It is no wonder that we question whether our modern wants, appetites, and aspirations are acceptable to our families. It can be unsettling to surpass our moms or challenge family norms, and our bodies are often where these conflicts are played out. Thinking back to our family's lessons about femininity and the proper place for women will help us to understand our current dilemmas.

Identity Development

Some families have difficulty tolerating individual self-definition or fostering healthy identity formation. Our sense of personal identity is formed by the integration of many parts of us: self-image, self-esteem, body image, body esteem, confidence, autonomy, and how we see ourselves as individuals and in relationships. Family naturally affects how these different aspects of our experience come together. If our families discourage (or even punish) our independence and growth as separate people, it is very difficult to develop the skills we need to feel strong, capable, and confident. If we take the path of least resistance and simply be what the family expects us to be, then our individual needs and wants go by the wayside.

It is hard for women to take a contrary path because we form much of our individual identities in relation to others and through these relationships. Even in the best of circumstances, we traverse a complex line between independence and interdependence as we develop our identity. But without sufficient self-knowledge and coping mechanisms, we are easy prey in a culture of body wars. Dieting, highly organized eating patterns, exercising, and other body obsessions can serve as a means of self-definition that also meet family and cultural standards.

Addiction

Children easily get caught in the cross fire of addictive families and often are blamed and made to feel responsible for problems they didn't create. The rules in a family with an alcoholic or other addicts boil down to: Don't talk. Don't trust. Don't feel. Families with even one addicted member tend to become addicted families. For example, if the mother is hooked on alcohol, the father and children become hooked on dramatic attempts to control or change her. These attempts are always futile, because only the addict can take the steps that actually break the addiction.

In this family type, the addiction is more important than the quality of the relationships. The parents are too needy to give, so children seldom get what they need. Underneath the addiction lies a great deal of pain, which chemically dependent people avoid by "self-medicating" with alcohol or drugs. Self-medication combines with deep denial to keep addicts from addressing depression, sexual abuse, trauma, or other severe disruptions common in the life histories of the chemically dependent.

In addictive families, feelings and perceptions become distorted, and fear of "setting off" the addict keeps emotions bottled inside. If we can't talk about what we feel or observe, can't question what is going on around us, and can't live in a denial-free reality, then we are forced to accept a family environment that makes no sense. Secrets abound, and telling the truth is risky under the pressure to conform to a system of denial. We begin to doubt our own perceptions, because if we speak with honesty (addiction's greatest enemy), then our family says we are wrong. Family loyalties (and maybe even our survival) dictate that we pretend this unhealthy family system is acceptable, normal, and not defective in any way.

Socialized to feel responsible for our families, girls easily get caught in the addictive family's web of impossible demands. We tend to become caregivers and caretakers at an early age, which undermines our ability to tolerate separation and autonomy. Without honest communication, we cannot feel truly close to others, so our relationships become pseudorelationships, more fake than real. Instead of feeling accepted and understood, we end up feeling alone and fraudulent. As we might expect, addictions are common in the family history of women with eating disorders and body image despair.

Abuse

Experiences of incest and childhood sexual abuse are also fairly common among women with eating disorders and body image problems. Frequently, perpetrators use food to manipulate their victims, giving special treats to reward them for submitting to the abuse. Food (especially the special treats) comes to mark the abuse for the survivor, and thus represents deep pain, fear, and violation. If we have suffered such trauma, we can turn against and even despise our bodies for having been tainted by or inviting abuse.

Constantly critical of the body, we reject our emotional and physical needs, and reject ourselves as unworthy. If we were violated by someone within or close to our families, we may feel we have no choice but to keep the abuse secret, especially if the perpetrator remains a powerful influence in our lives or holds power in the family. This secrecy makes the pain seem inescapable too. Bingeing, restricting, purging, and other self-punitive behaviors may become the ways we soothe our pain, set limits, and express anger. If we have survived abuse, we are unlikely to develop a peaceful relationship with food or our bodies until we deal with the pain, violation, and anger.

Martha was the youngest of three kids in an addictive family, and the only girl. Her dad was severely alcoholic, and her mom was passive and overwhelmed. Trying to keep the family together while dad spent money on liquor, mom worked long hours in a low-paying job. The home was chaotic, and Martha strove to make her parents happy, hoping her good grades would make up for all their other disappointments. While wanting to make her parents proud, she was also embarrassed by them and never had friends over. She felt alone and sensed that no one really knew her.

During their adolescence, as dad's alcoholism and the family situation worsened, Martha's older brother began sexually abusing her. No one was there to see or help, and she grew more ashamed and isolated. Martha starved herself, hoping someone would notice her distress. But because she also kept achieving and pretending that she was happy, no one responded. The abuse stopped only when her brother left home. Martha gradually began to eat more normally again and regained the lost weight.

Years later, as a thirty-nine-year-old dealing with her own teenagers, Martha relapsed into severe eating disorder behaviors. This time, she was able to get help. A bright and sensitive woman, Martha worked through the childhood traumas and began to feel more connected to herself and the important people in her present life.

Martha's husband, Harold, reacted as most partners of sexual abuse survivors do: he was very angry once he learned about and came to fully comprehend the sexual, physical, and emotional abuse Martha had suffered in the past. He even wanted to seek revenge. Working through such feelings is a great challenge to couples and families, but it can be done successfully. The process can draw a couple even closer together, and help a man grow. Harold says he is now more aware of how readily we let abuse and abandonment remain part of "what it means to be a man," and how those attitudes harm men, women, and children. Men like Harold often make up the bulk of male volunteers at sexual assault or antiviolence programs.

Eventually, both Martha and Harold saw her relapse as an inevitable result of the pain in her family, and an opportunity to finally address it. Paradoxically, Martha felt grateful that her relapse pushed her to make peace with herself and, in her words, transform "from a survivor to a thriver."

Obsessive attempts to develop a certain image of success and personal control are adaptive—if ultimately unhealthy—strategies to deal with our feelings of inferiority and inadequacy. Because troubled families don't manufacture self-esteem, food and body obsessions may act as ways for us to feel in control and feel good about ourselves, at least temporarily. The predictability of the rituals associated with eating disorders may serve to calm, soothe, and insulate us in an otherwise chaotic family. We get tacit support from the many people who view these as socially acceptable ways for women to express our distress.

Father Hunger

The residual issues, needs, and disappointments in our relationships with our parents live on even after we become adults. For example, what my adult clients often say about their relationships with their fathers isn't very different from what my teenaged patients say:

- My father was/is angry and irritable.
- He was/is self-absorbed and inattentive to others' feelings.
- He didn't/doesn't seem capable of praising or acknowledging my achievements.
- He can't understand my issues about food or weight.
- He hates fat people and continually comments about women's bodies.
- He can't stand it when I fail to meet his standards.

Whether adult or teen, a daughter's emotional responses are similar as well:

- I avoid issues or actions that might spark my father's anger.
- I don't allow myself to expect much from him.
- I still feel unsure of myself around him and other men.
- He makes me feel misunderstood or trivialized.
- I feel like I will always disappoint him in the end.
- I believe that my appearance, weight, or eating can please him.
- I constantly fear his displeasure with me.

As one patient said, "I'm in my fifties and I shouldn't still need my father's approval." But the fact remains that many of us suffer from what I call Father Hunger, which is a natural, universal, and intrinsic longing for a connection to Dad. When that hunger is not satisfied, we struggle with self-esteem and self-confidence, and we have more difficulty in our relationships with men and with life partners. Understanding how our fathers affect us can help free many adult women to move beyond issues dealing with eating and body image. It allows us to shape better intimate relationships (whether with men or women), working relationships with men, and relationships with our children.

Because our fathers and/or stepfathers set the standard for what we expect from men—and from intimate partners—we are easily drawn to partners and male friends who share similarities with Dad. We may even unconsciously pick a partner with whom we can work out unresolved issues with our dads (or mothers). Many of my father-hungry clients interact with men, including their spouses, in ways very similar to how they interacted (or still interact) with their own fathers: avoiding issues in anticipation of anger; not expecting much in order to avoid feeling disappointed; feeling misunderstood, trivialized, and unsure; fearing their disapproval; and believing that the "right" appearance will please them. These were not healthy patterns when these women were girls, and they are not healthy in adult relationships.

The language of fat and body image despair can be very appealing when we don't feel free to express ourselves emotionally or we expect to be let down, criticized, or disappointed. We can mistakenly believe that our bodies can fix the problems we have with our fathers, our partners, or other influential men in our lives. But they can't; trying to use our bodies to feed our Father Hunger only fuels disordered eating and appearance obsessions and leaves our true needs and hungers unmet.

———————— ∽ ————————

Dad and Relationships with Important People in Your Current Life

Take a few minutes and review the list of personal characteristics in the table below. Mark the ones that applied (or apply) to your father or stepfather, and those that apply to your spouse, partner, or significant other. (You can also substitute a male authority figure, boss, colleague, friend, or any man with whom you have felt some difficulty.)

He is/was:	Dad/ Stepdad	Partner
Often angry and irritable	☐	☐
Often self-absorbed and inattentive to others	☐	☐
Seldom able to praise or acknowledge your achievements	☐	☐
Seldom able to understand your issues about food or weight	☐	☐
Makes negative comments about women's bodies or about fat people	☐	☐
Often intolerant or impatient when others fail to meet his standards	☐	☐
Often avoids emotional issues or acts in ways to avoid his anger	☐	☐

I feel/felt:	Dad/ Stepdad	Partner
Like I can seldom expect much from him	☐	☐
Unsure of myself around him	☐	☐
Misunderstood or trivialized by him	☐	☐
Like I regularly fear his disapproval	☐	☐
That my appearance, weight, or eating can please him	☐	☐

Compare how many characteristics apply to both your father and the important men in your current life. Now take a few minutes to write down your answers to the following questions:

- How did you feel about the problematic characteristics your father had?

- How do you feel about them now?

- What was your reaction to those characteristics as a girl?

- What is your reaction to them today?

- How closely (if at all) do your reactions to your father parallel the reactions you have to the same characteristics in your spouse, partner, or other important men in your current life?

Write down your insights and share them in therapy or with a trusted friend to understand how you can begin to give up negative patterns and reinforce positive ones.

Mom in the Mirror

While our relationships with our fathers often reflect a chronic hunger that hasn't been satisfied, our relationships with our mothers and/or stepmothers are more varied. Sometimes we feel that Mom is smothering—too present in too many ways and making it hard to completely define ourselves as individuals. Some of us saw Mom's passivity with Dad create an unhealthy family environment and a negative role model for us as growing girls. We hungered for examples of self-assertion, self-confidence, and comfort with womanly appetites.

Recovery and a healthy adulthood require that we set limits on Mom's influence and reclaim more autonomy in our lives. Health and recovery also demand that we identify and legitimize our desires. We must learn that dieting, appearance obsessions, consumerism, and disordered eating cannot feed our true hungers—even if our mothers chose those routes. Instead, these unhealthy patterns leave us ultimately empty and unsatisfied.

Mother-daughter tensions often become entangled with competition around dieting and body image. Taking time to explore and understand how our mothers influence our feelings about our bodies and our eating can help us to gain healthy control of these issues, and avoid passing toxic patterns on to another generation.

Mom's Hand-me-downs

Many of our mothers channeled their frustrations and emotions into struggles with their bodies and food, creating a template for us as well. Mark the characteristics that were (or are) true for your mother, and for you.

She often did or does:	Mom/ Stepmom	Me
Talk about her weight	☐	☐
Go on and off diets	☐	☐
Weigh herself	☐	☐
Complain about the changes in her weight or appearance as she aged	☐	☐
Enforce strict rules on eating	☐	☐
Keep many nonfat, low-fat, or other diet products in the house	☐	☐
Label foods as good or bad	☐	☐
Have secret stashes of candy or other special foods	☐	☐
Seem conflicted or in denial about her appetites and hungers	☐	☐
Express remorse or guilt after eating	☐	☐

She often did or does:	Mom/ Stepmom	Me
Overeat or undereat when she appeared upset	☐	☐
Appear unhappy or dissatisfied with herself	☐	☐
Encourage others to diet	☐	☐
Criticize my body	☐	☐
Maintain a standard of perfection for herself	☐	☐
Maintain a standard of perfection for me	☐	☐
Judge others based on their weight or appearance	☐	☐

The more our moms spoke the language of fat, the more we are likely to speak it to ourselves and our own children. Now run through the list again, and see what example you may be setting for your daughters, sons, or other young people in your life.

Tracing the roots of our self-image can help us to be kinder and more forgiving to ourselves. The less self-blame we use, the easier it is to change our behaviors and develop better coping mechanisms.

Whether we are young or old, we all want the same things from our mothers and our fathers:

- to feel wanted and accepted unconditionally
- to feel respected as separate people
- to be able to differ from them without losing them
- to be acknowledged for who we are, not just for what we achieve
- to feel good enough as is
- to love and be loved.

We also crave these same feelings in our most important current relationships. The more lacking we feel, the more we may blame our bodies and try to solve our problems by changing our shape.

Whether or not our parents are alive, we can't change the

past. But as the personal stories in this chapter show, our original families still shape us long after we grow up and leave home. Her family's inability to identify and express emotion prepared Louise poorly for the complexity of life as she moved from childhood to adulthood. Joan's life was shaped by her father's intrusive and controlling style as well as by her mother's passive response to it. The unhealthy patterns of interaction in both families may have been unintentional and unconscious, but they still had long-lasting and damaging effects.

Until we begin understanding and making peace with such powerful influences, we can't learn from them—and we may remain at their mercy. It is important to remember that we *can* still make peace with that past (and our parents), find harmony in ourselves, and nurture strong current and future relationships by taking time to recognize how our pasts are shaping our current lives.

Through therapy, both Joan and Carol came to recognize that their parents did the best they could in light of their own lives and limitations. This helped them to forgive their parents, but that was only one step in the process. Carol and Joan also needed to understand the intricacies of these harmful family patterns in order to avoid continuing them with their own partners and children. Our adult challenge (for us and our families) is to tone down the negative childhood family dynamics and amplify the positive patterns.

The Shape of Our Current Family

The family we live in now also has a major effect on our body image, eating behavior, and sense of self. The personalities of our partners and children weave together with our own continually developing identity and the old dynamics from our families of origin to create new family dynamics. These multiple and complex forces affect whether we have an eating or body image problem, whether our loved ones recognize the problem, whether they contribute to it (knowingly or not), and whether they can help us to recover from the problem.

The Imposter Syndrome

Joan's family atmosphere was full of tension, unspoken emotions, and endless demands. Most of the time, her father's authoritarian style, her mother's passivity, and the family's high expectations for Joan played out over meals, so food became symbolic and problematic for her.

As she grew up, Joan developed impossibly high standards for herself and was thus never satisfied or felt good enough. Instead, she felt like an imposter frantically scrambling to keep from being discovered as a fraud. Her immigration into the modern Superwomen culture added to the underlying pressures. This degree of overdrive ultimately placed unbearable stress on Joan's health, well-being, and closest relationships.

Constantly pushing ourselves to do everything perfectly for everyone always backfires. We then can never truly meet anyone's needs, including our own. Nevertheless, many of us feel compelled to try and meet the impossible (therefore, unrealistic) standards we have set.

No matter how accomplished we actually are, we tend to feel like imposters. Because we don't live up to the Superwoman standard, we know that we are not what others think we are—or what we hope they think we are. Convinced we are imposters, we simply do not believe, accept, or allow words and gestures of praise and affection. We maintain a distance that limits satisfaction and intimacy—for ourselves and others—in relationships.

This merry-go-round is not merry at all, and it takes guts to decide to get off. Because we believe people value us only for what we do and how we look (not who we are), we also believe that accepting our imperfections will mean losing the affection or respect of others. But we are called "human beings" not human "doings" for a reason. It is who we are inside that counts, not what we do or how we look outside. Isn't that what we tell our children?

The Imposter Syndrome has far-reaching negative effects, especially if we are raising children. Believe it or not, children do *not* need perfect mothers. Girls in particular don't benefit from mothers who set impossible standards for themselves. Children learn from what we do more than from what we say, and girls are particularly good observers of their moms and other important female role models. No matter what we tell them about being "good enough the way you are" and loving themselves, our words are meaningless if we cannot embrace our own imperfect humanity.

To be positive role models for our daughters and other young women, we have to relinquish the Superwoman role and live as genuine and honest beings. If we do this, we also will be liberated from the debilitating Imposter Syndrome, no longer living in fear of being found out. Living genuinely makes our relationships, especially with our families, more real and more satisfying. Our loved ones will truly know us, and they'll actually love us more because they are getting the real thing, not some imposter.

Our perfectionism and Superwoman aspirations harm our relationships with our children and also wreak havoc on our marriages and other intimate partnerships. If we never feel good enough or satisfied with ourselves, we cannot be open and available in our closest and most important relationships. Husbands and partners who want a trophy wife (rather than a real woman partner) don't deserve real women—and don't deserve to have their warped standards influence how we value ourselves. A relationship based on trying to be someone we are not is no relationship at all. Real men and real women want to be with real women. As scary as it may be, when we let down our guard and risk being who we are inside, we offer our best to our intimate partners.

Superwoman Never Needs Help

We have many "bosses"—spouse, children, family of origin, work, in-laws, community—who have competing demands. Even if these multiple demands are not truly over-the-top, our Superwoman expectations may create a debilitating and paralyzing sense of pressure and failure.

Women are good at multitasking, but today's expectation that we can have it all by doing it all is simply a hoax. We cannot do all and be all without making ourselves vulnerable to stress-related illnesses and addictions. Something has to give; too often, it is us or our families.

We often decide that checking another thing off our endless to-do list is more important than the quality of our relationships. By living in a toxic culture, we believe that the perfect home, the perfect meals, and the perfect body will create a perfect family. Trying to cross the ever shifting goal line of being good enough is impossible as we try to outdo our neighbors in living, looking, and eating the right way.

Perfection is a myth; it simply doesn't exist (at least not in this world). When we strive to create that perfect family, real relationships suffer. Our spouses and children come to think that the symbols of perfection are more important to us than they are. Few of us are brave enough to admit that our appearance-first, perfectionist, cultural and personal standards for women are ludicrous. Like characters in "The Emperor's New Clothes," we pretend not to see the naked absurdity of trying to be Superwoman. Instead, our own lives become barren and naked as we obsess about being the ultimate wife, executive mother, master employee, and CEO chef.

From a very early age, most girls are trained to put others first. When making up our endless to-do lists, the deepest needs of others rank far higher than our own. That means many of us don't know how to nurture ourselves as women. For example, Joan's mother gave but never expected to receive. She never learned to recognize, let alone meet, her own needs. How could she teach her children, especially her daughter, to identify, understand, and satisfy their own hungers? In a healthy family, everyone, even a mother, is allowed to have needs, desires, and hungers and can expect to have at least some of them fulfilled.

Many of us have so many things going on in our lives, and so many areas where we are trying to prove ourselves, that we believe we cannot take any time for ourselves—whether for the simplest of daily mental health breaks or for life-or-death recovery from an eating disorder. Yet when someone we love has a serious illness, or even a cold, we make time and provide support for them. We don't expect them to take care of themselves without any outside assistance—in fact, we insist on doing everything we can to help the healing process. We simply cannot be healthy if we continue to live by this double standard. We must practice what we preach when it comes to caring for ourselves and reaching out for the help we need.

Spouses

When it comes to our issues with weight, food, and body image, most of us discover that spouses, partners, and significant others can be part of the problem, part of the solution, or both. Most adult women struggling with body and eating disorders have (or had) spouses or partners who fit into one of the following four types: the Controller, the Codependent, the Clueless, and the Committed.

The Controller tends to be unrelenting in his demands on us. He may contribute to self-image problems by criticizing our bodies and dispensing his approval only when we meet his standard for female beauty. He may criticize other areas of our lives, always wanting more and being dissatisfied with what we accomplish. Faced with these criticisms, we may use our bodies or eating to soothe ourselves or to feel a sense of personal control. Or we may believe that a perfect physique, diet, or style will finally please him.

A spouse may also play the Controller during our recovery. He may want us to get better fast, and to do it his way, insisting on simplistic solutions like "just eat!" He may expect us to follow his recommendations for eating and exercise, asserting that he is the expert on our body. He may also try to control our treatment, imposing his beliefs, needs, and timetable onto our therapeutic process. This approach interferes with our self-knowledge and is doomed to fail, but that may not stop a Controller.

Living with a Controller is difficult, especially when we need to focus on ourselves in recovery. Couples' therapy can often help with these hurdles. Some men prefer to work through their issues in individual therapy or in a men's group. The Controller needs to understand:

- How controlling he is.
- What life experiences lead him to rely so heavily on control.
- How his life is hampered by overreliance on control.
- How to temper his overcontrolling tendencies.
- How his tendency to overcontrol may exacerbate our eating and body image obsessions.
- How his tendency to overcontrol will hamper our ability to develop the internal control tools essential to recovery.

The Codependent tends to be very needy and may come from an addictive family where the children's needs weren't met. The Codependent bases his feelings, behaviors, and view of reality on how another person behaves—or how he thinks that other person will behave. He sacrifices his self to maintain the marriage or family equilibrium. The Codependent may unknowingly contribute to our problems by discouraging changes that threaten the existing balance, even if those changes make us healthier, stronger, or more independent—and stabilize the family. Uncertain how our recovery will change the rules of the relationship, the Codependent may subtly resist even small changes that we make in our eating or body management, despite his genuine desire for us to get better.

When one partner has a serious problem like anorexia, it's very easy for the other partner to organize his life and self-worth around attempts to manage it, without realizing how this codependent reaction may help keep the problem going. Codependents mean well and want to help, but their efforts tend to help keep everyone stuck. In a real sense, a codependent couple builds their relationship on the problem (addiction, eating disorder, and so forth), leaving little else to talk about or focus on. We have to assess whether codependency in our current family dynamic is hampering our attempts to get better. Again, marital, individual, or group therapy may help. If the Codependent is from an addictive family, Al-Anon and/or Adult Children of Alcoholics groups may also help.

Codependent's Checklist

Millions of people are affected by another person's eating or body image disorders. Read the following statements and check the ones that apply to your relationship with a sufferer.

I worry about someone else's eating behavior or ☐
appearance concerns.

I tell lies to cover up for someone else's eating or ☐
appearance behaviors.

If the person with eating or body image disorders ☐
really cared about me, she would stop her
destructive behaviors.

I blame her behavior on her relatives, friends, or ☐
companions.

Plans, meals, or holidays are frequently upset, ☐
delayed, canceled, or spoiled because of her eating
or body image problems.

I make threats, such as, "If you don't start eating, ☐
I'll leave you."

I secretly snoop around to discover whether she ☐
has been purging, restricting, or engaging in
other dangerous eating behavior.

continued

I am afraid to upset her for fear it will set off an ☐
episode of purging, depression, or other problems.

I've been hurt or embarrassed by her behavior. ☐

I search for hidden diet pills, laxatives, and other ☐
tools of her disorder.

I've refused social invitations out of fear or anxiety. ☐

I feel like a failure because I can't control her ☐
self-destructive behavior.

I think that if she stopped her eating or body ☐
obsessions, our other problems would be solved.

I have, even once, threatened to hurt myself to ☐
scare her.

I feel angry, confused, or depressed most of the time. ☐

I feel there is no one who understands my problems ☐
or our situation.

If you agreed with any of these statements, there is a very real possibility that you are responding in a codependent manner to your struggling loved one. Seek professional and other support in adopting the behaviors and attitudes most likely to support your loved one's recovery and your own well-being.

———————————— ✍ ————————————

The Clueless spouse is often very caring and loving but simply hasn't taken the time or developed the skills to figure out what being a woman today is all about. He is stuck in a narrow worldview reinforced by the cultural straitjacket of masculinity. Often feeling inadequate and inept when it comes to understanding women, a clueless spouse tends to avoid talking about or confronting personal or relationship problems. He genuinely wants us to be happy but isn't sure how to help, so he rarely inquires about our difficulties. The Clueless tends to ignore and simplify issues, not even knowing what questions to ask when he discovers we are struggling. He may not realize that problems related to food or weight even trouble us, despite years of being together. We may reinforce the Clueless response by covering up problems, hiding any sign of imperfection, and pretending that we are fine when we are not.

While both Joan's and Jennifer's spouses could be described as Clueless, they eventually did well in their efforts to support their wives' recovery. However, they needed a lot of direction from their wives and their therapists. Clueless spouses are not intuitive and may not be naturally inquisitive either. They tend to be passive and to feel out of their element when dealing with sensitive, emotional issues.

Like many women suffering from eating and body image issues, Joan and Jennifer were skeptical about involving their spouses in the recovery process. Their perfectionism made it hard for them to be seen as imperfect or needy. They also feared that their spouses might disappoint them by not caring or being unable to deliver. But their willingness to be open and honest paid off in the end. Too often, we assume that our spouses won't bother to understand or be able to help. However, most spouses do care. They want to be involved but often don't know how to do it well or usefully. Once they understand the dimension of the problem and how they can help, many Clueless spouses blossom into Committed spouses, just as Joan's and Jennifer's did.

The Committed spouse is able to support recovery, regardless of what it requires from him—and that requirement may be huge. Recovery sometimes brings major disruptions to a couple's life, especially if treatment requires the woman to leave home for a period of time. Jobs must be put on hold and family obligations and child care have to be rearranged, just as they would be for other serious or chronic illnesses. Committed spouses pitch in, shuffle their other commitments to share this burden, understand the depth of our problems, and recognize that there won't be any quick fix.

Louise's husband was surprised at how many people praised his commitment to his wife's treatment, which included residential treatment in a facility hundreds of miles away from their home. He said:

> I love her and was ready to do anything to save her. In my mind, I had no choice. This is exactly what I would have done had she been physically ill with cancer. All of us, Louise, me, the kids, did what we had to do. Sometimes, there wasn't a lot of support for the level of commitment we made, because there is still a lot of stigma surrounding emotional and psychiatric problem, especially eating disorders. Plus, contemporary culture promotes the idea that we should throw away a relationship as soon as it isn't perfect anymore, or we run into troubles. I'm glad we did it the way we did, and that we all have Louise back.

Having a Committed spouse helped Louise tremendously. After being sick for more than half of her life, she wonders if she would have recovered without his devotion, acceptance—and his openness to changing his life so she could concentrate on her treatment.

Any spouse can move from being a Controller, Codependent, or Clueless to being a Committed partner. It may be more difficult for the Controller or the Codependent to do this, but it is not impossible; it requires being open, willing to admit imperfections, and beginning to deal with difficult emotions. Many women fear that their spouses will disappoint or reject them, so they may not give their spouses the opportunity to truly know them and what they need. However, the opportunity to help is a very real gift to a partner. Our partners and friends need our help in order to help us.

The fear that our relationship will change if we get better can keep us stuck for a long time. We question if we'll be discarded once we reveal our true selves. Our spouses may wonder if they will still be needed, once we get well. It is important to remember that all relationships change (because all relationships are at least a little fluid) whether we get better or not, but remaining stuck in our old ways creates more and more distance between us. This distance may look very comfortable and familiar, but it is distance nonetheless. No matter how invested we are in making time stand still, it is not possible. If we are changing anyway, why not work to change in a way that will bring more honesty, spontaneity, and health into our lives and relationships?

Intimacy

If we are consumed by eating and body disorders, then rigid eating, purging, and body management rituals become the center of our lives. This inevitably destroys our most intimate relationships bit by bit.

Instead of sharing a relaxing meal at home or in a restaurant, eating becomes measured (literally and figuratively) and devoid of pleasure. Any break in routine, even an evening out, weekend away, or vacation with our partner, becomes a major stressor. The simplest things take on inordinate importance, and life is no longer fun, the way we or our partner once imagined. For some couples and families, depression and hopelessness set in as their world shrinks to fit inside the narrow limits of restricted eating and joyless body obsessions.

Sexuality and intimacy suffer profoundly in eating and body image disorders, both physically and psychologically. When we don't eat enough, the body's hardwiring triggers a plunge in our physical sexual energy. Our starvation survival mechanisms repress libido because sexual activity can lead to pregnancy, which in turn consumes energy that may be scarce during famine. That is why well-digested food is often the best tonic for low libido—a natural Viagra for modern women.

In addition to sapping sexual energy, body image despair and depression also psychologically disconnect us from opportunities to enjoy physical contact. If we cannot tolerate our bodies, we cannot enjoy anyone else touching them or seeking closeness with them. We may allow some sexual contact because we are afraid of being rejected or of disappointing our partners. But this contact is more likely to bring us conflict than satisfaction, joy, or pleasure. Our partners often sense this.

Keenly aware of our body's imperfections, we feel negative and worthless. We may feel devoid of sexuality or ashamed of any sexual appetite we do have. Shame over past abuse or violation can add to any anxiety or fear we feel in our present relationships, no matter how safe and loving our current partner is.

Creating an atmosphere of openness and honesty is the best way to improve intimacy. This takes time, trust, support, practice, and perhaps professional guidance. As with the rest of recovery, the appealing notion of a quick fix cannot solve problems this complex. The strength of couples who love each other unconditionally and commit themselves to working through such daunting obstacles is awesome and inspiring.

When Tracy first came to me for psychotherapy, she didn't meet the medical criteria for anorexia or bulimia. But she still spent years battling multiple conflicts with food, weight, body image, and exercise. Tracy was thirty-five, recently remarried, and knew her problem was getting worse, although she couldn't figure out why. Tracy felt her first marriage in her mid twenties failed because both she and her ex were too young, immature, and inexperienced to have a serious commitment to each other. She coped well with her divorce, pursued a career and graduate school, and was now with a new husband. She loved Tom deeply and saw him as her soul mate.

Despite this, Tracy started to feel more depressed in the months after her wedding. To make herself feel better, she exercised more, ate more rigidly, and obsessed about every aspect of her appearance. She even took laxatives and vomited every now and then when she felt desperate and fat. Tracy came to me because she was feeling more depressed, her methods of handling these feelings weren't working, and she was afraid her marriage would suffer.

Tracy was not instantly comfortable in therapy; she was used to handling things on her own. But gradually she revealed a history of childhood sexual abuse by a close family friend. She had never talked about this before; even her parents and sisters did not know. After each incident, and whenever she was upset about the abuse, Tracy used strenuous physical activity—usually running or biking—as her way to cope with her overwhelming emotions and anxiety. As she proceeded through high school and college, she obsessed about her weight and appearance, sometimes restricting, bingeing, or vomiting when these feelings swelled up.

While this behavior was disruptive to her, it had also become fairly normal. No one else ever commented on it, other than to compliment her on her appearance or her strict exercise schedule. Only recently had Tom questioned the frequency of her exercise and the rigidity of her eating habits. Despite this new and loving marriage to her soul mate, Tracy's symptoms felt more out of control than ever before.

As her relationship with Tom deepened, Tracy felt increasing shame about her past and tremendous anxiety about the possibility that her future children might be abused themselves. As Tracy gradually explored her sexual abuse history, she uncovered her fear that any intimate partner who discovered her past would reject her as damaged goods. Despite their deep trust in each other, Tracy feared that even Tom might react this way. Consequently, the marriage's growing intimacy paradoxically fueled Tracy's anxiety and self-loathing—causing her body obsessions to multiply.

Once she had talked about the events in her childhood and addressed her own self-blame and shame, Tracy agreed to have Tom join in therapy sessions. With me facilitating, Tracy bravely took the risk of telling Tom about her abuse and sharing her current struggles. Tom's emotions ran the gamut from sadness to rage at how badly Tracy had been hurt. He was especially angry that this could have happened without her family ever recognizing it. Despite these powerful impulses, Tom assured Tracy that he could handle his feelings, would do anything he could to help her, and would not leave her. Tom even understood when Tracy said she needed to temporarily back off from their sexual relationship while she worked through her feelings about the abuse.

Tom worked hard to understand how childhood sexual abuse damages adults and their partners. He read books and got information from self-help organizations and the Internet. He accepted my recommendation that he see a therapist to help him with his anger at Tracy's perpetrator and her family. Worried that they would be too upset by it, Tracy did not want to share the abuse with her parents. However, she did talk to her sisters, who responded with tremendous support and validation. Tracy feels closer to them and to Tom than she ever has. She also has forgiven her parents for not realizing what went on all those years ago.

Tracy has been able to heal in large part because Tom stood by her and remained committed to her and to their marriage. They now have a family of their own, and she is managing her anxiety about protecting her children. She no longer does anything harmful to her body, although appearance and exercise are still very important to her.

Tracy's story shows a universal truth: when it comes to body image and relationships with food, the family can be an asset, a liability, or (usually) both. Whether we examine our family of origin, current family, or extended family, we find forces that can help or hinder us in the search for a peaceful relationship with body, weight, and food.

Our larger culture also presents major self-image problems that even the healthiest among us must battle daily. Nowadays we spend as much time (or even more time) interacting with the culture than we do interacting with our families. So we'll now take a closer look at the influence of our culture on adult women's body image and attitudes about food.

Surviving Eating Disorders and Body Image Despair:
Ten Steps for Spouses

1. *Eating disorders and body image obsessions have tremendous power over your loved one.* She isn't trying to hurt you, and she isn't being resistant or stubborn out of spite. These are her own survival techniques and at times will overpower her logic and will. Recognize the disease's power and don't take her obsessions personally.

2. *Be compassionate.* She feels deep pain that she can only articulate through her body. Hopefully, in time she will have words for her emotions.

3. *Your loved one and her illness are not the same thing.* Remember the person who is covered up by these obsessions—she is still the person you love. Help her to recognize herself as well.

4. *Help her to see that there is more to her, you, and life than food, weight, and appearance.* Talk about other issues. Don't let the eating and body obsessions dominate your interactions and conversations.

5. *Admit your own anger, frustration, and helplessness.* Talk to others in similar circumstances. Join a support group for family members or spouses of people suffering from body image and eating problems. Read supportive books and visit support groups online for help and encouragement.

6. *Consider getting help for yourself.* You will feel overwhelmed, discouraged, tired, and angry at times. Working with a professional can help you to manage these feelings and deal with them constructively.

7. *You are her partner, not her treatment team.* No matter how much you love her, you cannot turn her problems around alone. Resist the impulse to battle over weight, food, and exercise. Help her to find a therapist, dietitian, physician, and/or treatment program so she has professional help guiding her.

8. *Ask how you can help, and listen for the answer.* At times, you can only be in the background, conveying love and support. Other times, she may need more direct help from you. This may be confusing, but she needs to be in charge of how you help her.

9. *These problems don't disappear overnight, no matter how hard someone works in therapy or how good a treatment program is.* Recovery is a long, winding road with lots of bumps and potholes. Don't expect her to be perfect in her recovery. Help her to take one day at a time—you do the same!

10. *Logic doesn't work: love does.* Endless debates about food, health, exercise, or weight do more harm than good. Help-

ing her to feel that she is loved and that life is worth living will do more than a thousand reasoned arguments. Some women who have recovered believe that the love of their significant other is what made them hope and believe that they could survive without the life preserver of their eating disorders and body obsessions.

7

The New Extended Family
How Culture Shapes Us

Women's widespread discontent with their body image is a cultural phenomenon that varies profoundly from culture to culture. In some present-day Arab countries, for example, rotund women are considered more desirable, and women fret that their husbands will leave them for larger women. As a result, women strive to be big, and some girls are actually force-fed to make them fat. It is a pattern that looks like an eerie mirror image of anorexia. Why do these women do it? Apparently for the same reasons Western woman do. As Jidat Mint Ethmane of Mauritania told the *Wall Street Journal*, "Beauty is more important than health."

The point is that our Body Myth is neither timeless nor inevitable; it is driven by arbitrary, external cultural standards. So why does it feel like a universal truth?

Perhaps it is because culture (especially in the form of the media) has taken over many functions that the extended family used to serve for earlier generations of women. In the past, the extended family had a profound influence on a woman's nuclear family and her individual identity. For millennia, grandparents, cousins, aunts, uncles, neighbors, and friends helped raise children and made clear what was expected from them and valued in them.

That was often a good thing, sometimes a bad thing, and usually a mixture of positive and negative. For example, when our grandmothers were girls, they may have spent little time away from their own grandmothers—an arrangement that probably felt down-right stifling some days. But, as a nineteenth-century woman, Grandma's grandma probably also demonstrated (in word and deed) to all of her grandchildren what the family valued most in women and girls: integrity, hard work, caring for others, and commitment to family. Rigid external standards of beauty seldom made the list because they were seldom relevant to survival or satisfaction in the days before the onset of mass electronic media.

The Culture as Extended Family

Today the influence of that human extended family has faded. Ours is a very mobile society—many of us no longer live near our families of origin. Even if we stay geographically close, we are likely to be wrapped up in the modern woman's life of multiple, demanding roles, which leaves little time for getting together with relatives. We miss the soothing ageless wisdom that springs from deep family con-nections and values through the informal mentoring given by older women in our families and communities.

Nowadays, the media-saturated culture fills the spot that the extended family filled for earlier generations of women. The nuclear family still plays a major role in creating our identity and guiding our development, but the culture has usurped the extended family in influence. Indeed, the culture may sometimes be even more powerful than the nuclear family in a woman's life, just as our grandmother may have been shaped more by her own grandmother than by her mother.

Meanwhile, Western culture is still ambivalent about the poten-tial, power, and changing role of contemporary women. Our increas-ing influence is met by a backlash of constantly changing (and unattainable) beauty standards that keep most women on edge and anxious about how others see us. In an earlier book, I coined the term *Body Wars* to define this systematic and relentless assault on our bod-ies by economic and social systems that benefit from suppressing women's economic and social power.

Because these assaults are so normal in our culture, we are unsure of ourselves and of what we really hunger or yearn for, no matter what our age. The Body Myth both erodes our capacity to fully realize the broader social influence and power we can attain in society and helps an ambivalent culture to "keep women in their place."

A hundred years ago, it was hard (although still possible) for a woman to escape her extended family and its standards, even though she could never entirely escape its influence on her development. Today, most Western women cannot escape the influence of the media and its promotion of the Body Myth. Every day, this culture-as-extended-family tells us that the most important and valuable thing about a woman is her external, physical appearance. That's a radically different message from the one our grandmothers got from their extended families.

In fact, none of our foremothers had to master nonstop media. This is another example of the way that we are immigrants into a foreign way of living life as women. Corporate-owned media culture is more inescapably *with* us than the human extended family was with our grandparents:

- The radio or TV is on as soon as we wake.
- We wear clothing with prominent logos and other marketing messages.
- Billboards and radio ads crowd our ride to and from work.
- Unbidden ads pop up on our computer screen.
- Ads literally envelop the food we eat for lunch.
- Back home at night, we read magazines and watch TV until we drop off to sleep.

Coursing through nearly every vessel of this commercial media octopus is the message that we don't measure up to the modern ideal of beauty. The culture's values and expectations about us as women are authoritarian, rigid, and unreasonable—just the way authoritarian parents and grandparents can be. You can negotiate with your parents (and even your extended family), but you can't negotiate with the culture.

It is as though a hyperactive, loud, overbearing, manipulative, and deaf grandfather shouts out nonstop, telling us who to be and what to do, regardless of who it is we actually are or what it is we actually need. On the occasions that we recognize the absurd, destructive notions about body image that Grandpa Media sells us, we can shout back at the TV screen in frustration. But the TV doesn't hear us. We never get a chance to say anything personal to it, or to hear it respond to who we are.

Facing such an unrelenting and rigid assault on our self-worth, even the hardiest among us sometimes succumb to self-doubt and self-hatred. No matter how absurd it is to expect a sixty-five-year-old woman to look like a fifteen-year-old girl, women of every age feel their value measured by a commercially generated standard of beauty.

Of course, there's a reason why Grandpa Media acts this way. The cultural extended family profits when we stay wrapped up in living the Body Myth and trying to meet an unyielding beauty ideal. The more wrapped up we are, the more we feel the need to buy products and services that we don't really need. Grandpa Media makes scads more money by making us feel bad about ourselves than a human grandpa can by sitting around his kitchen telling us family stories that help us cherish our heritage. In the cultural extended family, creating profit is exponentially more important than the pride and self-worth that a human extended family can create.

So while familial ties of the human extended family (as well as religion and community) are weakening, we must fight internal battles over body image, because the media, culture, and consumer value system are assailing our bodies and self-confidence.

This cause is not altogether and exclusively woman's cause. It is the cause of human brotherhood as well as human sisterhood, and both must rise and fall together. Women cannot be elevated without elevating man, and man cannot be depressed without depressing women also.

—Frederick Douglass

Bodies at the Turn of the Twentieth Century

Find a photograph or a print of a Pierre-Auguste Renoir painting in an encyclopedia, art history book, or online. You'll quickly see how differently we experience the female shape today than women and men did little more than a century ago, when Renoir painted. For example, take his 1895 *Seated Female Nude* or *After the Bath* (you can see it at New York's Metropolitan Museum of Art or online at www.metmuseum.org/special/Levin/3.L.htm). This painting shows how Renoir celebrated the sensuality and sexual attraction of a large, fertile woman. This was the cultural ideal beauty when our great- and great-great-grandmothers were in their prime.

But our great-grandmothers might never have seen the original *Seated Female Nude*, or even a print of it. That's because they lived in the last decades before electronic mass media exploded into our culture. Without radio, TV, or the Internet, they had radically different interactions with the culture, themselves, and the very concept of body image. Our great-grandmothers:

- were not exposed every day to thousands of mass media images

- often lived without mirrors into which they gazed critically at themselves every day

- lived in an economy that did not depend on them spending money daily to alleviate their body discontent

- Saw relatives, friends, neighbors, and other real women with diverse body shapes far more frequently than they saw idealized advertising images.

As a result, it was less common for 1890s women to be concerned if their bodies did not measure up to Renoir's *Sitting Nude*. The very notion of comparing themselves to mass-marketed beauty standards was as foreign as France itself. Our great-grandmothers spent vastly more of their time looking at real people in their natural extended families and neighborhoods than they ever did looking at ads, newspapers, magazines, and other commercially produced imagery. Their community culture held much less context or reason for obsessing about body shape.

Renoir once said that were it not for the female body, he never could have become a painter. This is clear: there is love for women in each detail of the canvas, and love for self, and there is joy, and there is a degree of sensual integration that makes you want to weep, so beautiful it seems, and so elusive.

—Caroline Knapp

Bodies of the Last Hundred Years

While today's framework of beauty may seem cast in stone, a look back across the last century shows that it isn't. For example, when the first fashion shows and beauty pageants began in the early twentieth century, participants averaged fifty pounds more than they do today—but were still considered the height of beauty. The past hundred years mark an epoch of increasing attacks on women's bodies through the media, which touts the latest product, procedure, or trend and promotes the notion that our ultimate value is our appearance.

The year 1920 was a pivotal one in media history and women's history. The first radio broadcast reported the 1920 presidential election, and within a decade, millions of homes had radio sets. The 1920 election was also the first one where women voted, since it came less than three months after ratification of the Nineteenth Amendment. But almost immediately, this growth in women's rights was met with a cultural backlash. For example, in 1921, the Miss America pageant began, signaling a rigorously shrinking ideal for women's bodies. During the Roaring Twenties, the popular beauty standard shifted to the thinner flapper image, with bound breasts and a penchant for dieting.

As women's movements continued to challenge traditions throughout the twentieth century, many believed that archaic narrow standards for female beauty would become obsolete. But it was not to be. Instead, beauty pageants flourished and, with the help of rapidly expanding mass media, fashion took on a more central role in women's lives.

When the so-called second wave of feminism generated major social change in the 1960s and 1970s, the beauty ideal shrank from buxom, full-hipped, size 14 Marilyn Monroe to matchstick Twiggy (five foot six and ninety pounds—only about 70 percent of the expected weight for her height and age). Fashion spreads and magazine covers favored models with the "starved" look. Weight Watchers and the dieting craze took off, joining the fashion industry to foster women's uncertainty about our worth. By the millions, we started looking for answers to life's questions in the mirror, on the scale, and amid the clothing racks.

By the late 1970s, U.S. women had won legal access to education, birth control, and sexual freedom unimagined by earlier generations of women. But while the opportunities to fulfill these appetites widened, our basic body appetites became taboo. Social liberation brought intense body shame and sanctions.

For example, only a tiny fraction of today's Miss America contestants fall in the healthy range of weight-to-height ratio. In fact, 60 percent of these young women fit a key diagnostic criterion for anorexia: they have less than 85 percent of the expected weight for their height. Pageant contestants average fourteen hours of exercise per week, with some working out as many as thirty-five hours. Their bodies aren't natural; they are crafted, sculpted, and starved in a subculture where fasting and purging are normal.

In the 1970s, the average fashion model weighed 8 percent less than the average American woman. By the 1990s, she weighed 23 percent less—hardly a model for the type of woman likely to throw her weight around in order to exercise power. We can trace some of that change to a slightly higher average weight for women, but most of the difference lies in a shrinking of the standard model. The gap between real and ideal continues to widen, festering great discontent for many women.

A few brave women in the fashion world challenge the domination of thin. Models with fuller (in reality, more normal bodies), like Emme, Carrie Otis, and Kate Dillon, show the guts to question the tyrannical standards of beauty, raise public consciousness about body image and eating disorders, and still succeed in their chosen profession. They courageously share stories of how they were pressured and threatened to shape their bodies into something smaller than their natures intended. These pioneers are admirable and we need more like them, but the fashion industry isolates them as so-called "plus-sized" models, even though their weight-height proportions are just plain average.

Today, only a rebellious woman could feel positive when her mirror reveals Renoir's 1895 ideal of ample, fertile, feminine contours. Most of us are ashamed of any softness on our bodies. We are supposed to be hard, bony, and muscular rather than curvaceous. We want to look more like a boy with breasts than a juicy Renoir woman. We are not supposed to look older, softer, rounder, and less angular. The body type dictated by our genes and ethnic roots has no relevance and gets no respect. By today's Body Myth standards, beauty is:

- singular, not diverse

- thin, not full
- crafted, not natural
- bought, not innate.

Beauty pageants continue to flourish across the United States and overseas each year. Women are expected (and we expect ourselves) to keep using arbitrary external beauty standards to judge our worth, while also assuming new social roles and work responsibilities. We want to feel part of the extended family that the culture represents, and we want its approval as well. No wonder we feel tired, confused, and distressed and are willing to manipulate our bodies endlessly, in hopes of feeling good enough.

Women and Wanting

A booming consumer culture requires that women want, because we make 85 percent of all purchases in the United States. Since our economy thrives on what we buy, it depends on manufacturing female desire—even if that manufactured desire puts us at war with our own bodies.

Consumer culture exploded in the 1950s when women needed a role after World War II, and factories needed new consumer products to replace military manufacturing. The number of magazines and the amount of advertising grew exponentially, pressuring women to want the perfect home, the perfect family, and all the products needed to complete this ideal picture. By the late 1990s, shopping malls made up over four billion square feet in the United States—about sixteen square feet per person. In order to support all of this shopping space, retailers need each of us to want a lot so that we'll purchase a lot. From many directions, we feel compelled to buy.

For example, within days of the September 11, 2001, terrorist attacks, we were told that the most patriotic thing to do was shop. Conspicuous consumption would stabilize our culture, prove our strength, and keep the terrorists from defeating us. Consumerism was once more enshrined as a central American identity and value. After decades of reinforcement, we've accepted that a central female role is to shop and consume, and that has been very good for our market economy's profit makers.

The Power of Money

Over the past fifty years, women have gained (through our own will and effort) unheralded advances in choice, opportunity, schooling, responsibility, money, expectations, and influence.

However, these advancements have produced a backlash, and we are now surrendering a great deal of our will, effort, and power to expectations that we take up less physical space and forfeit our strength of body. The more we submit to judging our worth by the world's standards about external appearance, the less power we have to make the world a better place for women—and for the men and children with whom we share this planet.

While women still make about one-quarter less than men for comparable work (and have fewer benefits), we pay out a much higher percentage of those earnings on our appearance than men do. We invest in cosmetics, beauty rituals, dieting, clothing, surgery, and other attempts to have our looks earn us status, acceptance, and self-worth. We feel compelled to buy products with no proven effectiveness, like the cellulite creams that cost U.S. women over $10 million in 2003 alone while failing to eliminate an ounce of cellulite.

Madison Avenue steers our purchases in trivial directions and relentlessly objectifies and pseudosexualizes the female body to sell goods and services. Advertising tells women that we are powerful and unstoppable (co-opting the positive results of the women's movement), but then sells the idea that a *product* will liberate or strengthen us as women. We are supposed to get "New Freedom" from maxi pads and obtain power through alcohol and tobacco.

Although we often seem blind to it, the irony drips from marketing like the campaign Philip Morris put behind Virginia Slims cigarettes. Tobacco products marketed to women have thin-related names—playing on our (false) belief that smoking will help us lose weight. For years, Virginia Slims ads featured highly sexualized photos of cigarette-smoking models proclaiming "You've come a long way, baby!"—manipulating women's hard-won social and economic progress to sell us a product guaranteed to shorten our lives. Philip Morris sells the myth of liberation, but if we buy the product, we're buying the captivity of addiction. A look at the increased rates of women's tobacco use since Philip Morris introduced Virginia Slims in 1968 shows that we've come a long way toward a dead end (literally).

Ad Addiction

Advertising is the most powerful engine of consumer culture. Many of us say, "I know about advertising, but it doesn't influence *me*." Such assertions are naive at best and self-destructive at worst. Corporations would not stay in business long if they spent billions of dollars on something that didn't turn a profit. Marketers spend more than $100 billion on advertising annually in the United States alone; they do it because it works. In her book *Can't Buy My Love*, Dr. Jean Kilbourne argues convincingly that the sophistication and ubiquity of today's advertising asserts an addictive power over people in a consumer culture. Marketing's multimedia, subliminal, and persistent methods get us to believe that some buyable thing will give our lives meaning and fulfillment.

Remember that a century ago, many women saw an ad only rarely, as they lived their daily lives with little mass media (none of it electronic). Today we rarely experience a minute without marketing's intrusion into our psyche. The average Western woman is exposed to as many as three thousand ads a day—more than two ads a minute (and more than three a minute during normal waking hours). That volume of consumption is extreme and makes our new extended family—the one based in our culture—look very much like an addicted family.

Your Personal Ad Volume

Here's a simple exercise to create awareness of how deeply advertising enters our lives.

When you wake up tomorrow, start keeping close track of the amount of time during the day when there is no marketing or advertising either visible or within earshot. Be sure to count any time spent when brand names and logos are visible; they are more widespread than many of us think. For example:

- If you are driving out in the country with the radio off, far away from billboards, the name and/or logo of the car you are driving is probably still visible on the steering wheel or dashboard.

- If you spend hours in the library, publisher's logos are visible on the spines and covers of books, while most books advertise the book's title on each page.

- Many pieces of clothing (including shirts, pants, shoes, jackets, and so forth) feature highly visible logos and/or brand names. For example, school names and logos on shirts and uniforms are a form of marketing.

At the end of the day, add up the time you spent free from any form of marketing. We've done this experiment, and our free time amounted to less than an hour. The exercise is not designed as an indictment of marketing, but rather as a way to raise personal awareness of marketing's ubiquity in our lives.

The imagery of these ads bombards us with increasing speed and intensity, making it nearly impossible to screen or filter them before they are absorbed into our consciousness. As recently as twenty years ago, thirty-second television commercials routinely had only a handful of edits; an image or shot could last ten, fifteen, or even then an entire thirty seconds. Next time you watch TV, count the number of edits or shots in today's commercials. It is now common for a thirty-second spot to have forty or fifty different shots, with images lasting a split second as they are machine-gunned into our heads. Commercials are quickly becoming shorter and shorter, as viewers' attention spans diminish. Meanwhile, marketers are subliminally "imbedding" products and name brands into regular programming and editorial content, blurring the line between ads and everything else. We are left without enough time, context, or information to analyze, consider, and decide whether to accept or reject a commercial message.

Most of us grew up watching television and were exposed to ads before we could even talk. Each year, marketing intrudes ever more deeply into our own children's lives. While a small handful of advocacy groups, like the Campaign for Commercial Free Childhood (www.commercialfreechildhood.org) and Dads and Daughters (www.dadsanddaughters.org) try to stem that tide, we seldom speak up against the worsening waves of marketing directed at adult women. No one seems to care that women of all ages, shapes, colors, and ethnicities are told to look like skinny, fair-skinned preteens. We spend years of our lives drenched in these images—they seep into the pores of our consciousness, subliminally shaping our decisions and perceptions. They ruthlessly attack our connection to our bodies, desires, and feelings—in the relentless pursuit of profit.

Women's and girls' magazines have a formula for profit requiring that the content of the magazine makes each reader feel like she doesn't measure up alongside articles and ads that promise she will fit in or feel better about herself if she buys an advertised product. The more the content drives *down* readers' self-esteem, the more it drives *up* magazine profits. The formula has worked for decades and is backed up by psychological research showing that the self-esteem of women and girls drops markedly after only a few minutes of reading a fashion magazine.

Most of the female images in ads and on the screen are not even real; they are airbrushed or computer "enhanced" (more accurately, computer distorted). Many of these mythical images are composites of several people, featuring the best feature of each. For example, the producers of *Pretty Woman* did not consider the body of box-office superstar Julia Roberts thin enough for the film's nude scenes. So those scenes were shot with another woman's body doubling for Roberts. With media image manipulation so common, many models, actresses, newscasters, and other public figures have regular cosmetic surgery. We mistake these pretty women for real women when they are not.

Big Questions

The next time you feel the desire to look like a mannequin or media image of an ideal woman, ask yourself these questions:

- Does she look strong enough to work in the fields?
- To operate machinery?
- To carry a child?
- To nurse the sick?
- To defend herself against sexual assault?
- To change a tire?
- To play professional sports?

- To compete with men in the boardroom?
- To coach a soccer team?
- To run for Congress—or maybe even president?
- Is it possible that smaller women are less of a threat to the status quo?
- Is it really possible to eat less but be more?

Even incredibly accomplished women get stuck in the Body Myth, spending immense energy, anxiety, and cash trying to change their bodies. For example, throughout Madeleine K. Albright's autobiography *Madam Secretary*, the first female U.S. secretary of state relates continual concerns about her weight and physical appearance. While her vast achievements were fueled by intense pride in her Slavic heritage, she felt chronically insecure inside the short, stocky shape of her Slavic body. Yet Albright's memoir includes no acknowledgment of how absurd it is for the country's most politically powerful woman to agonize over her natural appearance.

Many of us feel the same way: proud of our family but ashamed of the body that very same family gave us. The desire to feel more accepted by our culture dominates our daily lives and fuels an unconscious civil war between our body and our sense of self.

New Media; Old Battles

Proponents of the Internet promised that this new technology would create global and self-supporting communities to bring people together and help them feel good about themselves. In practice, the most visible communities for women have been commercially conquered.

For example, a Web site that promotes itself as the number one source of online information and everyday support for women is like a virtual mall, with nonstop ads (and direct, one-click links for) companies selling diet products, cosmetics, clothes, and other products promising to deliver us the right attributes. A quiz pops up asking if you are a good kisser, sexy enough, trying too hard, a great date, or a skilled lover. A top story promises a "Killer body now. Firm abs in 15 minutes. 30 days to a better butt."

While this site has hundreds of message boards on valuable topics like pregnancy, parenting, relationships, and work, these are outnumbered by links to gossip, astrology, entertainment media, dieting, and makeup. When we dig a little deeper into this Web site (the "investor relations" pages are ideal for this), we learn that its other properties include what the company euphemistically calls: "extensive databases of pertinent information to subscribing companies and members." When their privacy policy openly admits that "we frequently provide information and links to third party advertisers or partners," it is easy to see where information in those databases originates.

In other words, under the guise of building a community for women, this Web site actually sells information about those women to advertisers. As its euphemism-infused corporate profile puts it, the company "is recognized as an industry leader in developing innovative sponsorship and commerce relationships that match the desire of marketers to reach women with the needs of iVillage.com members for relevant information and services."

Because similar marketing techniques are so ubiquitous, it seems normal to accept them as the answer to women's needs, questions, and dreams. Instead of truly exploring women's hungers, we allow them to be packaged into retail products or sound bites.

The prevailing consumer culture leads us to believe that our power lies in purchasing. Now that we have our own money, we can join this new wave of consumer feminism and buy more of everything—bigger cars, houses, and wardrobes—for us and for our families. But these narrow choices are empty of the real nourishment our lives and spirits need. Drowning in the sea of marketing, we lose any inkling of what we really thirst for. Do we want a pair of designer heels promising to make us look taller and thinner—or do we want time to reflect, the power to influence legislation, and a chance to hold hands with a child, friend, or lover? Do we seriously think that the sisterhood of sharing community power can really be replaced by the sisterhood of shopping?

The Manufactured Body

In today's media and marketing culture, it is increasingly rare to find a woman's body that bears much resemblance to the female body's natural shape. The Body Myth creates an imperative that we redesign our natural shape. Constant exposure to designer bodies and designer faces makes even wise women with solid records of achievement succumb to the pressure of meeting these impossible standards.

For many years, legal correspondent Greta Van Susteren has used her smart, articulate, and analytical style to hold her own in the highly competitive world of TV news. She doesn't back down or defer, nor is she unnecessarily aggressive. She uses her brain, not her body, to successfully impress viewers.

The forty-seven-year-old, plain-looking, former defense attorney was at the top of her field in 2002 when Fox News Channel hired Van Susteren away from CNN to host her own prime-time news program, *On the Record*. That's when Van Susteren announced she would have a face-lift before starting her new show. Never confirming speculation that Fox required it as part of her contract, Van Susteren said that a month off between jobs gave her time to impulsively pursue cosmetic surgery. With the addition of a new hairdo, new hair color, and trendier fashions, Van Susteren had a younger, sexier, and hotter image. To her credit, Van Susteren made headlines because she is among the few public personas to admit having work done on her body.

Of course there is no connection between hot looks and quality journalism or insightful legal analysis. Van Susteren's story shows that the face we see on camera is not necessarily real. More important, it shows how our culture requires women to adhere to strict standards of beauty in order to be seen as successful—and how difficult (and often impossible) it is for women to be taken seriously, even when we display serious talent.

When we buy into this cultural requirement, the costs are immense:

- We live by the bigoted and false rules that our body's natural shape and appearance should determine how important we are and how seriously we should be taken.

- Attempts to alter our body's natural shape and appearance drain our mental, emotional, and spiritual resources.

- Even without the psychological price, the balance sheet racks up billions of dollars spent on beauty products and procedures that don't (and usually can't) live up to their promises.

- While we spend (for example, $20 billion annually on cosmetics), companies plow our money back into advertising to convince us that skin cream and hair dye can soothe our souls and solve the "problem" of aging.

- We risk losing our grip on who we are. Some of my clients are so afraid to be seen without these layers of protection that no one knows what they truly look like.

It used to be that women were considered narcissistic, unstable, or—at the very least—neurotic if they wore heavy makeup all the time or took radical steps like plastic surgery to change their real appearance. In today's climate, these same women are viewed as motivated and achievement oriented. Modern plastic surgery campaigns promote breast enhancement as safe, effective, and essential to women's mental health—just as they promoted breast *removal* as good for women's well-being in the 1920s, when the boyish flapper look was in style.

If women suddenly stopped feeling ugly, the fastest growing medical specialty [elective cosmetic surgery] would be the fastest dying.

—Naomi Wolf

In an age when more than 80 percent of women say they are dissatisfied with their bodies, it is no surprise that many of us believe the Body Myth's absurd notion that our psychological and emotional well-being is dependent on removing part of our stomach, chemically peeling our skin, or implanting synthetic sacs in our breasts. Of course, the widespread currency of this notion does not stop it from being absurd—and untrue.

However, the Body Myth does contribute to the cultural homogenization of beauty and to the growing insecurity among non-Caucasian women about their body image. The positive trend of cultural diversity in media and advertising actually complicates and intensifies issues about body image. For example, there is far greater diversity of body size and skin color among well-known male African American actors and models than there is among female ones (contrast Bernie Mac and Halle Berry). Especially in advertising, the black women most likely to appear are the ones with the lightest skin and the most "white" facial and body features.

This "white" aesthetic infects the self-image of noncelebrities as well. By 2003, 16 percent of cosmetic surgery patients in the United States were people of color. Among the most popular procedures are eyelid and nose reconstructions, which eliminate distinct genetic features to attain a more Western appearance. Women of African and Asian heritage face unique plastic surgery health risks with, for example, higher odds for scarring and fibrous skin tumors called keloids.

This trend depletes the essential cultural asset of real diversity. The homogenization of beauty—and the belief that a manufactured body is better than a real one—undermines respect for the countless ethnicities, religions, and races that enrich, and are essential to, the very life of our culture. Women who engage in plastic surgery also pass a deficit on to their families. Children of cosmetic procedure aficionados may not have a sense of how their own bodies should naturally look as they age—or even recognize earlier pictures of their parents in the family photo album.

Despite the multitude of downsides, body-altering procedures are common enough to be normal, even if they entail life-threatening operations. Patients tell me that they see it as comparable to coloring their hair—an ordinary experience for an ordinary woman on an ordinary day. Some of my patients, at the ripe old age of twenty-eight, have cosmetic plastic surgery with the sole purpose of looking younger.

One of every forty women in the United States has risky silicone gel-filled breast implants, even though the Food and Drug Administration banned their use for most women in 1992—and rejected an industry challenge to the ban in 2004. Several influences collude to pressure women into these decisions:

- Our sexual culture demands big breasts while our youth culture demands a young and perky body.

- The medical system often promotes procedures and materials later found unsafe, and then profits from follow-up surgeries and treatments to remove or correct the resulting problems.

- Through product liability cases, the legal system has helped right some of these wrongs, but the media's occasional coverage of the risks are outweighed by media glorification of unreal bodies.

Meanwhile, women still suffer from medical procedures about which they have very complicated emotions. A tragic example is Olivia Goldsmith, the successful, pop-feminist author of ten novels, including the best seller *The First Wives Club*, later a popular movie. While I was writing this book, Goldsmith died at age fifty-four from medical complications during a face-lift.

Investigations have shown deaths associated with liposuction and other cosmetic procedures, as well as autoimmune diseases from bursting or leaking breast implants. Risking one's life to fight off fear of aging may seem vain or unusual at first, but it's the logical outcome of a culture that degrades and ignores older women and their wisdom.

Plastic beauty is not beauty at all. Still our culture brainwashes many women into seeing it as the best remedy for our life concerns. Until we demand a culture that believes that women are okay as is, we will succumb to the constant pressures to look different, more fashionable, more attractive, thinner, and younger—in essence, to base our entire self-worth on our body's appearance.

Fashion and Fashism

> A Fashion is nothing more than an induced epidemic.
> —George Bernard Shaw

Fashion creates a big pressure to conform. While men are not totally immune, male fashion basics remain the same from year to year: suit and tie for white-collar work, casual shirts with slacks or jeans for everything else. For women, casual clothes are rarely casual—and work clothes are even more treacherous.

To be socially accepted as a real woman, we must adopt unrealistically shifting fashion trends at all times. Fashion's influence on the standards of femininity keeps us anxious, uncertain, and dependent. Sexism in fashion is dictatorial and unforgiving of individual variations in body shape and weight, or personal preference. It takes on a tone of "fashism," unapologetically sapping women's freedom, creativity, self-esteem, health, and wallets.

Fashism did not always have the widespread influence it enjoys today. Less than a century ago, most women made their own clothes, while more affluent women had dressmakers customize clothing to their individual shapes. The arrival of retail, mass-produced, ready-to-wear clothing in the 1920s ushered in a new era of anxiety about the shape of our body dimensions. We began to feel, on a deeply individual level, that the essential fashion problem was with our body, rather than with the standardized clothing we found on store racks. Alterations (if we can even get them at the store) cost extra for us; over in the men's suit department, alterations are free. The unspoken assumption is that a woman's body must change to fit into the garment, no matter how arbitrarily sized and styled, while the clothing itself is changed to fit whatever shape or waistline a man has.

Lookism and Ageism

Cultural perceptions of older adults remain unaltered as well. Our culture equates age with sickness, dependence, and helplessness, apparently blind to the millions of people who actively enjoy dynamic aging. Hundreds of thousands of older people travel to hostels and RV campgrounds, join exercise programs, return to school, or start second careers. With the media focus on deterioration rather than vitality, we lose sight of the fact that fewer than 5 percent of older Americans ages eighty and above have Alzheimer's disease. Nearly half of voters over sixty (many of them mobilized by AARP, one of the nation's most powerful political forces) go to the polls, while only about a third of younger voters do.

Fair-skinned blacks invented *passing* as a term, Jews escaping anti-Semitism perfected the art, and the sexual closet continues the punishment, but pretending to be a younger age is probably the most encouraged form of "passing," with the least organized support for coming out as one's true generational self.

—Gloria Steinem

While life expectancy increases, our ideas about aging and human potential remain stunted by perceptions reinforced by the mainstream media. One salient example is *New York* magazine, which devoted five pages to a feature story about Olivia Goldsmith's death. The remaining 200 pages of that same *New York* (the spring fashion issue) explain a lot about Goldsmith's beauty and aging angst. Page after page featured thin young women, most of them white, often in highly sexualized poses wearing revealing clothes. Even the ads for maternity fashion followed this formula.

New York's spring fashion issue is only one example of the thousands of ways that women become less visible and less valuable as we age. Living on such a toxic battlefield, it is no surprise that even accomplished women like Olivia Goldsmith are unhappy with their appearance. As we move from our twenties into our thirties, forties, fifties, sixties, and beyond, we see fewer and fewer women like us in the media.

Roles and opportunities in film, fashion, and television constrict radically for aging women in a way they don't for men. That is why it is unremarkable for Helen Hunt (born in 1963) to play a romantic lead opposite Jack Nicholson (born in 1937) in *As Good As It Gets*. However, it is a subject of great attention (not to mention the central joke of the movie) when Diane Keaton (born in 1946) plays a romantic lead opposite Jack Nicholson in *Something's Gotta Give*.

After a half-century of television news, a woman has never led the prime evening newscast on a broadcast network. In 1976, Barbara Walters briefly shared the *ABC Evening News* anchor desk with Harry Reasoner, before being dumped for a return to the male-only format. Female anchors on local and cable news are almost always coanchors with a man and are frequently selected for their looks.

The logical result of this looks-based career standard is this: women out-earn men only in occupations where practitioners directly use their bodies for income: modeling and prostitution.

Meanwhile, we ridicule women who challenge these realities, celebrate aging, and show more interest in power and fairness than in the power of having fair looks. We mock feminists, lesbians, and other "liberated" women for taking such "radical" steps as forgoing makeup and shaved legs. We mock men who wear makeup (unless they are under theatrical lights) or shave their legs (unless they are elite bicycle racers). When we judge an entire gender by its willingness to conform to arbitrary standards, we belittle and disempower all of us.

Steps for Aging Beautifully

- Develop a flexible body ideal. Remember that a negative body image is not a necessary side effect of getting older. Age can give you the confidence to create your own unique style.

- Identify with realistic role models. Find older, unglamorous role models who are truly magnificent, and hold them up as an image with whom to identify. Counteract your own ageism and lookism by trying to see older women as total women.

- Own up to your age. Age acceptance doesn't mean resigning yourself to the stereotype of ageism but redefining those myths as time redesigns your body. If you learn to see yourself in terms of your total assets, not merely in terms of appearance, the loss of youth's external beauty can be balanced by the accomplishments of age.

- Hang on to your sensuality. Indulge your body in all the physical pleasures you've earned by virtue of having lived this long. Keep enjoying the sensual side of movement, and keep challenging your body with physical activity.

- Use the wisdom you've acquired over the years. With maturity comes an understanding of what works well for you cosmetically, sexually, athletically, nutritionally. This knowledge can help you nurture your aging body with attention and respect.

Adapted from *Bodylove* by Rita Freedman.

Male Casualties

It may seem odd at first, but men and boys are also profoundly harmed by our culture's assault on the female body. A twenty-something female television reporter once interviewed my coauthor about a father's role in developing his daughter's body image. While chatting afterward, the woman (attractive by cultural standards) told how she and her most recent boyfriend broke up. The young man sat her down and said, "I like going out with you, but you're not pretty enough for me. You're only a seven or an eight and I need to be dating a ten."

While this boorish comment was outrageous and hurtful to the young woman, take a moment to consider how completely this young man has absorbed the twisted standards of our culture-as-extended-family. He is going through life with a pornographic view of the world. He doesn't believe he is succeeding unless he is with a supermodel. He is missing the entire point of being human—making genuine connection. He is walking around with a huge void in the center of his life.

Most disturbing of all: he doesn't even know the void exists. We may not realize it, but the culture's values shower men and boys (including our sons) with the belief that how a woman looks is more important than who she is. Such pornographic objectification of women distorts men's reality and cripples their (and, therefore, our) ability to fully experience the depth and thrill of true intimacy.

This is the central reason why men have a huge stake in how our culture views and treats females. Men have their own serious issues about body image—overcoming the false notion that success means landing a good-looking female and that men will feel inadequate if they don't have washboard abs. Men may not see it readily (unless they have daughters), but they pay too high a price for the Body War objectification of women. The way our culture views women warps what we expect from men and how men see themselves.

A boy who grows up believing the lie that the size of a woman's cleavage and waistline are more important than the size of her heart and brain is ill prepared to have a lifelong intimate relationship with anyone.

Turning the Corner

If we hope to help ourselves and our children live in healthful ways that foster good relationships, then we have to cast off the Body Myth and make peace with our bodies. As we saw in chapter 6, families and loved ones may be willing to change to help support women who are struggling to free themselves from obsessions with weight, food, and body image. But the extended family of Western culture reacts cruelly and critically when women try to regain control of their lives and their self-esteem.

I wish our culture's relationship with women reflected the luscious vibrancy in Renoir's paintings of female nudes. Instead, as we've just seen, the picture of women's body image is quite a bit bleaker.

Despite that, women *can* extricate themselves (and one another) from the toxic extended family of commercial media culture. As we move into chapters exploring treatment and recovery, we'll look at the deeply personal work women must do to make peace with their individual bodies. But we'll also explore the more collective efforts we must all make to create a cultural extended family that embraces women as they are, rather than making war on their bodies.

8

The Shape of Recovery

So what do you do if it looks or feels like you or a loved one might indeed have an eating disorder or suffer from body image despair?

There is no one simple answer. These multifaceted problems must be addressed from a number of angles, and each woman has to create a unique blend of what works best for her. Much of recovery happens outside formal treatment, when we begin to take chances in life by putting into practice what we learn in therapies. Recovery builds on the willingness to do things differently. Just like love, it is a cluster of small things, not just one "aha."

In the throes of eating disorders and despair over body image, we translate our pain, disappointments, and anguish into the Body Myth's language of fat. Recovery means putting those feelings into the language of words instead. Fortunately, we don't have to do this alone. There is help available, and isolation only makes pain grow like an untreated tumor, spreading, metastasizing, invading, and taking over more and more of life. On the other hand, sharing eventually shrinks the pain.

Talking about our pain and despair may feel just as frightening as undergoing chemotherapy for cancer—it is strong medicine that might make us feel worse before we feel better. Some of my patients say they would rather have a physical illness like cancer than a psychological one like eating disorders or body image obsessions. However, effective treatment works because we get guidance and support from others, so that we no longer feel alone with our problems.

At first, it may be hard to believe that recovery can work for us. Most of my adult patients apologize for needing my time, saying that their problems just aren't important enough. They apologize even more when they begin to talk about the issues underlying their symptoms. These women have completely absorbed the cultural values suggesting that their true hungers, needs, appetites, and feelings are less legitimate and important than the shape of their appearance.

> Pain festers in isolation, it thrives in secrecy. Words are its nemesis, naming anguish the first step in defusing it, talking about the muck a woman slogs through—the squirms of self-hatred and guilt, the echoes of emptiness and need—a prerequisite for moving beyond it.
>
> —Caroline Knapp

This chapter will explore the process of recovery from eating disorder or body image obsessions. Recovery is not an easy on/off switch. It requires a process of building motivation and readiness before any change can actually take root. Many women with eating and body image issues get discouraged and give up because they aren't able to make major shifts right away. In reality, no one takes giant steps without taking a lot of baby steps first. Always remember that recovery is possible.

Can Things Change?

Women with eating disorders often wonder if they can survive without their disease because they don't see or feel any separation between the illness and their sense of self. Some of my patients feel that everyone and everything else in life has let them down or caused too much pain, leaving the eating disorder as their old reliable. On the other hand, a woman's eating disorder might mobilize previously unseen (or even nonexistent) support and concerns from partners, friends, or family. Afraid of losing this comfort and positive attention, she may resist letting go of the problem and being left alone in the background once again.

Some women feel hopeless, convinced that they cannot get better because they have been sick for so long. Too afraid to hope, they feel sure that they will fail at recovery, and then feel even worse about themselves. Their hopelessness and ambivalence are self-protective. Others believe they deserve to be punished and that God (or some other Power) will not allow them to be happy or feel better. Patients who are skeptical or ambivalent about recovery frequently tell me:

- What if I work really hard at getting better, I gain weight, and I still die? I don't want to die, and I especially don't want to be fat.

- I don't deserve to feel better. I have messed up my life and have no one else to blame. This is my punishment.

- Nothing has ever worked out for me, why should I believe I can get better?

- If I gain weight but don't feel any better, then what will I have?

This ambivalence and despair are powerful, and they are fueled by the obsession's self-defeating Voice and the depression caused by malnutrition's impact on brain neurotransmitters. Together, these factors can make it feel nearly impossible to take the leap of faith necessary to begin recovery.

There is no denying that recovery from these illnesses is hard work, requiring major changes in how we think, feel, and live. Many women who have recovered found it helps to break down recovery into smaller pieces or stages:

- *Contemplating change.* I'm aware there is a problem, but I'm waiting until later to do anything, or I feel ambivalent about whether to do anything.

- *Preparing for change.* I'm getting ready to do something soon, or I recently began to try some new attitudes and behaviors.

- *Taking action.* I'm working to overcome the problem by actively altering my behavior, self-perceptions, beliefs, and/or my surrounding environment.

- *Preserving change.* I'm taking steps and getting support to prevent relapses and maintain my new positive, healthy life pattern.

Looking at things this way, we can see ambivalence as a *part* of recovery. It is a stage of change rather than a stubborn resistance to it. We also recognize that maintenance of recovery is a process of ongoing change and growth. We realize that the road of recovery is a healthy journey, not a Nirvana destination.

———————————— ✑ ————————————

Readiness for Change

If you are struggling with issues about eating or body image, this exercise can help clarify your next steps. In each group of statements, pick the one (or ones) that best describe where you are right now.

1. ___ A   I don't think there's anything wrong with how I feel about food or my body.

   ___ B   I need to do something different—this really isn't working for me.

   ___ C   I'm going to do something about this soon.

   ___ D   Reading fashion magazines makes me feel worse about myself; I'm giving them up.

2. ___ A   Other people badger me about this; they don't know what they're talking about.

   ___ B   When I'm ready, I'll be able to do something about this.

   ___ C   I am discussing this problem with my partner, friend, or doctor.

   ___ D   I am going to start eating regular meals every day.

3. ___ A   It's normal to obsess about weight and food and not be able to think about anything else.

   ___ B   I am afraid others will think less of me if I gain weight or look different.

   ___ C   I'm going to get professional help—I can't do this alone.

   ___ D   I won't buy any more fat-free foods (or diet pills, laxatives, etc.)

4. ___ A   I'm fine—other people are just jealous of my self-control.

___ B   I'd like to be able to order off the menu without making any changes.

___ C   I'll read the self-help book that helped my friend.

___ D   I am throwing the scale out.

5. ___ A   Exercise is more important than having friends.

___ B   I'd like to be able to have more balance in my life.

___ C   My New Years' resolution will be to eat better.

___ D   I'm posting positive affirmations on my mirror so I won't be as negative about my body.

A answers indicate you are in the precontemplation stage, not sure that there's anything wrong.

B answers indicate that you are contemplating making some changes but haven't quite started yet.

C answers are signs that you are preparing to change.

D answers indicate that you have already started to take action.

If you picked a blend of these letters, you are moving from one stage to the next. Ambivalence about change is common among women recovering from eating or body image disorders. Motivation to change is not a black-or-white thing—it evolves. Even reading this book could be the beginning of a change process!

The Shape of Treatment

A serious eating disorder or body image obsession affects all dimensions of the sufferer's life—identity, spirituality, relationships, work, family—and every biological system in the body itself. Effective treatment uses multiple strategies to address these disparate elements together, rather than approaching them individually, in isolation. An individual session with a psychologist may include conversations about emotions, family, medical issues, and the sufferer's relationship to her body. Consultations with a physician might include discussions of emotional struggles, nutrition, and pressing medical concerns.

Discussions with a nutritionist may explore family history, work environment, and meals. While effective treatment may look incomprehensibly interwoven, it eventually makes sense—and leads to recovery.

Eating disorders expert Dr. Anita Johnston, author of *Eating in the Light of the Moon*, describes the treatment process as a labyrinth: a single pathway that often loops back toward itself while moving forward at the same time. She writes that women working their way through recovery

> follow a twisting, turning, winding path to their centers. . . . to leave behind old perceptions of themselves that they had adopted from others and to reclaim their inner authorities. . . . to listen to the voice from within to give them guidance and support as they searched for their true thoughts, feelings, and desires. . . . letting go of all expectations of linear progress, disengaging the rational mind, and embracing the power of their emotions and intuition.

On this journey, Johnston says, women will sometimes feel

> trapped, lost, bored, disoriented, frustrated, or anxious, but they keep on going, placing one foot in front of the other. Finding their centers, the essence of who they are as women, was not the end of the journey. They then had to exit the labyrinth, integrating this new vision with a new way of being in the world.

Recovery's leap of faith eventually blossoms into a willingness to explore new places in ourselves, our relationships, and our world. Some steps on the journey are slow and tentative, others come more easily—but each can be taken only one step at a time.

How Long Does It Take?

When beginning treatment, most of my patients ask, How long will this take? My nearly twenty-five years' experience treating women with eating disorders and body image problems teaches that it is impossible to accurately guess. No matter how wise or experienced, a professional can never predict precisely how long it will take a particular woman to recover from her particular crisis. Each woman is different, no matter how similar her symptoms or problem behaviors may be to those of other women. In the end, it is crucial to remember that, like life itself, recovery isn't a race.

As long as we look at recovery as a continuum, rather than as a single destination or a cure, there is plenty of reason to hope and to anticipate how we can actually improve our lives, be less tormented, and become healthier—even if we've been struggling for years. It helps to give up old black-and-white reasoning that equates worth or good only with perfection. Recovery is progress, not perfection, and that is the formula that holds the real promise of peace.

Recovery is hindered when we judge ourselves harshly by someone else's progress; our problems are the only ones we can ever fully understand—and even that is a challenge. On the other hand, a healthy comparison with someone doing well in recovery can inspire us and help us see that recovery is achievable. Remember that if we have suffered for years (or even decades), we won't get better with just a handful of therapy sessions, visits to the doctor, or consultations with a nutritionist. And treatment alone won't do it—it's what we do outside of treatment that matters most. Change does not happen instantly. As a wise woman once told me, "A tincture of time is the best medicine."

Some of my former clients simply did not believe they could ever change how they saw themselves or treated their bodies. After entering treatment, however, they allowed themselves to hope instead of be hopeless, to share their stories and their pain instead of isolating themselves, and to rely on other human beings for help instead of continuing their lonely Superwoman stance of needing no one.

Since the larger culture is seeped in the Body Myth and at war with women's bodies, it provides little positive support for recovery. While we can't change our culture overnight, we can change our reaction to the culture and learn to take better care of ourselves. I never promise new patients that they are going to feel great about their bodies, even though some do eventually embrace their bodies fully. But even the women who remain occasionally haunted by that bad-body Voice *can* find ways to turn down The Voice's volume, tune in more positive voices, and focus on other, more important pleasures in life.

If in the past you had a negative experience when seeking treatment or just felt it didn't help, try again. You may be more ready now because you're at a different point in your life. It may be that a new and different approach will work better for you.

How Does It Work?

Like length, the how of treatment depends on the patient and the professionals. Minimally, an adult woman suffering from these problems needs an individual therapist who is experienced in eating disorders, body image, and women's health to assess the situation and make recommendations about the continuum of care she needs. Usually *individual therapy* is vital to the ongoing process of treatment because it helps uncover the deeper issues below the symptoms. In this one-on-one therapeutic relationship, a woman gets understanding and support as she takes the brave steps toward change, gradually removes the mask of perfection, and learns to be her true self. As she gains confidence in the safe confines of therapy, she grows more assured in her other relationships. A skilled therapist also helps a patient to begin changing her behaviors, set reasonable goals, and work through the anxiety engendered by giving up old habits.

Finding the Right Help

The cornerstone of treatment for eating disorders is developing a trusting relationship with a primary therapist—the person we work with most closely. Usually this is a trusted individual therapist, specializing in eating and body image issues, who can direct us to other necessary services. Of course, we can't measure trust on a scale—it is a feeling. Still there are some guidelines to use to find that person.

First, ask for recommendations from friends who have had similar experiences, a medical provider, or other professionals you trust (clergy, nurses, social workers). Resource lists may also be available on the Internet, or from local mental health associations and hospitals. (We also list some resources in the appendix.)

Once you have some therapists' names, call (or visit the therapist's Web site) and ask for basic information such as:

- Are you a specialist in eating and body image problems?

- How long have you specialized in this area?

- What other problems do you treat?

- What degrees and licenses do you have?
- What are your fees? How do you handle payments and insurance reimbursement?
- What is the availability of appointments?
- What is your evaluation process?
- Will you need any medical information prior to my appointment?
- How do you develop a treatment plan and how do we know if it is working?
- What is your treatment approach or philosophy?
- What form of family involvement should I expect?

The first appointment should be an evaluation on both sides. It helps to talk about our motivation for treatment, what we have tried in the past, and how successful those past efforts were. We should discuss treatment options and other forms of therapy that might help. We should talk about how we will evaluate progress, determine whether a different level of care is needed, and what to expect in terms of the course and duration of treatment.

After the first session, reflect on the following questions and answer them honestly:

- How do I feel about the therapist and the surroundings?
- What is my comfort level?
- If I'm uncomfortable, is it due to the therapist or to the feelings stirred up by seeking help and being honest about my behaviors and emotions?

A good individual therapist can help us decide how and when to include other family members. Sometimes arranging *marital* or *family therapy* with a separate professional is best, so that we can keep dedicated attention on our own personal growth in individual therapy. In other cases, we may be able to integrate our spouse, partner, children, or other family members into occasional sessions with the individual therapist. One way or another, marital and family sessions help break negative patterns that keep us stuck in unhealthy relationships with food and our body, while helping our partner and family understand what we are dealing with and how best to support us.

Being in *group therapy* with other women facing body image and eating problems can dramatically decrease a woman's sense that no one really understands, or that others will judge and condemn her. It is easier to take risks when we see our peers doing the same, and we can draw strength from their shared experiences and successes. Group therapy can also provide noncompetitive relationships with other women, which is a joyful and life-altering comfort. However, group therapy also has the potential to accentuate negative competitive behaviors (who's thinnest, who exercises the most, who's sickest?), so it's important to be in a professionally led group or to talk regularly with one's primary therapist about whether the group is actually helping.

Nutritional counseling is essential for eating disorders recovery, and very useful for addressing body image issues. It is easier to make major changes in how and what we eat when we understand the true physical and health consequences of those decisions. A dietitian or nutritionist trained in problems resulting from disordered eating assesses our nutritional intake and can quickly identify areas where it is deficient—and how those deficiencies keep our eating disorder going. Many of my adult patients eat fairly regularly—they just don't eat enough, they eat things that don't sustain them, they binge and purge, or they burn up nutrition too quickly through excess exercise. These behavior patterns keep their lives and bodies focused on food (another demonstration of how the body instinctively defends itself against starvation). While dietary counseling alone is seldom enough to change these behaviors, it can increase our motivation, provide accurate information about our nutritional needs, correct some of our misguided beliefs about food, and reduce fears about making the change.

Body image, movement, and creative arts therapies use a variety of experiential approaches to help heal the conflict between body image and self-image. Talking therapies are essential, but therapeutic body movement and art expression can profoundly alter old patterns, perceptions, feelings, and bodily sensations. This helps us to actually feel more connected to our bodies, and to find a new way to relate to ourselves and others. Most specialized eating disorders treatment programs include art and/or movement therapy, but it can be difficult to find these services outside of a formal program.

Medical treatment is a critical component of recovery. We need early and regular medical evaluations to find out if any of our symptoms stem from underlying diseases like malignancies, chronic infections, diabetes, thyroid disorders, kidney dysfunction, or inflammatory bowel diseases. When the overall treatment process begins, an assessment of how our eating or body disorders have affected the body's systems and organs will determine the level of immediate medical care necessary. Minimally, an electrocardiogram and blood work should be done at the outset of treatment (and regularly thereafter) to prevent life-threatening heart attacks or other potentially debilitating problems. The therapist, dietitian, and medical provider must collaborate periodically to assess any immediate physiological danger.

Psychiatric medications help some women during the course of recovery. When appropriately prescribed and monitored, antidepressants can often help control compulsive behaviors and mood, especially early in treatment, when changing behaviors is so unsettling. Antianxiety or sleep medications are sometimes prescribed, but in many cases, improved nutrition does more than any drug to improve the mood, anxiety, and sleep disorders that accompany eating problems and poor nutrition. So it is wise to give careful consideration to what (if any) medications are used as tools in recovery.

Western medicine has a history of excessively medicating women. Because it is cheaper and less time-consuming to medicate eating and body disorders than it is to treat them comprehensively, HMOs, insurers, and physicians sometimes provide prescriptions (with little or no monitoring of their effectiveness) rather than the multifaceted therapy necessary for recovery. One adult woman was taking fifteen prescription medications when she entered an eating disorders program; her treatment professionals evaluated and closely monitored her, quickly reducing the number to two helpful prescriptions. The bottom line: psychiatric medication alone can't fix eating and body disorders.

We must take an active part in decisions about all aspects of our treatment, whether medical, nutritional, or psychological. The insight gained through therapy and the resultant changed perceptions of self, relationships, and the world are the most important tools for making progress in recovery.

Spiritual growth supports and weaves through all aspects of recovery. Many women struggling with body and eating disorders say they don't have any spiritual beliefs or support systems. To recover, we must nurture our faith that things can change for the better, trust in our professional helpers, hope for the future, and believe that there is more to life than the body. If we don't believe, relief won't come. Spiritual growth can come from formal religious traditions or from less organized forms of faith. We all have spirituality that (like our physical health) needs attention and nurturance to make it work for us the best it can.

Many who recover from eating and body image obsessions are drawn to a *political and cultural awareness* about the role women play in society and the negative messages about body issues we continually receive. This consciousness gives a larger context for why we battle our bodies so severely, which helps us feel less sick or crazy. In her recovery, Jennifer began finding her voice and feeling more personal power when she started lobbying against Web sites that glorified eating disorders. Although these Web sites didn't contribute directly to her illness, she understood how they endorsed and encouraged extremely unhealthy behaviors that endanger others. After recovering from bulimia, Louise started a foundation to help women access eating disorders treatment. Becoming an activist was critical to her recovery and makes her feel that something positive is resulting from her years of pain.

Treatment Philosophy

Therapists and treatment programs tend to emphasize one or more ways of conceptualizing eating and body image disorders, and this section briefly describes the most common viewpoints. It is important to ask therapists what underlying philosophy or philosophies guide their work. These various models can be, and often are, integrated. For example, my therapeutic approach is primarily feminist. But I worked for years in a hospital-based treatment program, so I'm very familiar with the medical model. I can also draw on therapeutic tools from my training and experience in family therapy, my knowledge of 12-step programs, and my familiarity with psychodynamic theory, existential and humanistic psychology, object relations, and attachment theory, as well as cognitive and behavioral treatment principles.

In general I recommend that women struggling with eating and body image concerns work with therapists and programs that respect the tenets of feminist theory and acknowledge the unique pressures on women in today's culture. This does not rule out working with a male therapist—men can be feminists, and male therapists working in this field usually are.

The Medical Model: The body is sick. The Medical Model focuses on the body itself and will develop treatment goals based on gaining weight, eating correctly, and controlling symptomatic behaviors. The Medical Model sometimes pays little attention to the patient's underlying issues or how she experiences the treatment. Medical intervention is essential in order to get an acutely ill patient out of danger, but as treatment proceeds, the medical model alone has limited effectiveness in treating eating disorders.

The Behavioral Model: The behavior is sick. The behavioral approach also focuses on the symptoms rather than on the underlying issues. A strict behavioral approach manages symptoms with rewards and punishments for progress and problems. This was a common eating disorders treatment model in the past, but it did not prove effective over the long term and may sometimes even be harmful. If a woman feels forced to change a behavior too quickly, she may regress, or else develop new disordered behaviors to cope with the stress. If a woman with anorexia is pressured to gain weight without exploring and understanding the reasons for her food obsession, she may put on the pounds but then begin purging for the first time to relieve her unaddressed emotional disturbances.

The Cognitive Model: The thoughts are sick. Instead of focusing on behavior, the Cognitive Model attempts to redirect and reshape the thoughts that initiate and support the eating disorder or body image obsession. This systematic approach is often used in group therapy and can be found in printed manuals and online treatment packages. The Cognitive Model identifies and then challenges maladaptive beliefs and thoughts, on the theory that this will in turn change the maladaptive behavior.

The Addiction Model: The woman is hooked. Eating and body image obsessions share some similarities with addictions like alcoholism, but there are some important differences too. Some aspects of eating disorders are addictive, like the physical dependence on laxatives or diuretics described in chapter 5. Both illnesses share frequent denial, the need to hit bottom before seeing the need to get help, powerlessness over the problem behavior, the possibility of relapse, and the need to grow spiritually in recovery.

The Family Systems Model: The family is sick. This model is built on understanding how family dynamics can help create and feed psychological problems. Family systems therapy targets interactions, boundaries, and multigenerational patterns within our family and/or families. The philosophy is that improving family system patterns will enable the person with symptoms to stop her harmful behaviors and achieve recovery.

The Feminist Model: Cultural expectations for women and our appearance are sick. Like the Family Systems Model, the Feminist Model does not believe that eating disorders and body image despair are rooted exclusively in the individual. It takes a more cultural and global view, seeing eating and body image behaviors as coping mechanisms that women of all ages use to deal with sexism, racism, weightism, lookism, consumerism, sexual abuse, and other forces that harm and limit female lives. While other models tend to place the therapist in the role of expert, the feminist approach leans more toward a partnership between therapist and client, setting mutual goals and helping the client to find healthier ways to relate to herself, others, and the larger world.

Where Is It?

Body image and eating disorders treatment programs operate in a number of different physical settings, which work best when matched properly with the severity of current symptoms. Unfortunately, the final decision is often determined by the sufferer's insurance coverage and ability to pay, rather than by which resources are most effective for the particular patient.

Outpatient treatment works best for someone who is medically stable, has an adequate support system, and is motivated to work on problems while continuing to live at home and function normally at work, home, and socially. It may consist of separate appointments for individual, family, or group therapy, and nutritional counseling, or it may be an intensive outpatient program blending these services together through session in the evenings and/or on weekends.

Inpatient treatment takes place in a hospital or medical center. The most expensive setting, it is usually aimed at sufferers who need acute medical facilities close at hand because they are physiologically unstable (with depressed or fluctuating vital signs, very low weight or significant weight fluctuations, electrolyte imbalance, complications from other illnesses such as diabetes, and the like) or psychiatrically unstable (with rapidly worsening symptoms, severe symptoms that aren't yet responsive to other treatment, suicide risk, and the like).

In *residential treatment*, patients live at a facility dedicated exclusively to eating disorders therapy. Residential programs are usually not in a hospital building, although some are housed on hospital grounds. This setting is suitable for patients who are psychiatrically unable to respond to partial hospital or outpatient treatment but are physiologically stable enough to go without daily acute or intensive medical care.

In a so-called *partial hospital* program, patients are treated for many hours a day inside a hospital but then return home in the evening. Partial hospital works for patients who still need daily monitoring of their medical status (but are not at immediate risk) and who are psychiatrically impaired (unable to function in their normal daily roles and/or still engage in their symptoms daily). This setting provides intensive treatment, which the person gets to take home and practice for a few hours before returning for the next day's intensive therapy.

Eating and body image issues pose particular challenges to the traditional *self-help recovery* model. These challenges are not well understood by many well-meaning people who, for example, expect the 12 steps of Alcoholics Anonymous to transfer easily to the treatment of eating disorders. Such notions are understandable, since eating disorders share many similarities with addiction. But the differences between alcoholism and anorexia are profound, making it potentially dangerous to use alcoholism's recovery tools on anorexia, or vice versa.

The most basic difference, of course, is with abstinence. Abstinence from chemical use is the core of drug and alcohol addiction *treatment*, but abstinence from food lies at the core of anorexia's *symptoms*.

Recovery from drug or alcohol addiction requires wrenching changes in the addict's every relationship, routine, and habit. People with eating disorders must make similar changes in order to achieve recovery. But an addict's body won't die if she completely abstains from drugs or alcohol. On the other hand, no one's body can survive complete abstinence from food. There is no healthy escape from our daily physical need to eat or the necessity of living every moment inside our bodies. Since abstinence isn't a recovery option for eating and body image disorders, we have to find other ways to make peace with our body, body image, and food.

Programs built on the 12 steps help millions of people overcome addictive behavior and regain their health. While a 12-step approach can be very valuable in eating and body disorder recovery, we must consciously and carefully shift our mind-set away from traditional concepts of abstinence. Some eating and body disorder treatment programs incorporate 12 step practices but change the language to better reflect the realities of eating disorders.

Take AA's first step, which reads "We admitted we were powerless over alcohol—that our lives had become unmanageable." A woman with anorexia would have to reframe and reword that step for it to help her recovery. Instead of admitting that she is powerless over the *external* substance of food, she would find the source of her powerlessness in her *internal* qualities like perfectionism, a tendency to take care of others before herself, or constant self-shaming. Thus, instead of abstaining from food, she would strive to abstain from the negative ways she treats herself. In a sense, women with eating and body disorders are addicted to how they see and treat themselves, more than to the external elements of the illness.

Overeaters Anonymous, a 12-step fellowship for people struggling with compulsive overeating, may seem like a logical place to get support for eating and body image problems. However, some OA meetings may seem so focused on eating that they reinforce the dangerous good food–bad food dichotomous thinking that supports eating disorders. Still, OA's fellowship, with its physical, emotional, and spiritual approach, is helpful for some people. If 12-step programs have helped you with past life problems, work with a therapist on the best way to integrate those principles into your journey of recovery from food and body disorders.

Obstacles to Getting Help

Ambivalence, denial, and the stubbornness of eating and body image disorders are not the only barriers to recovery. Insurance often covers mental health very differently from the way it covers physical health, and that can be a rude awakening for someone seeking help.

If you follow the right procedures and get the proper referrals, insurance generally covers medical visits and procedures with little trouble. But you can expect annual or lifelong caps on the number of dollars an insurance company will reimburse for mental health treatment. State insurance laws vary, but these caps can be as low as $10,000 for inpatient and $2,000 for outpatient treatment, or can just permit a certain number of visits or days of treatment regardless of the person's actual needs (if an employee self-insures, state regulations may not apply). Hospitalization for an eating disorder can burn through benefits rapidly, barely long enough to stabilize a patient, much less make any significant progress toward recovery.

Some insurers actually pay less for eating disorders treatment than they do for other mental illnesses (like alcoholism treatment), or they even exclude coverage completely. Because eating disorders treatment takes a substantial amount of time, it is expensive, and insurers are not willing to bear the cost, opting for profit over people. Also many people (including policy makers) still don't understand eating disorders and don't take them seriously. For example, insurance practices seldom acknowledge that anorexia poses a greater mortality risk than most other psychiatric disorders. Despite the fact that a woman's medical status improves as therapy resolves underlying psychological issues, insurance often covers only the medical expenses.

In the current era of managed care, an insurance policy's list of endorsed providers may not include anyone specialized in the treatment of eating and body disorders. This is often a catch-22: if insurers aren't willing to cover eating disorders therapy, there is little incentive for a therapist to specialize in eating disorders. This leaves substantial areas of the country without specialists. So even if an insurance company decides to cover treatment, there may not be any professionals nearby for a woman to see.

To fight back, we suggest going to the human resources department, union, or whoever ultimately holds the contract with your insurance company to request help in advocating for adequate treatment. When an insurance company stands to lose a contract, it may suddenly find ways to be flexible. Most women who recover from these disorders had to fight hard to obtain the treatment that addressed their particular needs. One woman who succeeded in getting coverage says, "When someone at the insurance company says no, assume that he's really saying 'I don't know,' and don't stop asking until you hear a yes you can use."

Strong advocacy has persuaded some insurance companies to pool mental health and medical benefits to cover necessary treatment. After being denied coverage or care, some women have hired lawyers, recruited state attorneys general, and lobbied legislators to challenge the inequity. In the meantime, we have to get help anyway we can. This takes a fair amount of energy, but it can be a good job for a family member, especially one who struggles with knowing how else to help.

My Web site, www.thebodymyth.com, has guidelines on how to fight the system and get help. "Securing Eating Disorder Treatment: Ammunition for Arguments with Third Parties" provides ten positions to take with an insurance provider, including research citations that document the proven benefits of proper care. "Eating Disorders Survival Guide: How to Afford Appropriate Treatment for an Eating Disorder: A Guide for Patients and their Families" suggests ways to advocate for the treatment most likely to enhance recovery.

In the meantime, many organizations of professionals and families are banding together to fight for better coverage for eating disorders through the Eating Disorders Coalition for Research, Policy, and Action (www.eatingdisorderscoalition.org). The coalition advocates in Washington, D.C., for more federal treatment resources, access to treatment, and funding for research, education, and prevention. Eating disorders and body image obsessions now represent a major public health problem, primarily affecting women, which should get federal recognition and support. The coalition has ways for individuals and families to lobby for such support at the federal level, and the National Eating Disorders Association (www.nationaleatingdisorders.org) has similar opportunities at the state and local level.

New Ways to Shape Your Thinking

While there is no one way to achieve recovery, some universals do exist, such as the need to avoid self-blame and the importance of changing distorted thinking about our body, weight, and food.

Eating and body obsessions don't follow an A-causes-B-causes-C kind of pattern with simple, clear conclusions. Instead it helps to imagine our life and problems as one of those "connect-the-dots" children's puzzles. Connecting two dots doesn't solve the puzzle, but the more dots we connect, the more sense we can make of the total picture.

We have to accept that we will never understand everything that led to an eating or body obsession, but it still is important to appreciate that these complicated behaviors started out as survival techniques. They acted as a life preserver because, at a gut level, we felt that we would drown if we let go of them. Instead of berating ourselves for using an obsession to stay afloat, we can learn how it functioned in our life—and then release it as we build sturdy, wide, and new ships in which to sail healthfully through our future.

> All suffering is bearable if it is seen as part of a story.
>
> —Isak Dinesen

As women enter and work through recovery, they rely on those who have gone before them to help show them the way. Here are some short descriptions of common steps other women have taken in achieving and maintaining recovery:

Develop your life story. Acknowledge the people and events that shaped your life, both positively and negatively. Discover how often or seldom you met your real needs and hungers, and how that relates to obsessions about weight, food, and body image. As you come to understand your life story, you will naturally become less critical and harsh with yourself; you may even learn to empathize with yourself. This, in turn, will make you less likely to think negative and self-blaming thoughts that open the gates for the self-punitive behaviors of restricting, overexercising, overeating, or purging.

Add up the balance sheet. In addition to understanding how eating and body obsessions functioned as flawed life preservers, begin to explore the price you paid for using them. When you felt good about being thin, was there anything else you truly enjoyed about your life? What was the quality of your relationships with others? These obsessions always take sufferers away from real people and real pleasure. As you progress through recovery, relapse looks less attractive when you periodically reflect on such questions.

Self-knowledge never ends. There are many paths to insight. Insight is never a fixed state or end product. It is an ongoing process of self-awareness that grows richer and deeper as you proceed. Continued individual therapy can help uncover ongoing insights. Family therapy or informal discussions with family members can help uncover family secrets and patterns that give context to your experience. Group therapy can uncover new understanding about your own experience as you and your peers share life stories, strategies, and future hopes.

Make time to reflect. We can't develop insight or nurture ourselves if we maintain Superwoman schedules that leave no time to reflect or process our experience. Instead of avoiding thinking about the shape you're in by always keeping busy, reserve daily time to stop moving, sit down, and be quiet with yourself through meditation, journaling, or other self-awareness strategies. Writing in a journal can be a great way to develop a deeper appreciation of your goodness and foster insight into your problems. If you allow yourself to write down perceptions without filtering and critiquing them, you will learn a great deal. The more frequently you make time for reflection, the more helpful it will be.

Remember that fat is not a feeling. Whenever that three-letter *f* word comes up in conversation or drifts into your mind, it is a signal to dig deeper and find out what you are really feeling in that moment (journaling can help a lot with this). It might be sadness, anxiety, fear, loss, inadequacy, loneliness, or other difficult emotions. Women aren't taught that our feelings are legitimate, so it is often difficult to accept or express them. Since we learn to measure ourselves by our appearance, it becomes easy to use the word *fat* to describe any and all negative or painful feelings. It is hard to stop speaking the language of fat and figure out all these complicated feelings. But the insights and rewards are great when you move out of your head and into your heart to trust your gut feelings and intuition.

It is normal to feel worse before we feel better. For years, an eating or body disorder masked and numbed feelings of pain and joy. When the disease's symptoms start to fade, you will actually feel emotions more intensely than you have in ages. This may be the first time you ever address some life issues head-on. It will not be easy, but these feelings will not last forever. All feelings change, so cherish the good ones when they are present and recall them fondly when they go. Meanwhile, remember that the difficult emotions will also pass in time if you let them. Now is the only time you have. Planning how you're going to feel next week is a real waste of time and energy—plus it may keep you from realizing it when you *actually* do feel better.

Never fear feelings. Covering up emotions does much more harm than meeting them head-on. Louise, whose severe eating disorder controlled her life for more than twenty years, says she binged to get away from bad feelings, then purged because she felt bad about the bingeing. This led to feeling bad about her purging, which she avoided by bingeing again. This vicious, destructive cycle spun on the avoidance of other bad feelings that Louise eventually had to confront anyway to recover. She says:

> The pain of my eating disorder was measurable; I knew what it would be. It was my system to keep me safe. I was scared of everything else. I thought all those bad feelings would be too much for me. It turns out I was wrong. I went through treatment more than once and had to face up to those emotions. I would want to run away again, and sometimes I did. But in the end, those feelings didn't kill me, or even keep on hurting me. I survived, and now, for the first time, I get to really experience the good feelings too, because they got pushed down and away just as much as my bad feelings did.
>
> Louise used her eating disorder like a cocoon to separate her from difficult emotions and problems. In recovery, she learned to cope with tough feelings and challenges by breaking them down into what she had to face in the here and now. Frequently, my advice to patients is to just deal with "what's in your face" because that is stressful enough. We don't have to solve all of our problems at once.

Respect the shadow. Everyone has angry and brooding thoughts and feelings. Don't fear or judge them. Because women are taught the myth that aggression and anger are not feminine, we tend to reject these very natural feelings and criticize ourselves for having them. In fact, powerful feelings like anger can be creative, constructive, and transforming, if harnessed wisely and well. Think of how angry Rosa Parks was about having to give up her seat to a white man on a Montgomery, Alabama, bus in 1955. Her refusal helped to launch the civil rights movement, which gradually challenged and transformed race relations in the United States. Consider Mothers Against Drunk Driving. Founded by women whose grief and anger about intoxicated drivers killing their children, MADD has changed laws and increased conviction rates nationwide. Even the group's name, MADD, is a powerful example that anger in the service of love can be very constructive. Let your shadow of angry feelings work for you instead of against you.

Recognize and trust appetites. Our culture confuses women about their appetites, teaching that calories and fat grams are more important than joy and passion. Taught to want a constricted body instead of a full spirit, our intuitive sense of our needs and hungers begins to fade. Figuring out what you really want becomes a dumbfounding challenge. The next time you feel a food binge or a shopping frenzy coming on, stop and ask: What am I really hungry for? It may be harder to answer than you imagine, but that answer is what will truly satisfy your appetite for living.

Adjust your aging attitudes. There is no denying that growing older means losing your youth, but these years can also bring a gradual liberation from youth's dependency on others' opinions and approval (with all the concerns about how others see us). Mark Twain wisely observed that in his youth, he worried continually about what people thought about him, but when he got older, he realized that nobody was thinking about him—they were busy thinking about themselves! Letting go appears to be the mantra of healthy and happy folks who thrive as they age. Adopting an attitude that embraces the feelings and experience of being alive can replace the old control junkie and make you a lot happier.

As we age, many of us have more influence at work and in our communities. We have more expendable income to support good causes, pursue our hobbies, travel, and enjoy other well-earned pleasures. With better medical treatment and knowledge about disease prevention, we can expect to live longer and to stay well. With good health and less pressure to prove ourselves, we may find renewed energy for relationships, personal challenge, spirituality, renewal, and contentment. Some women enter politics or start their own businesses at midlife, tapping renewed sources of ambition and aggression. Since we have less estrogen and more testosterone, we can blend the masculine and feminine in a way we never have before. We may even get comfortable being seen as different or a little eccentric, welcoming comparison to a grandmother or aunt who was seen as a character, complete with odd habits and gray hair.

Make relationships feed you. Many women develop patterns of selflessness in intimate relationships, which leaves them hungry for their own needs to be met. You may worry that others won't like you anymore if you presume to meet your needs, and not just theirs. While you may think this approach makes you an expert on what others feel, it actually leaves you feeling incomplete, alone, misunderstood, and hungry for more. A relationship is pretty shallow if only one person's needs are being met. In recovery, you must tune in to your feelings and needs in a relationship, paying at least as much attention to your needs as you do to the other person's. You can be assertive, ask for what you want, and say how you feel. You can choose relationships wisely, spending more time with friends who help you to feel good about yourself and little (or no) time with people who put you down or bring out your sense of competition and negativity. You can have intimate friendships with other women that don't include competing over weight, dieting, appearance, or anything else.

Getting a Journal Started

A journal is yours. You don't have to worry about sentence structure, punctuation, or legibility. As long as a journal makes sense to you, it has accomplished its goal. So let go of any hang-ups you have about writing; this is therapy, not school!

- Set aside ten minutes each day to write in your journal. Some days you won't need all ten minutes and other days you may run over. You can always find ten minutes for yourself no matter how busy you are.

- Tell others to leave you alone during your journal time. Unless the house is on fire or someone needs to go to the emergency room, nothing horrible will happen without you during those ten minutes.

- Consider writing your life story, from your earliest memories up until now. Let this take as many days or weeks as feels comfortable.

- Reflecting on your life story, identify times when you became aware of being uncomfortable or unhappy in your body. Write about those memories and what was happening in the rest of your life at that time.

- Trace the lifeline of any symptoms that arose from obsessions with eating and your body. Try to identify the periods when you had the most body image difficulty, and record the surrounding circumstances of your life. What might you have been hungering for at each of these points?

• Reflect on how other family members handled food, weight, and body image and how this affected you then and now.

• Write about what is happening in your life currently to encourage eating or body image struggles. What is behind these struggles, and how can you support yourself better?

This short list of suggestions may keep you and your journal busy for weeks or months. From this point forward, use your journal to tune in to how you are feeling that day, identify recurring patterns in your life, and give yourself support and validation.

9

Thinking and Coping in New Ways

To develop a positive relationship with food and our body, we have to translate our feelings from the Body Myth's language of fat into the language of emotion and words. We also have to move our *thoughts* out of the language of fat and into the language of reality.

Our thought patterns actually shape our emotions in powerful ways. The Body Myth trains us to see every situation and phenomenon in black-and-white terms, and this sets us up to feel overwhelmed, defeated, and incapable of changing anything in our lives. But if we teach ourselves to see shades of gray, we can cope—and feel—much better.

Minding the Mind

When we think of everything as one side of a dichotomy, we virtually eliminate the ability to make progress. For example, if we perceive every situation or thought as either a complete success or a complete failure, we can't learn from our mistakes. Mistakes serve only as failures, not as lessons, teachers, and opportunities to change. Black-and-white thinking convinces us that we are total losers if we ever slip up.

This kind of thinking is part and parcel of eating and body image disorders. Women with these disorders judge their lives as all one way or all the other: success/failure, thin/fat, in control/out of control. When it comes to the body, they know how to judge and deprive themselves. They know how to do too much of something, but not how to act in moderation.

Because we are human, we will make mistakes. If we believe every mistake is a total failure, then we inevitably believe that we will continue failing forever. This is a recipe for hopelessness and unhealthy behavior, rather than for growth and progress. Dichotomous thinking also makes us fear *success* because it represents a radical change and departure from the safety and predictability of what we know—even if all we let ourselves know is failure. We lose a lot by staying in a dichotomous world—it may seem safe, but it is really very dangerous.

Changing entrenched patterns of dichotomous reasoning takes practice, but it opens the door to self-forgiveness, patience, and an appreciation that life (and recovery) is a process. More realistic reasoning brings insight but not always immediate changes in our behavior or symptoms. Insight is always easier than behavior change. New self-knowledge may even set our behavior back a bit as we process the new information before moving forward again. We must be patient with ourselves, even if our patience only lasts ten minutes. The best approach to recovery is one day at a time, sometimes one hour at a time or one meal at a time, just putting one foot in front of the other and doing the next right, healthy thing.

Restructuring Cognitive Distortion

Black-and-white reasoning is deeply intertwined with The Voice of eating and body image disorders we discussed in chapter 5. The Voice and dichotomous reasoning keep us feeling bad all the time—that's called *cognitive distortion*. Here are cognitive distortions known to fuel eating disorders and obsessions about body image:

- *Personalization.* We blame ourselves for things that are not our fault, take everything too personally, and see ourselves as responsible for things that have nothing to do with us.

- *Terminal uniqueness.* We think that our problems and situation are unique. We believe this leaves us all alone and that no one can ever understand our lot in life.

- *Dichotomous thinking.* Everything we see and experience is either black or white, all or nothing. For example, we only see ourselves as either perfect or worthless, fat or thin.

- *Selective attention.* We pay attention only to things that support a negative view of ourselves. We filter out facts, opinions, and voices that contradict our negative view or dichotomous thinking. We hear criticisms but seem deaf to compliments.

- *Oversimplification.* Everything revolves around food, weight, size, and shape. Nothing else about us is important.

- *Superstitious thinking.* We believe in cause-effect relationships where none exist. We may feel that God is punishing us through our eating disorder, that we cannot get better, and that we deserve the castigation. We continue to hold these beliefs even after they are proven invalid.

Such thinking bends and twists our perception of reality, which is why it is known as cognitive distortion. The solution is a technique called *cognitive restructuring*, which helps us to reframe our thoughts to better reflect reality.

For example, when we hear the negative words and thoughts of The Voice or the Body Myth, try writing them down. If we write down the negative thought, we are literally getting it out of our head, where we can examine it more coolly and subject it to these critical questions

- Does this thought affect my behavior around food and my body? How?

- Where did I learn this thought?

- Is this thought logical?

- Is this thought actually true?

- What am I getting right now out of listening to The Voice or the Body Myth?

- Do I want to pay that price?

Once we've written down the thought and the answers to our questions about it, the thought itself will look different because we've reexamined it in a new light. Usually, we find that it is wrong and illogical. In this simple and concrete way, we start to alter our thinking process.

The next step is to write down a *corrected* thought. We come up with a new thought based on logic, truth, and reality. This cognitive restructuring process takes lots of practice before it starts to feel natural—after all, we are undoing years of old, negative, dichotomous thinking patterns. And we must remember that logic and truth alone can't magically change deeply ingrained negative behavior or symptoms. We still have to work hard on our behavior, but now we have a new and powerful tool. Plus we can take comfort in knowing that we are starting to change one very important behavior: our thinking itself.

> Unless you feel beautiful inside, you will not see your outer beauty, let alone believe it or enjoy it. Feeling lovely is more central than looking lovely. The inner shift precedes the outer change.
>
> —Marcia G. Hutchinson

As we learn to correct The Voice and its destructive reasoning, we can also use a technique called *thought stopping*. When we begin to hear that negative Voice or an illogical thought, we catch ourselves and imagine a big red stop sign that brings the thought to a halt. This brief pause makes it easier to redirect our reasoning toward a corrected thought.

Finally, we can develop some quick and easy *positive retorts* to our negative thoughts. I encourage my clients to write short, simple affirmations (like "I am beautiful inside and out!) and tape them up in prominent and problematic places around the house. Hanging in my office are mirrors that say these positive messages to my clients:

- She believes in herself.
- She reaches for the stars.
- In her dreams, she can fly.
- Dream.

After years of hearing The Voice, cognitive distortion becomes second nature. The good news is that with daily practice, restructured, positive thinking patterns can also become second nature. When we tune in to our negative self-talk, we become more quickly aware whether cognitive distortion has kicked in. That is an opportunity to rebut The Voice and correct its distortions. Some women take a satiric approach; because they don't think The Voice deserves respect, they sass back at it. Others let lose their anger and shout back at it. No matter what our approach, we are building a real alternative to The Voice. We must develop a voice of our own and use it often.

Identifying and Correcting Negative Self-Talk

Here is one example of how we can take some common negative thinking from The Voice and creatively convert it into our own reality-based voice and take back control of our thinking.

Negative Self-Talk (Cognitive Distortion)	Rebuttal (Cognitive Restructuring)
They all think I am fat and disgusting.	I don't know what they really think. I am not fat and disgusting. I'm just unsure of myself right now.
I always embarrass myself in social situations.	Not true. Absolute statements like "I always . . . " are the kind of all-or-nothing thinking that causes me trouble. In social situations, I am actually good with other people and show a lot of caring.
Everyone is going to stare at me. I'll ruin everything if I don't look right.	They won't really care about how I look. I'm not responsible for other people, their thinking, or their feelings. Besides, no one's outward appearance has the power to determine whether or not an event is ruined.
I ate like a pig last night. Everyone will think I'm weak and out of control.	I ate a normal meal of food that my nutritionist recommends. People are actually more focused on themselves and may not even notice me.
I lost it last night. I should never have eaten that. I'll have to starve myself today.	I can't change yesterday, so I need to start over today. I don't have to punish myself for eating.

continued

Negative Self-Talk (Cognitive Distortion)	Rebuttal (Cognitive Restructuring)
I overheard them talking about exercise. They must think I'm fat and need to lose weight.	The world does not revolve around me. They weren't talking about me, they were talking about themselves.

Developing a Fuller Perception of Who We Are

Because the Body Myth is so deeply entrenched in our culture (and so many people's psyche), it is easy to believe that other people care about us only for the shape our body is in. We often use that belief as a rationalization for making our body shape into the only thing we care about too. But there is a lot more to us—and to other people— than how our bodies look.

To live a healthy life, we must take time to conceptualize who we really are. This takes practice, just like cognitive restructuring does. We start with concrete steps to make ourselves conscious of our non-physical attributes—which are far more numerous (and important) than the physical ones.

Attribute Inventory

If you write down information about your personal qualities, you literally see those traits in a new light. Write one- or two-sentence answers to the following questions. Brief answers may help you avoid convoluted rationalizations, cognitive distortion, and other habits that denigrate your attributes. If the list of questions seems overwhelming, break it up into smaller chunks, doing a few each day.

- How do I relate to others?
- What are my particular strengths in my relationships with my partner, friends, family, coworkers, strangers, and acquaintances?
- What are my weak spots in these relationships?

- How do or would other people describe me?
- How does my view of myself fit with how other people tend to see me?
- What words best describe my personality?
- In what ways do I function at work?
- What are my work habits?
- What are my strengths and weaknesses at work?
- In what ways do I handle my responsibilities at home?
- In what ways do I handle my responsibilities for self care and meeting my personal needs?
- In what ways do I handle my responsibilities for my family's needs?
- What are my intellectual strengths and weaknesses?
- What are my emotional strengths and weaknesses?
- What are my spiritual strengths and weaknesses?
- What are my hobbies, special talents or expertise?
- What do other people seem to like about me?
- What do I value about myself?
- What are all the things I do in a normal day? (Make a list.)
- What am I really like?

Your answers to these questions can help you begin to appreciate who you really are. Each day be aware of these important personal attributes. Be aware that you are more than the Body Myth says you are. Recognize that you can decide to connect your self-esteem to your many rich and precious internal attributes—and disconnect your self-esteem from your appearance.

Can I Get Better?

Yes, women with eating and body image disorders can get better. But eating and body image disorders are complicated in all their aspects, including the part about getting better. That means we must first talk about what we mean by *better*, *worse*, and *recovery*. For example, women working on overcoming eating disorders often expend great effort trying to figure out if they have completely recovered. But that may not be a fruitful use of our time and energy.

On the one hand, there is no consensus regarding the criteria for recovery. Most academic research focuses on physical parameters like restoration of menstrual cycles or a certain weight-to-height ratio, but not the quality of life. Using these limited criteria, studies find that about 40 percent of women "recover" from anorexia and bulimia. Another 35 percent see improvement, but not enough to meet the "recovery" criteria. The remaining 25 percent stay ill or die from the illnesses.

In general, research on eating disorders recovery is done by experts who work with the most severely ill patients, so their numbers may not reflect the whole picture or how more typical eating disorders look. When it comes to body image obsessions, we have very little outcome research at all. Plus the criteria for recovery from body image disorder are murky because our culture makes body dissatisfaction and obsession the norm, not the exception. All of this limits what we can learn (at least so far) from research on recovery.

On the other hand, a woman with eating disorders and body image obsessions can still get much better than she is right now, both physically and mentally—even if she has struggled with these problems for decades. These disorders include a continuum of complex difficulties and stages of progress that make it hard to nail down one single point that can unmistakably identify whether or not someone has reached recovery.

In practical terms, it may be more useful to think of ourselves as recover*ing*, rather than recover*ed*—recovering as an ongoing progress instead of recovered as a single, relatively arbitrary, immovable standard. Eating and body image disorders already involve a lot of measuring of ourselves against external standards that don't reflect reality very well, so we may not benefit from repeating that pattern by trying to measure recovery in exact, all-or-nothing terms. The most important thing is to work on getting healthy again.

Life itself is a continuing process, rather than an immutable point in time, so we'll make more headway if we think of recovery in similar terms. As soon as we take our first steps toward breaking the cycle of eating and body image disorders, we are on the recovery road. The bottom line:

• We have every reason to believe that we can and will get better.

- We have every reason to believe that our life will improve if we get help and refuse to give up.

Sarah experienced the entire range of eating disorder symptoms and began treatment for the first time when she was in her early forties. She was convinced that she could never make peace with her body image. It was a struggle, but she kept at it and started to see glimmers of hope. About a year into therapy, Sarah had a transforming experience while getting ready for a holiday party. As she pulled on her panty hose, she began her usual and familiar negative self-talk of "your family is going to ridicule you behind your back because your thighs are too fat. You look terrible in this dress; no one will like you." Somehow, in the next moment, she looked in the mirror and let go of The Voice. She replaced its corrosive messages by speaking aloud: "Margo is right: I am a goddess."

This was a concrete example of the new ways therapy helped Sarah to understand her life. Treatment was teaching her that she no longer had to punish herself through her eating disorder or blame herself for family problems she did not cause. After months of hard work, soul-searching, and verbalizing things she had never shared, Sarah found that she no longer had to translate difficult feelings into the language of fat. Instead she could deal with them directly. In turn, she could start seeing herself for who she really is. Life hasn't stopped sending challenges her way, but Sarah no longer needs to use the rituals she developed around body image and eating to cope with life's challenges. She can face them head-on instead. And she is much happier.

Sarah's experience echoes what I have heard from clients over the past twenty-five years, and what I learned while interviewing women in recovery for my doctoral dissertation. When I ask women in recovery what helped them to get better, the most common responses are:

- My therapist didn't give up on me.
- I didn't feel alone anymore.

The keys to recovery—connection and hope—ring through these words. We can't do this alone. We don't have to give up. There is safety in numbers. We can get better.

Believing

Because recovery is a long and paradoxical process, it can be hard to imagine that there is light at the end of the tunnel. I sometimes advise patients or their families to believe in recovery just as blindly as they once believed in the tooth fairy. This is a big leap of faith for women after years of living with the underlying conviction that they deserve the pain and misery of their eating and body image obsessions. It may seem like they're being gullible to believe in recovery, but every one of us deserves to believe, just as we deserved the right to believe in Santa, and reap the rewards of that innocent trust each December.

Therapy is essential in teaching us to believe that we can have a less conflicted—or even a peaceful—relationship with food. Recovery can be a discouraging process, with a step or two forward and then a slide back. It is too daunting to attempt entirely alone. An experienced therapist can help us figure out the reasons for our slips and learn from them, instead of letting them defeat us. With this guidance, experiences that once crushed us become opportunities to reshape our self concept, worldview, beliefs, and behaviors. When things look dark or we feel ambivalent, it helps to remember the 12-step saying "Don't give up five minutes before the miracle."

Louise had every reason to give up on herself after suffering from severe bulimia for well over twenty years, since college. She went through two treatment programs, including a year-long intensive outpatient treatment that had her getting better. Louise and her husband devoted a lot of energy and financial resources to her recovery. But then she had a severe relapse when life events became extremely stressful.

Somehow she didn't give up. Louise decided to take a bigger step and enter residential treatment, even though it would be difficult for her husband and school-age sons to have her so far away from home. Finally, this last chapter of treatment helped her to break the hold bulimia had on her for over two decades. Louise is now living fully on the recovery road, as vibrant and alive a woman as can be. Her recovery still requires attention, and she does not take it for granted, but she is grateful that she never gave up.

Life Is Not a Dress Rehearsal

It is normal for people to occasionally wish they were younger, looked different, or were someone else. It's healthy to have such passing fancies, but not healthy to make them your life story and build your life around them. Our wishes and fantasies usually represent a deeper appetite. Say you are fifty-five and, one day, you are smitten with the desire to be twenty-three again. That wish probably springs from a longing to rekindle a warm new emotional tone in an important relationship, or resurrect the youthful freedom to explore any life direction without encumbrances.

Understanding these hungers helps us from getting stuck in the initial fantasy and moving backward in life. If we are missing a sense of connection with our partner, we don't need a time machine to transport us back to our first date. We need to use our experience and hope to recharge the relationship so we can then travel together to new heights far more satisfying than puppy love. After all, life is a cumulative process; each year builds on the last. Our experience gets richer if we move forward with a willingness to learn and change. Trying to freeze time or live in the past doesn't work and brings no satisfaction.

Learning how to move on is easier when we can admire the paths blazed by women before us. Some of those pioneers are people we know. Others are famous and historical women we can learn from too (more on this in the next section).

I wasn't yet thirty when my friend Caroline turned forty. Back then, forty seemed pretty old to me, but Caroline's perspective was liberating. She proudly announced: "I no longer feel compelled to buy all the back-to-college fashion magazines each August!" Her words were a great gift to me, because I saw a lively, optimistic woman embracing her age as a positive reality. I am now at an age when forty sounds pretty *young*, but I still cherish the perspectives of my vibrant female elders. No matter how old we are, it helps to find ourselves some Carolines!

Another friend of mine has struggled through multiple bouts of breast cancer. Phoebe relies on the following mantra for recovery and life: "This is not a dress rehearsal!" Her brushes with cancer put Phoebe's concerns about weight and appearance in stark perspective. She no longer cares that she can't fit into clothes she wore thirty years ago. Instead, she has a true carpe diem approach to life.

When it comes to good recovery and health, we need to have this same attitude. Yes, firmly entrenched bad habits can seem to have a life of their own. But we all know that putting off a decision only makes the decision harder. We can change injurious habits, and because our life is not a rehearsal, there is simply no good reason to wait.

We are dreaming if we postpone work on unhealthy food and body behaviors until some elusive morning when we might wake up to find a supernatural switch that turns off our obsessions. Pie-in-the-sky epiphanies may happen in made-for-TV movies, but they seldom occur in real life. If we continue to wait for some magic moment of motivation to strike, we risk dying before we seize the opportunity to recover. Please don't wait.

Paradoxically, recovery from eating disorders and body image despair requires us to have a sense of urgency about our condition, along with the permission to take the necessary time to make the difficult life changes that recovery demands. While paradoxes are often quite challenging and confusing, remember that life itself is filled with them. Paradoxes are no excuse for not living life as fully as we can. Remember the words of that wise cancer survivor: "This is not a dress rehearsal." Today may be your best chance at recovery; take that chance now or as soon as you possibly can.

The Women We Admire

What women do you look up to? Few of us give credit to other women for their contributions to our world; men are not the only ones to ignore or dismiss the importance of women's work. Acknowledging the value of adult women can help us feel more positive about getting older ourselves.

Make a list of the older women in your life that had an important influence on you. Then ask yourself these questions:

- What were the influences these women had on me?
- What do I value in adult women?
- Who is an example of the kind of woman I would like to be as I get older?
- How important is that woman's appearance, shape, and weight to my opinion of her?
- What does "aging gracefully" mean to me?
- What could I do to honor the contributions of women?
- What can I do to emulate positive ideals rather than media images?

New Ways to Look at Women

Our culture is starving for visible role models who age gracefully and confidently. Such women exist, but they can seem invisible because they get so little attention and public praise for aging with pride.

The popularity of the movie *Something's Gotta Give* speaks to how much we want and need a different approach to women's aging. Diane Keaton won a Golden Globe for her role as the mother of a young woman dating an older man (Jack Nicholson). Eventually Keaton and Nicholson become involved in a comedic romance that contrasts refreshingly to the rigid Hollywood formula of May (female)–December (male) romances.

At nearly sixty, Diane Keaton is also a great real-life role model for aging gracefully. Happier since giving up her self-proclaimed dependency on romantic relationships with men, she adopted two children in her fifties and describes her life as more complete and full of love than ever. An extremely accomplished woman, Keaton began acting in comedies, then progressed to dramatic roles, and now directs and produces theatrical and television films. Meanwhile she has edited photography books, restored houses, and succeeded in Hollywood without cosmetic surgery. As she told *More* magazine:

> I'm stuck with this idea that I need to be authentic. My face needs to look the way I feel. . . . I don't know what's the matter with women; maybe they don't want to think of themselves as being the age they are. Are they going to support the reality of what it is to be 58, or do they just want to pretend that they aren't 58 and run away from it? I feel like you have to be inclusive about who you are, like, not perfect.

Keaton, who coincidentally was one of the stars in Olivia Goldsmith's *The First Wives Club*, reminds us that women need to support these realistic images. Actors-turned-producers like Keaton and Geena Davis have trouble finding backing for realistic films about women of all ages—what studios disparagingly call chick flicks. But we have a role to play too. If we want different images and realities for women, we must vote with our wallets. Consumer feminism could be a powerful and transforming force if we aimed it in directions like this!

Publisher Katherine Graham is another great example of someone who came into her own as a mature woman. After her husband's suicide, Graham felt totally unprepared for running the family's news media conglomerate, including the *Washington Post* and *Newsweek*— while also raising her children. But she forged ahead and succeeded. Graham's courage in backing the *Post*'s ground-breaking coverage of Watergate had an impact she never imagined beforehand.

There is only one *Washington Post* to run, and we can't all win an Oscar. But Keaton and Graham (along with Maya Angelou, Mother Teresa, Alice Walker, and others) show us how women can keep growing and mastering the challenges of adulthood. They are far more useful role models than any fashion model!

Women of substance help us remember what really counts: the inner self, values, beliefs, morals, and the ability to love. With this insight, we may gradually see our entire female experience differently and consider letting go of our food, weight, and body image obsessions.

Sure, he [Fred Astaire] was great, but don't forget that Ginger Rogers did everything he did . . . backwards and in high heels!
                                              —Bob Thaves, *Frank and Ernest* cartoonist

---

Next time we are tempted to pick up a fashion magazine, choose a book on women's history instead. Learn more about the history of women—it will help a lot more than the latest articles about how to be sexier, skinnier, and "more successful."

Granted, it is harder to find books about important women than ones about famous men (and harder to find than fashion magazines). Historically, Western culture has ignored the contributions of women. Below are a few facts about U.S. women. See how far this snippet of women's history can go toward helping us see what is really important about being a woman—it is not our weight or dress size!

- Women were central to indigenous life in North America.

- Women were among the first permanent European settlers in the 1600s.

- George Washington's army was supported with money raised by women.

- Women have served in every U.S. war. They flew thousands of missions as pilots in World War II and serve today in prominent and dangerous posts.

- In 1833 Prudence Crandall opened the first school for African American girls, in violation of Connecticut law. This drew national attention to the abolition movement.

- Also in 1833, Lydia Maria Child wrote the first antislavery book in the United States.

- In 1850, Harriet Tubman escaped slavery and then returned to free 300 other slaves.

- In 1852, Harriet Beecher Stowe wrote *Uncle Tom's Cabin*, the most widely read antislavery book in the United States.

- Victoria Woodhull was the first woman to run for president— in 1872.

- A hundred years later, Shirley Chisholm became the first African American woman to run for president.

- In 1874, Mary Ewing Outerbridge introduced tennis to the United States.

- Women invented (among many other things): submarine lamps; suspenders; windshield wipers; life rafts; fire escapes; and Kevlar.

Entire social movements have been started by women, including:

- In 1843, Dorothea Dix exposed the treatment of the mentally ill in hospitals and paved the way for more humane treatment of psychiatric patients.

- Clara Barton founded the Red Cross in 1881.

- Jane Addams won the Nobel Peace Prize in 1931 for promoting mediation during World War I and for her leadership of the Women's International League for Peace and Freedom.

- Alice Hamilton was the first physician to study occupational disease, leading to today's Worker's Compensation laws.

- In 1924, women founded the Parent-Teacher Association.

- In 1955, Rosa Parks refused to give up her seat to a white man on a bus in Montgomery, Alabama. Her arrest prompted a boycott against the municipal bus company and helped launch the modern civil rights movement.

- In 1962, Rachel Carson's writings stimulated the development of the environmental movement.

- After being forced to retire at sixty-five, Maggie Kuhn founded the Gray Panthers in 1970 to challenge discrimination against older people.

This is a tiny sampling of what women have done (and still do) to enhance the shape we're in as a society. However, contemporary culture's obsession with the Body Myth tends to keep these contributions invisible. That is why women's history is so useful in changing how we see ourselves. When we replace the narrow cultural view of women with a new appreciation of our many historic accomplishments, we start changing the standards by which we judge our own success and value.

Scanning the Past

Our own family history can go a long way in helping us live healthfully and in recovery. Look over old family photos, portraits, or videos to learn what the bodies in our family are supposed to be like and what our genetic heritage means for our sense of self. This historical research is instructive while also being a lot of fun!

As you look at images of your ancestors, consider these questions:

- What are the women's body types like?

- What relative do you most resemble in body type or appearance?

- What stories of female accomplishment can you see or remember when you look at the images?

- What do the women's bodies say to you?

- What relative do you most resemble in personal characteristics and accomplishment?

- What do your relatives and their stories teach you about being female?

- What do they teach you about attractiveness?

- What do they teach you about getting older?
- What do they teach you about sexuality?
- What do you feel about these people?
- What do you feel about their bodies?
- What do you feel about your own body as you look at theirs?

We have a lineage of accomplishment, body shape, and true beauty. Seeing photos of relatives we love or admire can help us to love and admire the parts of us they passed down to us. Images in the family photo album can offer a far better reflection of reality than magazines or TV shows. Appreciate the bodies, beauty, and accomplishments of our female ancestors. That can do a lot to help us appreciate ourselves.

10

Embracing Our Selves

Life is not a destination but a journey of self-discovery. It is a journey of self-care, doing things to stay well and to improve our emotional and spiritual state. It is never too late to start this journey. But we must recognize that this process happens over time and can't be endlessly evaluated as an either/or success or failure. Whether we're thirty or eighty, we still can decide to overcome the Body Myth, reclaim our life, focus on our own values and desires, and embrace our shape and self.

Question the Questions

Many factors help us get and keep a healthy body image—starting with the values and core beliefs that guide us. These life fundamentals are best revealed in the fundamental questions we ask ourselves each day. Being immigrants in a culture at war with our bodies and confused about our true hungers and needs, do we focus on the quick fix of our appearance as a measure of our personal self-worth as well as of our public success? Do we gaze critically at our bodies and at other women's bodies, looking for answers that cannot be found there and only leave us empty and hungering for more?

Far too many of us simply ask the wrong questions about the shape our life is in.

We must abandon the Body Myth's false questions, which only can be answered by the mirror. We must replace fundamental questions like "How do you think I look?" with "Who do I want to be?" and "What do I really want?"

When our questions move away from the mirror, our whole perspective changes for the better. Our mission in life shifts from pleasing other people through our appearance. Instead, we focus on contributing to the world and pleasing ourselves through our core being. Only then can we embrace our selves and our lives, and live fully.

The Right Stuff versus the Real Stuff

Our consumer culture seduces us into thinking that if we have the right stuff, we'll be happy, satisfied people, able to fulfill our lives and our potential. The opposite is really true—we need to be who we are first, and then we'll know what we need. But because the marketing onslaught is powerful and plays on our insecurities, many of us live our lives backward.

While the right stuff might be available for purchase at the mall, the real stuff isn't. We must remember the truth that you can't buy happiness, no matter what we've been told. No product or look will (or can) give our lives meaning.

So what *is* it that makes us happy, keeps us happy, and gives life meaning?

Is it a walk with a friend, or a trip to the mall? A talk with your partner or your child, or a couple of hours at the gym? Weighing a pound less, or nurturing deep connections with others?

Many of us are much better at preparing to live than actually living. Instead of waiting until we get the right stuff (or the right body), we can start living more fully with what we have, and in our present bodies, right now. This real stuff will displace the power that dissatisfaction with appearance (including eating disorders and body image despair) hold in our lives. In turn, we will be able to embrace our real body and live more fully.

Life's fundamental questions are actually pretty simple, but they are not easy—especially in today's culture. We have to find ways to avoid being distracted by the right stuff and discover the real stuff that is really important to us.

Children's books can hold excellent perspectives on life's fundamental questions. Here is a famous discussion between children's toys in Margery Williams's classic *The Velveteen Rabbit*.

> "What is REAL?" asked the Rabbit one day. . . . "Does it mean having things that buzz inside you and a stick-out handle?"
>
> "Real isn't how you're made," said the Skin Horse. "It's a thing that happens to you. When a child really loves you for a long, long time, not just to play with, but REALLY loves you, then you become Real. . . . It doesn't happen all at once. . . . You become. . . . It takes a long time. . . . Generally, by the time you are Real, most of your hair has been loved off, and your eyes drop out and you get loose in the joints and very shabby. But these things don't matter at all, because once you are Real you can't be ugly, except to people who don't understand."

The Legacy We Leave

One simple (but not easy) way to decide what's important in life is to consider the epitaph we want on our tombstone, or what we hope our obituary will say. Do we want to be remembered as "a good dieter," or as "a great friend"? Do we want "she slimmed down to a size 6," or "she used her boundless energy to make the world a better place"?

Today it is easy to feel inconsequential as our busy world races by, filled with people, things, and events. We reduce our importance to whether or not we meet the beauty ideal. But we are not inconsequential. We affect people in big ways and in little ways, especially the ones we love. (If you think little things don't matter, just remember your last mosquito bite.)

We each need to decide what mark we want to leave on this earth and on the people we touch. How do we want to be remembered? Let's imagine our future legacy and be sure to create a life that meets it.

A Moment's Peace

We are the first generation with cell phones, voice mail, email, instant messaging, beepers, laptops, and other telecommunications miracles. We are plugged-in pioneers, expected to manage all kinds of input and stressors we couldn't even imagine twenty years ago.

As contemporary women, we have come to accept being beeped or interrupted as normal. We feel that if someone needs anything from us, they can access us instantly to get it. We are always on call and seldom have someone to take our place.

Access to twenty-four-hour-a-day international news is also stressful; we have to deal with our day-to-day responsibilities while also witnessing what is happening all over the globe. Bad news from everywhere seeps into our consciousness and often creates vicarious trauma. Living in a state of hyperarousal, even the smallest and most mundane issues may take on undue significance and a sense of urgency.

While there are advantages to all this sophisticated instant access, moments of calm, peace, or reflection are few and far between. Some of us actually keep ourselves hooked into all those electronics specifically to avoid ourselves and how we really feel. This keeps us from knowing any of our true hungers because constant distractions cloud our inner feelings.

We each have to find ways in our life to create quiet time for reflection. In fact, former patients sometimes tell me that being able to "sit by myself and do nothing" was an essential ingredient in recovery. We need to find a moment's peace on a regular basis to embrace our selves and reclaim our lives.

Mindfulness

We are mindful when we pay attention to ourselves and our world fully, purposefully, and without judgment. A key to meditation, mindfulness is a practice that makes us more aware, in tune, and in touch with each moment. Many spiritual practices (including Buddhism, Taoism, Christianity, yoga, Native American spirituality, and transcendentalism) hold mindfulness as a concept central to spiritual growth. When we practice being in touch with, or at one with, our inner world and senses, we begin to awaken to our own true nature.

Although mindfulness is part of formal meditation practices, it is also a very simple method of awareness. Buddhist thinking describes a "beginner's mind" as giving us a fresh way of looking at the world, with eyes wide open to notice and appreciate what is around us. With awareness of our surroundings, we can better see the miracles and beauty in our world. This is a great way to offset the input from the media and other distractions. It can actually make us feel grateful for the many little things we take for granted each day—like the sky, the wind, trees, and all the natural beauty on this earth—including our miraculous bodies. Mindfulness also helps us to become more spiritual and appreciative of the importance of intangible things, like love.

Paradoxically, mindfulness means thinking a little less and being more aware of what we are sensing. In essence, it is a way to link the body and the mind. It can help us to grasp the concept of our selves as human "beings." Too often we see ourselves as human "doings," only worthwhile for our accomplishments. But we are valuable for who we are more than for what we do—which is why we are human beings.

Most of the time, our bodies are doing one thing and our minds are thinking about something else. Through mindful breathing, the two can come together. Here's a simple technique to begin this process. Sit or lie quietly, and then:

- Breathe in slowly, deeply, and say "in."

- Breathe out slowly and say "out."

- After doing this for a few minutes you will feel calmer and clearer, more mindful.

- Or, upon breathing in, say, "Breathing in, I calm my body."

- And upon breathing out, say, "Breathing out, I smile."

The more mindful we become, the more we can choose our responses to situations. Since we are more aware of what we feel and what we are reacting to, these feelings don't have to ambush or over-whelm us. We choose to react consciously, rather than reflexively.

Mindfulness also enables us to focus on the present, instead of rehashing the past (the food we should not have eaten) or worrying about the future (the pounds we plan to lose). In the end, happiness is really only possible in the present, because we can't change the past or control the future. Thus, through our mindfulness, we help to create happiness.

We actually design our own reality in many ways. For example, if you choose to smile, you relax hundreds of muscles throughout your entire body. Buddhist teacher Thich Nhat Hanh calls smiling "mouth yoga" because it calms our nervous systems and can instantly change our experience.

The next time we look in the mirror, let's remember to stay in the present, not berate ourselves for what we have done to our bodies in the past, nor plan new attacks on it in the future. Smile and accept the smile back in return.

Balance

Modern women live hectic and overloaded lives with long lists of have-tos and shoulds. The list of Body Myth "shoulds" alone seems infinite. Trying to do it all and have it all is a great formula for exhaustion and burnout, making it easier to revert to the soothing and numbing rituals of disordered eating and body image distress. If we "should" all over ourselves and try to do it all, we throw our entire life out of balance.

Creating balance in our lives starts with basic self care. We may have every cosmetic product for creating a youthful appearance and every household appliance for a perfect home but still be negligent in truly taking care of ourselves. There's no better setup for emotional, physical, and spiritual crisis than being exhausted and spent. Rest and relaxation have to be part of our daily self-talk and schedule, not just something we advise others to do, or only do ourselves during a rare vacation. Many of us talk the talk of self nurturance, but we don't walk the walk.

It may sound impossible to build relaxation time into our days. But we need to reject all-or-nothing formulas of needing to do every-thing perfectly, including relaxation and recovery. Even if some days leave little time for us, we can usually capture a few minutes to do one healthy, soothing thing for our souls. If we have a particularly hectic day or week with work or family, take downtime at night and on weekends. It can be as simple as having a second cup of coffee, reading the newspapers leisurely, or another simple indulgence that helps us rest, rejuvenate, and relax.

The Three Rs: Rest, Rejuvenate, Relax

Here are some rest, relaxation, and rejuvenation activities most of us can do without taking too much time or trouble. Add some of your own.

- Buy a coloring book and crayons, and then color like you did when you were a kid.
- Listen to your favorite music. Let yourself feel the rhythm. Dance!
- Go for a walk outdoors.
- If you can't leave home, imagine one of your favorite outdoor scenes and take a virtual walk.
- Call a friend or family member that you enjoy talking to.
- Read poetry—or write some.
- Take a nap.
- Watch your favorite TV show.
- Buy flowers for yourself. Admire their beauty and yours.
- Have a cup of tea or other soothing, warm drink—but not too much caffeine!
- Play solitaire.
- See a play, a movie, or a concert.
- Visit a museum or read a book about a favorite artist.
- Pray.
- Sing some old favorite songs with no one listening.
- Meditate.
- Stretch.
- Swing on a swing set.
- Watch children play at a playground.

- Beat a drum.
- Indulge in a warm bubble bath.
- Burn a candle in one of your favorite scents. Stare at the flame and relax.
- Daydream.
- Watch the sun come up or go down.
- Star gaze.
- Spend time outside. Let Mother Nature awe you.
- Listen to the birds.
- Read for pleasure.
- Plan or plant a garden.
- Spend time with a favorite pet or go to the humane society and pet a lonely animal.
- Go to a park or nature preserve.
- Return to an old hobby that you enjoyed.
- Make a list of hobbies that you have wanted to pursue, and then try one.
- Visit a library or browse through a bookstore.
- Make a collage.
- Write in your journal.
- Make a list of your favorite people. Remember a fun or special moment with each of them.
- Look at photos of family, friends, or a happy memory. Soak up that energy.
- Smile.

The Essentials

Sleep deprivation not only causes us to be overtired, but it also confuses our internal body about its states and needs. It is easy to think we're hungry when we really need sleep, or to think we're sleepy when we really need food. The only way to avoid this confusion is to be sure we are getting adequate amounts of both rest and food. In fact, the healthiest older people have very steady habits of eating and sleeping. Our bodies seem to handle these essential life processes better when we give them certainty and sameness, rather than chaos or irregularity.

Routine sleep patterns are especially important in maintaining recovery—going to bed and getting up at similar times helps our bodies to get into a rhythm more conducive to sleep. Turning the world off at a reasonable hour is difficult to accomplish these days but still essential. Let friends or colleagues know how late you will accept calls, and let voice mail answer the phone more often. Turn off the cell phone or beeper; if something is truly an emergency, people will find you the way they did before cell phones.

It helps to end our household tasks at a reasonable hour as well. Even if we have children at home, we can make some quiet time after they are in bed to do nothing or to do something mindlessly enjoyable. Forget about housework—it'll be there in the morning. We need to rest even during menopause's sleep-disrupting hot flashes and night sweats, or during other emotionally straining times when sleep is elusive. If we wake up early and can't get back to sleep, we can enjoy the hours we have to relax in bed before the day starts, or use some of the breathing and relaxation exercises described in this chapter.

Priorities, Priorities, Priorities

We tend to live in a state of urgency about many things, but very few of them are really life-and-death. Stop and think about where you were one year ago today. Can you remember specifically and in detail the biggest worry you had that day? Most of us can't, because most days don't bring truly earth-shattering crises. It helps us keep perspective about today's worries when we realize that we probably won't even remember those worries a year from now.

As we survey the many demands and opportunities of life, we often anguish over what our top priorities should be. But we don't always realize that setting priorities means setting limits and developing the ability to say no. Creating priorities and establishing limits are major steps toward living healthfully and preventing relapse into disordered symptoms.

For example, most of us work both inside and outside of our homes. But research consistently shows that women carry far more of the load around home than men do, even in dual working couples.

When working women feel guilty about the time taken from the family, what our homes and families "look like" can be another source of undue pressure. We may feel our house must constantly look perfect, lest it (and us) be judged poorly by others. That makes housework feel like an endless priority and task, especially on a sunny day when you can see the dust and cobwebs. A healthy, balanced life usually requires setting priorities and limits about things like housework, giving up the futile compulsion for a perfect-looking home. If we try setting that limit and bending our "perfect home" priority, we soon see that the world does not come to an end if we go outside on a sunny day, rather than use it to clean cobwebs.

Another simple limit-setting tactic is making a list with our partner or roommate, agreeing about all the things we feel have to be done around the house over the next two weeks. When we negotiate how frequently each task needs doing, we:

- Gain perspective on how important the task is to the running of our home (and how important it is to the other person, who we may think needs us to be compulsive about the house).
- Establish a shared priority list.
- Make it much easier to share the responsibility equally with the other person.
- Get newly freed time we can take regularly for ourselves.

Too often we make housework a way to avoid other more important issues. We can't know what we really want when we keep ourselves in constant motion accomplishing inconsequential missions. We don't have to live in a hyperalert state in our homes. Our physical appearance isn't as important as what goes on inside us—it isn't even close. The same holds true for our home—it is what happens inside that counts, not how it looks.

Learning to Breathe

Watch a baby breathe. Her belly goes visibly up and down, naturally feeding her brain adequate oxygen. All of us are born knowing how to breathe fully. Over the years, we lose this natural ability as shallow breathing becomes the norm, especially for women.

By preadolescence we were taught to "hold your stomach in," constantly contracting our abdominals in preparation for a lifetime of body consciousness and self-criticism. Negative body consciousness isn't our only problem when we don't reclaim our right to breathe deeply and abundantly. If we don't breathe fully, we don't get adequate oxygen to our brains. This causes a chain reaction: without sufficient oxygen, we can't relax and our anxiety increases, even if we don't consciously recognize it. In fact, most of us don't—after years of holding our stomachs in, feeling anxious and short of breath seem second nature to us.

Understanding the physiology of breathing helps us to recognize its importance. When we inhale, oxygen comes into the body, crosses the lung's membranes, and enters our bloodstream. Our red blood cells, rich with oxygen, engage in intracellular respiration. Our cells use the oxygen to grow, repair, and replicate. At the same time, carbon dioxide is moved out of our bodies and exhaled. The quality of our breathing affects every process in our bodies.

We'll feel better both physically and emotionally if we learn to breathe more fully. Even a short period of deep, slow breathing can lower blood pressure and reduce our anxiety level. Taking ten deep breaths before we react to a demanding or irritating situation always brings some level of calm and perspective. When we are nervous, slowing down our breathing helps us speak clearly and truly. We can do this anywhere, anytime, and it improves the quality of our lives.

Breathing better and more fully feels good, once we learn how to retrain our bodies. We can also practice deep breathing in preparation for stressful times. If we still struggle with anxiety about eating, using one of the breathing techniques described below before meals may help.

Belly breathing—reengaging our diaphragms rather than keeping the stomach sucked in—can make a world of difference both emotionally and physically. Allowing our belly to rise and fall with each breath will bring much more oxygen into our lungs, and our whole body will benefit. Learn from the wisdom of babies.

Better Breathing Made Easy

Deep Breathing

Lie on your back, palms up, legs relaxed (the corpse pose in yoga). Consciously release all the muscles in your body. Slowly inhale and exhale, paying attention to the sound of your breath. Notice your belly rising and falling with each breath. Start with five minutes and gradually extend the time period whenever you do the exercise. You also can do this sitting in a chair, cross-legged on the floor, or by putting your forehead down on a table.

Three-Part Breathing

Sit in a chair or on the floor, with your spine straight. Inhale by expanding the abdomen. Move the breath up to the rib cage and then into the upper chest. Exhale doing the reverse, beginning at the collarbone and emptying the breath down to the stomach. Expel everything in your lower abdomen, pushing the air out by contracting these muscles. Let your breath rise and fall, placing your fingertips on your torso to direct the breath. Begin with one minute, then increase to four to five minutes.

Do *not* try to do these exercises perfectly. Don't judge how well you are following the directions or how well you are doing it compared to someone else. The goal is to *practice* relaxed breathing so that you can do it easily and discreetly. Try to practice one of these techniques each day.

Building Breathing Room

Learning to breathe fully is one thing, but creating more breathing room in our lives is another. Both are essential to getting and staying well.

Some people may be shocked or disappointed if we start setting limits and reclaiming more of our life and energy. But none of us can be all things to all people. True friends and loved ones will respect our limit setting, especially if we explain the journey we are on and the reasons for the changes we are making. As difficult as it may be, staying consistent with these limits will actually help others to accept and respect the breathing room we are working to establish.

Most of us grew up learning to acquiesce to other people's needs, leaving our own to pale in importance. But we have the right to say yes and to say no to the demands in our lives. In fact, we have many rights in our life and our relationships that we may not have exercised yet.

Exercise Your Own Bill of Rights

Pick some of the rights listed here, add some of your own, and personalize your own Bill of Rights. Review your rights periodically and be sure that your life reflects them; if it doesn't, make some changes.

I have the right to:

- speak my mind
- ask for what I need
- ask for what I want
- change my mind
- make my own decisions
- have my own values, beliefs, and priorities
- express my feelings, even if others won't like it
- experience a whole range of feelings
- be honest
- expect honesty from others
- be angry
- make mistakes
- not be perfect
- only be responsible for my behavior and no one else's
- set limits
- say no when others ask or expect me to do things that interfere with meeting my own needs at that time
- feel safe in my relationships
- feel respected by others
- be healthy
- be in charge of my own life
- be happy
- pursue my own dreams and desires

- change and grow
- live my life to the fullest
- feel good in my body and about my body.

In order to fully say yes to life, women have to be able to say no. After all, saying no is sometimes the definitive way to care for yourself.

Setting the boundary of no is a repetitive theme in the treatment and recovery process for women with eating and body image issues. That's because we lose track of our own basic needs for food and self nurturance when we are always responding primarily to others.

My father frequently said, "If you are strong enough to act on your beliefs, then not pleasing other people is just part of life." He would also paraphrase Abraham Lincoln's famous quote and say, "You can please all the people some of the time, and some of the people all the time, but you cannot please all the people all the time."

Although my dad usually made these statements in conversations about public or political stands, I gradually applied the message to my internal and interpersonal life. It continues to help me balance the pressure between pleasing others and pleasing myself. My dad and Abe Lincoln were right. We simply can't please all the people all the time, even if we are taught that we should. Take that great gift from my dad and keep it in your heart too.

A New Relationship with Food

If we are suffering from eating or body image disorders—or even if we've only been indoctrinated with the Body Myth—we need an entirely different relationship to our body and food in order to be healthy again. We have to learn how to see our food and our body as what they truly are—just two necessary givens.

We may think we have successfully proven that we don't need or want food because we've gone without it for long periods of time. But thinking doesn't make it so. We do need to eat, and we do need to accept our bodies for what they are. Many adult women in recovery continue to struggle with their feelings about food and with strong desires not to eat. Their challenge is to manage those emotions and make a daily commitment to eat and to take care of themselves.

It can and does work. Both Beth and her mother struggled with eating disorders for decades. But after hard work and commitment to getting better, Beth is controlling her feelings about food, rather than having them control her: "Now I eat because it's the right thing to do. Not because I want to—I don't. But I know it's the right thing to do. For me. For my daughters. It's still hard and sometimes I absolutely hate food. Maybe I always will. But I eat because it's right."

Some women recovering from eating disorders tend to become overly rigid about food intake, setting up all kinds of rules because they feel a need to eat perfectly at all times. This may help very early in the recovery process, but as time passes, rigidity backfires. If we don't build in flexibility, we will still feel remorse and guilt when we give in to cravings or eat more than our bodies can handle easily because it tastes so good. That easily restarts a cycle of restriction, more backfires, and renewed negative feelings.

The rigidity has to go. When it does, we discover that all those rules weren't really about the food. Instead they manifested the deprivation we impose on ourselves, our discomfort with our natural desires, and the complicated emotions that food, weight, and eating have masked for so long.

Most of my patients are frightened when I suggest that they loosen up the rules and allow those outlawed or forbidden foods back into their lives. It can take a long time to become convinced that there's no such thing as good food or bad food.

Dichotomous thinking about food can be very dangerous. I often see examples of too much of a good thing, when women eat only good foods like vegetables or fruits and end up with orthorexia's severe medical problems: no muscle stores, exhausted immune system, unsafe blood chemistries, gastrointestinal problems, and a weakened heart.

Healthy living and eating includes an overall balance in our nutritional intake. Unless we are allergic to a certain food, we can incorporate all kinds of food in our diets and still be healthy. If most of our food choices are healthy, it is fine to periodically eat richer or less nutritious foods. And if we get adequate calories and an adequate balance of fat, carbs, and protein, we'll be less likely to overdo it with one of those less healthy choices.

The human body has been functioning in balance for millennia. We have to:

- Trust the innate knowledge of our long genetic history.
- Trust our bodies to use up what they take in.
- Trust that our appetites will normalize if we loosen up our rules a bit.
- Trust that our relationship to food will improve.

Instead of trying to be perfect (a standard that does not exist), we need to set flexible goals, such as choosing to make 75 to 80 percent of our food choices "healthy" and have some "forbidden" foods in the remaining balance. Despite the initial apprehension, many women feel more satisfaction and fewer cravings after such a change in thinking. This is a change we can live with, unlike the impossible script of perfect eating that can literally kill us.

A New Relationship with Our Bodies

No matter how hard we try (or what the Body Myth would have us believe), we cannot stop the changes that age brings to our bodies. Our lives are different from what they were twenty years ago, and so are our bodies. It is unhealthy to believe that we can look twenty-five when we're forty-five, or even when we're thirty-five. We need body goals and lifestyles that fit this healthy reality, instead of a recipe for weight loss and disaster.

I frequently encourage all of my patients to accept their body "as is." Recently an anorexic patient on the road to recovery added an important piece of wisdom to this phrase: "I must accept my body as is and as it will be." She was right—her body will continue to change, and she needs to accept that change—even if it means naturally gaining weight.

We help ourselves accept our body "as is and as it will be" when we remember the awesome abilities of women's bodies—menstruation, ovulation, pregnancy, childbirth, and lactation. And remember the miraculous things every human body does on its own to stay in ongoing balance and health:

- Skin replaces itself each month.
- The stomach lining re-creates itself every five days.

- Our livers reline themselves every six weeks.
- Our skeletal system replaces itself every three months.
- And within one calendar year, 98 percent of our atoms are replaced.

Our bodies are walking, talking miracles. Be awed by their magic.

Another simple act that can help recovery and healthy living is to wear clothes that fit. Clothes that are too tight always make us uncomfortable with our bodies. We have to let our clothes change as we change—an outfit that fit normally three years ago may be too small now due to the natural aging process, when middles get a bit thicker. That's a good thing, because it's a sign of how our bodies are growing to meet our changing needs!

We can even make a celebratory ritual during which a friend or kindred spirit helps us dispose of clothes that don't fit. We especially need to purge from our closets and psyches those outfits we sometimes use to punish ourselves, with thoughts like "I'm a failure because I can't fit into that dress anymore." We can also take a dose of retail therapy, treating ourselves to some clothes that fit and feel great. All of it helps us enjoy this body "as is and as it will be."

Twenty-five Ways to Love Your Body

We have to work to make peace with our bodies. Spend at least five minutes a day reflecting on this list by yourself, with your partner, or with family and friends. Share your reactions and experiences as you think about the amazing things our bodies do.

1. We are born in love with our bodies. Watch an infant sucking her fingers and toes, not worrying about body fat. Imagine being in love with your body.

2. Think of your body as a tool. Make an inventory of all the things you can do with it.

3. Notice what your body does each day. It is the instrument of your life, not an ornament for someone else's enjoyment.

4. Create a list of people you admire who have contributed

to your life, your community, or the world. Was their appearance important to their accomplishments?

5. Consider your body as a source of pleasure. Think of all the ways it can make you feel good.

6. Enjoy your body: stretch, dance, walk, sing, take a bubble bath, get a massage, get a pedicure.

7. Put signs on mirrors saying things like: I AM BEAUTIFUL INSIDE AND OUT.

8. Affirm that your body is perfect just the way it is.

9. Walk with your head high, with pride and confidence in yourself as a person, not as a size.

10. Don't let your size or appearance keep you from doing things you enjoy.

11. Remember that your body is not a democracy—you are the only one who gets a vote.

12. Count your blessings, not your blemishes.

13. Replace the time you spend criticizing your appearance with more positive, satisfying pursuits.

14. Every year, 98 percent of our atoms are replaced. Your body is extraordinary—respect and appreciate it!

15. Be the expert on your body. Challenge fashion magazines, cosmetic companies, and weight tables.

16. Let your inner beauty and individuality shine.

17. Be your body's ally and advocate, not its enemy.

18. Every morning when you awake, thank your body for resting and rejuvenating itself so you can enjoy the day.

19. Every night when you go to sleep, thank your body for what it helped you do throughout the day.

20. Find a method of exercise that you enjoy and do moderate amounts of it regularly. Don't do it compulsively or to lose weight—do it to feel good.

21. Think back to a time in your life when you liked and enjoyed your body. Get in touch with those feelings now.

22. Look at family photos. Find the beauty, love, and values in those bodies and faces. Hold them close to your heart.

23. Ask: If I had only one year to live, how important would my body image and appearance be?

24. Make a closet inventory. Do you wear clothes to hide your body or just to follow fashion trends in lockstep? Keep the clothes that give you feelings of pleasure, confidence, and comfort.

25. Beauty is not just skin deep. It is a reflection of your whole self. Love and enjoy the person inside.

A New Vision for Our Bodies and Health

Many of the barriers between us and healthy living are built on the confused and mistaken associations between health and weight that we discussed in chapter 2. Some health care professionals and activists have begun to challenge those barriers with a new movement called Health at Any Size or Health at Every Size. This movement rejects the focus on dieting and thinness as keys to health and happiness. It promotes the evidence that we can be fit and healthy at any size, while the biggest health risks stem from poor nutrition and low physical activity.

While the dieting industry pressures us to reach the mythical ideal weight, the Health at Any Size movement (http://d.webring.com/hub?ring=anysize) encourages us to be healthy in our lifestyle, rather than focusing on a certain weight goal or specific diet program. Health at Any Size is health centered instead of weight centered. It focuses on improving health through eating well and being physically active rather than food restriction. It promotes self-acceptance, self-respect, and appreciation of the diversity of our natural bodies. The movement recognizes the risks of obesity but challenges war-on-obesity scare tactics that prompt many people to take risky steps to lose weight.

While based on common sense and comprehensive research showing that our health is based on our physical, mental, and social well-being, not on our weight, this is a radical movement. Leaders see it as an extension of the other recent social change efforts like the civil rights movement and the women's movement. We now need a body movement that will free women to embrace our full, natural, and powerful selves.

Thanking Our Bodies for Their Magic

Every now and then, let's thank our bodies for all they do for us. Pick something from this list or come up with other ideas. Find the things that feel good to your body and arrange them as regularly as your budget and schedule permit.

- Have a massage or some other form of therapeutic touch such as acupressure.

- Have a facial.

- Have a manicure or pedicure.

- Enjoy a sauna, steam bath, or whirlpool (if this is safe for you; your doctor can determine if these are too stressful for your heart).

- Take a class in movement, tai chi, qi gong, or Pilates.

- Practice yoga. (We recommend hatha yoga or gentle yoga, which are less stressful to the body than other kinds.)

- Experience Reiki or another form of energy medicine.

Safety in Numbers

Going it alone is part of an eating or body image disorders illness process. Believing that we need no one or that no one else understands our problems can be seductive and keeps us stuck in our obsessions. Recovery and health happen and continue when we connect with others.

We do this by joining with others, through group therapies, support groups, and organizations that fight back against the Body Wars or address other women's health issues.

Jennifer found great satisfaction and self-worth in her efforts to get proanorexia Web sites off the Internet. She joined the National Eating Disorder Association and volunteers in its campaigns to improve girls' and women's lives through education about body image and eating disorders. The energy, dedication, and clarity of others in the organization help her to fight back against The Voice and the impulses of her eating disorder. Many other women in recovery join these and other efforts, and find that connectedness and activism strengthen their resolve in recovery.

Avoiding Relapse

Living stressful lives in our appearance-obsessed culture presents a serious risk to women in recovery from disordered eating and body image despair. We can learn from other women's experience about the recognizable red flags indicating attitudes and actions that often lay the groundwork for relapse into old, dangerous symptoms:

- More frequent obsessive thoughts about food, weight, and appearance.
- Weighing yourself more often.
- More frequent negative self talk, self-defeating, and derogatory statements.
- Either/or, dichotomous self-perceptions (success/failure; thin/fat; good/bad).
- Desperate need to be in control all the time.
- Striving for perfection and believing that the perfect weight/ size/body/grade/life will solve all your other problems.
- Feeling more competitive with peers regarding who is the most attractive, thinnest, or the best dieter.
- Believing that you can restrict just for a day or purge just once without hurting yourself.
- Knowing that you are fat and unattractive even when others say you're not.
- Needing to rely on no one else, proving you can handle everything on your own.
- Becoming more isolated and less involved with others.
- Choosing exercise over time with friends or other activities.
- Constantly checking yourself out in mirrors.
- Being unable to look in the mirror.
- Making multiple clothing changes before you leave the house.
- Being unable to relax or to do nothing.

- Not sharing dark thoughts in therapy or with friends.
- Reverting to ritualistic eating habits or restricting.
- Drinking more water, coffee, diet soda, or tea to fill you up and cope with hunger.
- Feeling more hopeless and depressed but covering this up with others.
- Avoiding therapy or other relationships that tend to keep you honest.

If you find yourself agreeing with many of these statements, you are on the road to relapse. Even agreeing with a few of them shows your vulnerability and the importance of addressing the shape of your inner life so that you do not succumb to the dangerous cycle of basing your worth on the shape of your external body.

Getting well is only the first step in recovery. Staying well and embracing life make up all the other steps. Those steps include incorporating positive attitudes and activities into everyday life.

Fortunately, women's experience has revealed simple, healthy strategies that work if taken seriously and practiced daily. Try to do the following things every day:

- Do something that you love for at least ten minutes.
- Eat foods that you enjoy.
- Wear clothes that fit and feel good.
- Loosen up when feeling rigid or perfectionistic.
- Say yes and say no; don't just let life happen to you.
- Be mindful—take time to reflect daily.
- Do nice things for your body.
- Count your blessings.
- Make a daily gratitude list at least five items long.
- Stay connected with positive people in your life.
- Declare: "My body is not a democracy—I'm the only one who gets a vote." Believe this with all your heart.

Most of all, we need to find hope in our search for recovery. A woman with an eating or body image disorder needs to believe that she can in fact recover and can call on lots of resources to keep herself going. The words of this Tibetan prayer capture the thoughts and feeling needed to move forward and stay well:

May I be at peace.
May my heart remain open.
May I know the beauty of my own true nature.
May I be healed.

Embracing Ourselves

Writing about her recovery from bulimia and body image obsessions, actress Yeardley Smith (the voice of Lisa on *The Simpsons*) says she used to see her body as her enemy:

> I have things more in perspective now. [For example,] I don't regret my plastic surgery, but I do regret feeling at the time that I couldn't live without having it. I've learned to accept who I am, thank God, because there is so much energy that goes into that self-loathing of how come my hips aren't a size 36 or whatever. All of those feelings of failure are completely in my own head. I finally get it.

No matter where you were when you started this book, you now know that the desire for a perfect body is not an immutable force of nature. In fact, it is not even a true desire. The search for a magic shape is in our own heads and in the toxic values of the Body Myth.

No matter where you were when you started this book, I hope that you are now more convinced of the need for every one of us to embrace ourselves fully. Even if you're that rare woman who never in her life had a bad body-image day, your role is just as important as anyone else's.

Whether or not we have an eating disorder or body image problem, we can help one another by challenging the Body Myth, refusing to speak the language of fat, and showing one another that the shape we are in is not determined by the shape of our bodies.

I am not my body. You are not your body. Each of our bodies is an important, lovable vehicle, but it is not the journey or the destination. Nor are our bodies the enemy.

Your body is worth respecting and appreciating, no matter how it looks or how you think it looks. Even more important, your life is worth respecting and appreciating. So let's agree to embrace our bodies and our lives—along with the bodies and lives of every other woman.

Appendix

Resources for Eating Disorders and Body Image Despair

My Web site www.thebodymyth.com has easy links to all of these Web sites and books, as well as other information and resources.

Web Sites

www.about-face.org
About-Face promotes positive self-esteem in women of all ages through media education, outreach, and activism.

www.aedweb.org
The Academy for Eating Disorders is a professional organization that provides training and education to clinicians and dedicates itself to improving the research, treatment, and prevention of eating disorders.

www.ANAD.org
National Association of Anorexia Nervosa and Related Disorders provides information, referrals, education, and support groups regarding eating disorders.

www.andreasvoice.org
Andrea's Voice is a moving Web site dedicated to a young woman who died from bulimia, with critical and helpful information for sufferers and their families.

www.annawestinfoundation.org
The Anna Westin Foundation, also dedicated to a young woman who died from her eating disorder, advocates for insurance coverage and provides support to families.

www.bulimia.com
Sponsored by Gurze Books, this Web site is both a bookstore and a resource for information about eating disorders.

www.cswd.org
The Council on Size and Weight Discrimination advocates for people of all sizes and provides education/information on fairness, weight bias, and media images.

www.dadsanddaughters.org
Dads and Daughters is the national advocacy nonprofit that helps men advocate for girls' and women's issues, including body image portrayals in marketing.

www.eatingdisorderscoalition.org
The Eating Disorders Coalition for Research, Policy and Action advocates at the federal level for the recognition of eating disorders as a major public health problem.

www.edreferral.com
The Eating Disorder Referral and Information Center has free information and referral lists for treatment of eating disorders.

www.freedfoundation.org
Founded by Gail Schoenbach, this foundation raises money for treating eating disorders and providing public information about them.

www.healthyweight.net
The Healthy Weight Network provides up-to-date information on eating and weight research and diet quackery, and promotes the Health at Every Size movement.

www.hedc.org
Sponsored by Harvard University, the Harvard Eating Disorders Center provides training and educational programs.

www.iaedp.com
The International Association of Eating Disorders Professionals provides education and training to professionals.

www.mentalhealthscreening.org
This organization sponsors screening, education, and outreach program for eating disorders (the National Eating Disorder Screening Project).

www.mwsg.org
My practice's Web site (Maine & Weinstein Specialty Group) provides helpful information and links to other sites.

www.nationaleatingdisorders.org
The National Eating Disorders Organization is the largest national organization providing educational materials and referral information, sponsoring the annual Eating Disorders Awareness Week, offering educational programs and materials. A great resource for both the public and professionals.

www.redwinggogirls.com
Red Wing Go Girls shows the power of young women advocating against negative media images that promote eating disorders and pressuring the media to foster more realistic images.

www.somethingfishy.org
Something Fishy is a wonderful Web site full of information and resources for anyone concerned about eating disorders or suffering from them.

www.theelisaproject.com
The Elisa Project is dedicated to a young woman who succumbed to eating disorders. This foundation sponsors education and outreach programs in the Dallas, Texas, area.

www.winsnews.org
We Insist on Natural Shapes provides education and media advocacy programs to prevent eating disorders and body image distress.

Books

Berg, Francie. *Women Afraid to Eat: Breaking Free in Today's Weight-Obsessed World*. Hettinger, N. Dak.: Healthy Weight Network, 2001.

Borysenko, Joan. *A Woman's Book of Life: The Biology, Psychology, and Spirituality of the Feminine Life Cycle*. New York: Riverhead Books, 1996.

Brumberg, Joan Jacobs. *The Body Project: An Intimate History of American Girls*. New York: Random House, 1997.

Chernin, Kim. *The Hungry Self: Women, Eating and Identity*. New York: First Harper Perennial, 1994.

Costin, Carolyn. *The Eating Disorder Sourcebook: A Comprehensive Guide to the Causes, Treatment, and Prevention of Eating Disorders*. Lincolnwood, Ill.: NTC Publishing, 1996.

Domar, A. D., and H. Dreher. *Self-Nurture: Learning to Care for Yourself As Effectively As You Care for Everyone Else*. New York: Viking, 2000.

Durek, Judith. *Circle of Stones: Woman's Journey to Herself*. San Diego, Calif.: LuraMedia, 1999.

———. *I Sit Listening to the Wind: Woman's Encounter within Herself*. San Diego, Calif.: LuraMedia, 1993.

Fallon, P., M. Katzman, and S. Wooley. *Feminist Perspectives on Eating Disorders*. New York: Guilford, 1993.

Fodor, Viola. *Desperately Seeking Self: An Inner Guidebook for People with Eating Problems*. Carlsbad, Calif.: Gurze Books, 1997.

Freedman, Rita. *BodyLove: Learning to Like Our Looks and Ourselves*. Carlsbad, Calif.: Gurze Books, 2002.

Friedman, Sandra. *Body Thieves*. Vancouver, B.C.: Salal Books, 2002.

———. *When Girls Feel Fat*. Buffalo, N.Y.: Firefly Books, 2000.

Gaesser, Glenn A. *Big Fat Lies: The Truth about Your Weight and Your Health*. Carlsbad, Calif.: Gurze Books, 2002.

Hall, Lindsey, ed. *Full Lives: Women Who Have Freed Themselves from Food and Weight Obsession*. Carlsbad, Calif.: Gurze Books, 1993.

Hall, L., and L. Cohn. *Bulimia: A Guide to Recovery*. Carlsbad, Calif.: Gurze Books, 1999.

Hall, L., and M. Ostroff. *Anorexia Nervosa: A Guide to Recovery*. Carlsbad, Calif.: Gurze Books, 1999.

Hutchinson, M. G. *Transforming Body Image*. Freedom, Calif.: The Crossing Press, 1985.

Johnston, Anita. *Eating in the Light of the Moon*. Carlsbad, Calif.: Gurze Books, 2000.

Kabat-Zinn, Jon. *Coming to Our Senses: Healing Ourselves and the World through Mindfulness*. New York: Hyperion, 2005.

———. *Wherever You Go, There You Are*. New York: Hyperion, 1994.

Kearney-Cooke, Ann, and Florence Issacs. *Change Your Mind, Change Your Body: Feeling Good about Your Body and Your Self After 40*. New York: Atria Books, 2004.

Kilbourne, Jean. *Can't Buy My Love: How Advertising Changes the Way We Think and Feel*. New York: Simon and Schuster, 2000.

Kingsbury, K., and M. E. Williams. *Weight Wisdom: Affirmations to Free You from Food and Body Concerns*. New York: Brunner-Routledge, 2003.

Knapp, Caroline. *Appetites: Why Women Want*. New York: Counterpoint, 2002.

Koenig, K. R. *The Rules of "Normal" Eating: A Commonsense Approach for Dieters, Overeaters, Undereaters, Emotional Eaters, and Everyone in Between*. Carlsbad, Calif.: Gurze Books, 2005.

Lerner, Harriet. *The Dance of Anger: A Woman's Guide to Changing Patterns of Intimate Relationships*. New York: HarperCollins, 1985.

Maine, Margo. *Father Hunger: Fathers, Daughters and the Pursuit of Thinness*. Carlsbad, Calif.: Gurze Books, 2005.

———. *Body Wars: Making Peace with Women's Bodies*. Carlsbad, Calif.: Gurze Books, 2000.

Manheim, Camryn. *Wake Up, I'm Fat!* New York: Broadway Books, 1999.

Nasser, M., M. A. Katzman, and R. A. Gordon, eds. *Eating Disorders and Cultures in Transition*. New York: Brunner-Routledge, 2001.

Northrup, Christiane. *Women's Bodies, Women's Wisdom: Creating Physical and Emotional Health and Healing*. New York: Bantam Books, 1998.

Piran, Niva, ed. *Preventing Eating Disorders: A Handbook of Interventions and Special Challenges*. Philadelphia, Pa.: Taylor and Francis, 1999.

Rabinor, Judith R. *A Starving Madness: Tales of Hunger, Hope, and Healing in Psychotherapy*. Carlsbad, Calif.: Gurze Books, 2002.

Radcliffe, Rebecca. *Hot Flashes, Chocolate Sauce, & Rippled Thighs: Women's Wisdom, Wellness, and Body Gratitude*. Minneapolis, Minn.: Ease Publications, 2004.

———. *Body Prayers: Finding Body Peace*. Minneapolis, Minn.: Ease Publications, 1999.

———. *Dance Naked in Your Living Room: Handling Stress and Finding Joy*. Minneapolis, Minn.: Ease Publications, 1997.

Roth, Geneen. *When Food Is Love: Exploring the Relationship between Eating and Intimacy*. New York: Plume Books, 1991.

Sarasohn, Lisa. *The Woman's Belly Book: Finding Your Treasure Within*. Asheville, N.C.: Self Health Education, 2003.

Sheehy, Gail. *Passages: Predictable Crises of Adult Life*. New York: Bantam, 1977.

Steinem, Gloria. *Revolution from Within: A Book of Self-Esteem*. Boston: Little Brown, 1992.

Waterhouse, Debra. *Like Mother, Like Daughter: How Women Are Influenced by Their Mother's Relationship with Food and How to Break the Pattern*. New York, Hyperion, 1997.

Wolf, Naomi. *The Beauty Myth: How Images of Beauty Are Used against Women*. New York: Perennial, 2002.

Zerbe, Kathryn J. *The Body Betrayed: A Deeper Understanding of Women, Eating Disorders, and Treatment*. Carlsbad, Calif.: Gurze Books, 1993.

Notes

Introduction

1 *the national press has periodically asked me to discuss* For example, Ginia Bellafante, "When Midlife Seems Just an Empty Plate," *New York Times*, sec. 9, March 9, 2003.

1 *one-third of its residential patients are now over thirty, a historical shift* Personal communication, Dr. William N. Davis, vice president, The Renfrew Centers.

4 *"a woman's individual preoccupation with weight often serves as a mask"* Caroline Knapp, *Appetites: Why Women Want* (New York: Counterpoint, 2003), 17.

Chapter 1. The Changing Shape of Womanhood

10 *"the language of fat"* Sandra S. Friedman, *Body Thieves: Help Girls Reclaim Their Natural Bodies and Become Physically Active* (Vancouver, B.C.: Salal Books, 2002).

12 *Extensive studies reported in the Journal of the American Medical Association* Glenn A. Gaesser. *Big Fat Lies: The Truth about Weight and Your Health* (Carlsbad, Calif.: Gurze Books, 2002).

12 *A 1983 Glamour magazine survey of 33,000* "Feeling Fat in a Thin Society," *Glamour*, February 1984, 198–201, 251–52, cited in Richard A. Gordon, *Eating Disorders: Anatomy of a Social Epidemic* (Malden, Mass., Blackwell Publishers, 2000).

13 *Twenty years older now, this generation of women is still saddled with a distorted body image and body dissatisfaction.* See L. H. Clarke, "Older Women's Perceptions of Ideal Body Weights: The Tensions between Health and Appearance Motivations for Weight Loss," *Ageing and Society* 22 (2002): 751–73; Francie Berg, *Women Afraid to Eat: Breaking Free in Today's Weight-Obsessed World* (Hettinger, N. Dak.: Healthy Weight Publishing Network, 2001); and M. M. Hetherington and L. Burnett. "Ageing and the Pursuit of Slimness: Dietary Restraint and Weight Satisfaction in Elderly Women," *British Journal of Clinical Psychology* 33 (1994): 391–400.

13 *That's why traveling to another country so often produces culture shock—the anxiety and disorientation of not knowing how to communicate* Dr. Carmen Guanipa, Department of Counseling and School Psychology, San Diego State University (1998), http://edweb.sdsu.edu/people/CGuanipa/cultshok.htm.

14 *However, research finds that up to half of women using commercial weight-loss* L. T. Goldstein, S. J. Goldsmith, K. Anger, and A. C. Leon. "Psychiatric Symptoms in Clients Presenting for Commercial Weight Reduction Treatment," *International Journal of Eating Disorders* 20, no. 2 (1996): 191–97.

16 *Collectively, U.S. women spend as much on cosmetics every five days as George W. Bush raised to become president in 2000* Based on data from www.fec.gov, http://cspan.

politicalmoneyline.com/cgi-win/x_candpg.exe?DoFn=P00003335*2000, and www. itds.treas.gov/cosmetics.html. The U.S. cosmetics industry has at least $15 billion in annual sales ($41 million per day). George W. Bush's presidential campaign received $194 million in donations between 1/1/1999 and 12/31/2000. If you divide $194 million by $41 million, then you get 4.73 days.

19   *In her book Passages: Predictable Crises of Adult Life, Gail Sheehy*   G. Sheehy, *Passages: Predictable Crises of Adult Life* (New York: E. P. Dutton, 1976), 242.

20   *Storyteller Lise Lunge-Larsen calls this threshold when you pass between phases of life "liminal" time*   Joe Kelly, "Calling Our Daughter's Name," *New Moon Parenting*, June/July 1993, 13.

21   *Naomi, a New York public relations executive, is no teenager*   Bellafante, "When Midlife Seems Just an Empty Plate."

22   *Step Back Exercise*   Inspired by a ritual in Stanley Krippner and David Feinstein, *The Mythic Path: Discovering the Guiding Stories of Your Past—Creating a Vision for Your Future* (New York: Jeremy P. Tarcher, 1997).

Chapter 2. Fact versus Fiction

24   *bingeing does not cause dieting*   J. Polivy and C. P. Herman. "Dieting and binge eating: A causal analysis" *American Psychologist*, 40 (1985): 193–204. Cited in Gordon, *Eating Disorders*, 157.

26   *Before puberty, a girl's body*   Debra Waterhouse, *Like Mother, Like Daughter: How Women Are Influenced by Their Mother's Relationship with Food and How to Break the Pattern* (New York: Hyperion, 1997).

26   *Only 10 percent of women die*   Debra Waterhouse, *Outsmarting the Female Fat Cell after Pregnancy: Every Woman's Guide to Shaping Up, Slimming Down, and Staying Sane after the Baby* (New York: Hyperion, 2003).

28   *In her book Transforming Body Image*   Marcia Germaine Hutchinson, *Transforming Body Image* (Freedom, Calif.: Crossing Press, 1985).

28   *Researchers have known for decades that diets can't fool Mother Nature*   Kathy Kater, *Real Kids Come in All Sizes* (New York: Broadway, 2004), 138–39.

28   *more than 104,000 book titles on Amazon.com*   Search conducted August 30, 2004, by author.

29   *the mortality risks related to obesity have been grossly oversimplified*   See Berg, *Women Afraid to Eat*; and Gaesser, *Big Fat Lies*.

29   *But researchers find that health problems among the overweight poor are due more to being poor than to being fat*   E. D. Rothblum, "Women and Weight: Fad and Fiction," *The Journal of Psychology* 124, no. 1 (1990): 5–24.

30   *As California psychologist and body image expert Dr. Debbie Burgard*   Mary Duenwald, "Body and Image; One Size Definitely Does Not Fit All." *New York Times*, sec. 15, June 22, 2003, www.nytimes.com/2003/06/22/health/womenshealth/22DUEN.html.

30   *Nutritionist Francie Berg has researched diet trends*   Personal communication with author, April 2004.

31   *Glenn Gaesser's book Big Fat Lies: The Truth about Your Weight and Your Health*   Gaesser, *Big Fat Lies*.

32   *During our transition to menopause*   Waterhouse, *Like Mother, Like Daughter*.

32   *Normal menopausal women gain eight to twelve pounds*   Ibid.

33   *Women who gain a moderate amount of weight during menopause*   K. S. Losconzy, et al., "Does Weight Loss from Middle Age to Old Age Explain the Inverse Weight Mortality in Old Age?" *American Journal of Epidemiology* 141 (1995): 312.

33 *A review of multiple studies indicates that extra weight in women may actually bring them benefits*   Gaesser, *Big Fat Lies*.

34 *Healthy adult bodies are hardwired to burn more*   W. Bennett and J. Gurin, *The Dieter's Dilemma: Eating Less and Weighing More* (New York: Basic Books, 1982).

34 *Science has repeatedly proven this phenomenon through animal research and human twin studies; twins raised apart grow up to have similar weights regardless of how much their adoptive parents weigh.*   Ibid.

34 *even though health care professionals and researchers treat the BMI as a well-founded*   Berg, *Women Afraid to Eat*.

35 *The National Heart, Lung, and Blood Institute recently changed the BMI*   Ibid.

35 *The new agency guidelines*   Ibid.

38 *Exercise: What Happens When We Diet to Lose Weight?*   Adapted from Margo Maine, *Body Wars: Making Peace with Women's Bodies* (Carlsbad, Calif.: Gurze Books, 2000).

Chapter 3. Women's Bodies, Women's Lives

46 *For example, many historic cultures had something called a Red Tent, set away from the village.*   Anita Diament, *The Red Tent* (New York: Picador, 1998).

46 *The pioneering research of Dr. Carol Gilligan*   Carol Gilligan and Lyn Mikel Brown, *Meeting at the Crossroads: Women's Psychology and Girls' Development* (Cambridge, Mass: Harvard University Press, 1992). Also, see Carol Gilligan, *In a Different Voice: Psychological Theory and Women's Development* (Cambridge, Mass.: Harvard University Press, 1993).

46 *Renowned anthropologist Margaret Mead*   Helen Fisher, *The First Sex: The Natural Talents of Women and How They Are Changing the World* (New York: Random House, 1999), 185.

46 *Germaine Greer saw menopause*   Ibid, 182.

46 *Writer Betty Friedan calls aging*   Nancy Friday, *The Power of Beauty* (New York: HarperCollins, 1996), 494.

48 *"Though [the] excessive visibility"*   Germaine Greer, *The Change: Women, Ageing and the Menopause* (London: Hamish Hamilton, 1991), cited in Friday, *The Power of Beauty*, 507.

52 *On the other hand, our culture has a denial of death, which both reinforces and feeds on its overglorification of youth.*   Ernest Becker, *The Denial of Death* (New York: Free Press, 1997).

52 *Writer Marilyn Karr was shocked*   Personal communication with Joe Kelly, December 2003.

56 *Listen to the murky path one female Realtor must constantly tread*   Personal communication with Joe Kelly, July 2003.

57 *A 2000 AFL-CIO survey finds that more than half of mothers with children*   AFL-CIO Working Women Survey, 2000," cited in Knapp, *Appetites*, 151.

57 *A 2003 New York Times Magazine cover story profiled affluent women*   Lisa Belkin, "The Opt-Out Revolution," *New York Times Magazine*, October 26, 2003, 42.

58 *Appearance discrimination is an embedded concrete reality*   For example, see Tolerance.org, "Sizing Up Weight-Based Discrimination" May 2002, www. tolerance.org/news/article_tol.jsp?id=505; Steven L. Gortmaker, Aviva Must, James M. Perrin, Arthur M. Sobol, and William Dietz, "Social and Economic Consequences of Overweight in Adolescence and Young Adulthood," *New England Journal of Medicine* 329 (September 30, 1993): 1008–1012, 1036–1037; and Esther Rothblum, Pamela Brand, Carol Miller, and Helen Oetien, "The Relationship

between Obesity, Employment Discrimination, and Employment-Related Victimization," *Journal of Vocational Behavior* 37, no. 3 (December 1, 1990): 251–66.

70   *We still teach young boys more about how to maintain what men's activist Jackson Katz* Jackson Katz, *Tough Guise: Violence, Media and the Crisis in Masculinity.* A film directed by Sut Jhally (Media Education Foundation, 1999).

70   *a man who claims to bolt a marriage because of his partner's body shape is lying to himself* Adapted from Joe Kelly, *Dads and Daughters: How to Inspire, Support, and Understand Your Daughter* (New York: Broadway Books, 2003).

71   *As veteran divorced mother Sarah puts it* Personal communication with Joe Kelly, July 2003.

Chapter 4. The Shape of Eating Disorders

76   *Kitty Westin, attended the premier screening and reception* Personal communication with Joe Kelly, January 2004.

79   *in centuries-old documents, medical historians find regular mention of symptoms that are recognized today as eating disorders.* Gordon, *Eating Disorders.*

80   *People with anorexia nervosa can* Unless otherwise noted, material for this chapter's descriptions of specific eating disorders is drawn from clinical experience and the National Institute of Mental Health publication *Eating Disorders: Facts about Eating Disorders and the Search for Solutions* (NIMH, 2000). See www.nimh. nih.gov/publicat/eatingdisorders.cfm.

81   *5 percent of women with anorexia are likely to die* American Psychiatric Association, "Practice Guideline for the Treatment of Patients with Eating Disorders (Revision)," *American Journal of Psychiatry* 157, no. 1 (2000, January Supplement): 1–39.

81   *Alcohol abuse among women with eating disorders increases mortality risk* D. B. Herzog, D. N. Greenwood, D. J. Dorer, A. T. Flores, E. R. Ekeblad, A. Richards, M. A. Blais, and M. B. Keller. "Mortality in Eating Disorders," *International Journal of Eating Disorders* 28, (2000): 20–26.

82   *There is no quick-fix for anorexia* M. Strober, R. Freeman, and W. Morrell. "The Long-term Course of Severe Anorexia Nervosa in Adolescents: Survival Analysis of Recovery, Relapse and Outcome Predictors over 10–15 Years in a Prospective Study," *International Journal of Eating Disorders* 22, no. 4 (1997): 339–60.

83   *Researchers estimate that between 1 and 4 percent of women develop bulimia* American Psychiatric Association, "Practice Guideline (Revision)."

86   *Orthorexia* See Steven Bratman, *The Orthorexia Home Page*, 2003, www. orthorexia. com.

89   *In her thought-provoking book* Waterhouse, *Like Mother, Like Daughter.*

90   *The average woman today eats two hundred calories less* Ibid.

92   *Body Dysmorphic Disorder* American Psychiatric Association. *Diagnostic and Statistical Manual of Mental Disorders*, 4th ed. (Washington, D.C.: American Psychiatric Association, 1994); K. A. Phillips, *The Broken Mirror: Understanding and Treating Body Dysmorphic Disorder* (Oxford, England: Oxford University Press, 1998); and www.nimh.nih.gov/studies/2anxdisocd.cfm.

95   *Here is a list I created* Maine, *Body Wars.*

98   *The New England Journal of Medicine and the National Task Force on Prevention and Treatment of Obesity recommend* G. D. Curfman. "Editorial: Diet Pills Redux," *New England Journal of Medicine* 337, no. 1 (1997): 629–30.

98   *By the late 1990s, more than nine million adults* Gaesser, *Big Fat Lies.*

98   *The Food and Drug Administration warned the public about phenylpropanolamine*

"FDA Issues Public Health Advisory on Phenylpropanolamine in Drug Products" (FDA, 2001), www.fda.gov/fdac/features/2001/101_ppa.html.

98   *Similarly, the FDA banned continued U.S. sale of fen-phen, the diet drug combination* F. M. Berg, "Fen-phen Tragedy Triggers Uproar," *Healthy Weight Journal* 12, no. 2 (1998): 17–32. Also, "Reports of Valvular Heart Disease in Patients Receiving Concomitant Fenfluramine and Phentermine." (FDA, 1997), www.fda.gov/cder/news/phen/phenfen.htm.

98   *After numerous studies, the Food and Drug Administration banned ephedra*   G. Condon, "Study: Ingredient Worsens Ephedra," *Hartford Courant*, January 14, 2004, B1; and "Sales of Supplements Containing Ephedrine Alkaloids (Ephedra) Prohibited" (FDA, 2004), www.fda.gov/oc/initiatives/ephedra/february2004/.

99   *Over-the-counter cathartic laxatives like Dulcolax can be very dangerous when used in excess*   B. D. Wadholtz, "Gastrointestinal Complaints and Function in Patients with Eating Disorders," in P. S. Mehler and A. E. Andersen, *Eating Disorders: A Guide to Medical Care and Complications* (Baltimore, Md.: Johns Hopkins University, 1999).

99   *At colonics retreat spas we can pay up to $3,500 a week*   See www.juicefasting.com/programs.htm; Vanessa Grigoriadis, "Rest the Tummy, Restore the Soul," *New York Times*, sec. 9, August 24, 2003; and Karen Robinovitz, "No Talking. No Fun. It's Called a Vacation," *New York Times*, January 16, 2004, http://travel2.nytimes.com/mem/travel/article-page.html?res=9E01E5DF1E30 F935A25752C0A9629C8B63.

100   *In 2003, 45 percent of cosmetic surgery was performed*   American Society for Aesthetic Plastic Surgery, "Cosmetic Surgery National Data Bank: 2003 Statistics" (ASAPS, 2004), www.surgery.org/download/2003-stats.pdf.

100   *The American Society of Plastic Surgeons (ASPS) calls this elective surgery* "Reconstructive Surgery Procedures at a Glance," American Society of Plastic Surgeons (2004), www.plasticsurgery.org/public_education/procedures/ReconstructiveSurgery.cfm.

100   *More than ten thousand people attended casting calls*   "Extreme Makeover: About the Show," ABC TV (2004), http://abc.go.com/primetime/extrememakeover/show.html.

101   *culminating in what the producers call "a climactic unveiling"*   Ibid.

101   *Each week, contestants go through a boot camp regimen*   "The Swan: Info," Fox TV (2004), www.fox.com/swan/home.htm.

101   *According to ASPS, the 2002 ratio of elective to reconstructive*   "2000/2001/2002/2003 National Plastic Surgery Statistics, Cosmetic and Reconstructive Procedure Trends," American Society of Plastic Surgeons (2004), www.plasticsurgery.org/public_education/loader.cfm?url=/commonspot/security/getfile.cfm&PageID=12552.

101   *According to ASPS statistics, more than 8.7 million elective cosmetic surgeries*   Ibid.

103   *In one study, 83 percent of women with BDD had either no improvement*   K. A. Phillips and S. F. Diaz, "Gender Differences in Body Dysmorphic Disorder," *Journal of Nervous and Mental Disease* 185 (1997): 570–77.

103   *In another more recent study, the number was 93 percent.*   K. A. Phillips, J. Grant, J. Siniscalchi, and R. S. Albertini, "Surgical and Nonpsychiatric Medical Treatment of Patients with Body Dysmorphic Disorder," *Psychosomatics* 42 (2001): 504–10.

103   *Concerns about body image and weight also increase adult women's cigarette use*   E. Stice and H. Shaw, "Prospective Relations of Body Image, Eating and Affective Disturbances to Smoking Onset in Adolescent Girls: How Virginia Slims," *Journal of Consulting and Clinical Psychology* 71, no. 1 (2003): 129–35.

103   *Although the number of U.S. women who smoke declined*   Statistics, trends, and other helpful information available in "Women and Smoking: A Report of the

Surgeon General," Centers for Disease Control and Prevention, U.S. Department of Health and Human Services (2001), www.cdc.gov/tobacco/sgr/sgr_forwomen/ataglance.htm#Health%20Consequences.

103 *Few of us would consciously choose to manage* Ibid.

103 *Women who smoke weigh an average of four pounds less* Naomi Wolf, *The Beauty Myth* (New York: William Morrow, 1991).

103 *The National Institutes of Health reports that not everyone gains weight* "You Can Control Your Weight as You Quit Smoking," The National Institute of Diabetes and Digestive and Kidney Diseases of the National Institutes of Health (2003), www.niddk.nih.gov/health/nutrit/pubs/quitsmok/index.htm.

104 *Extinguishing the Smoke* Adapted from "How to Quit Smoking," National Women's Health Information Center, U.S. Department of Health and Human Services (2002), www.4woman.gov/QuitSmoking/howtoquit.cfm.

106 *I thought I should know, intuitively* Knapp, *Appetites*, 148.

Chapter 5. So Why Do People Do It?

111 *However, research indicates that black women* Deborah Schooler, et al., "Television's Role in the Body Image Development of Young White And Black Women," *Psychology of Women Quarterly* 28 (2004): 40.

112 *Centers for Disease Control statistics on high-risk dieting practices among adolescents* "Youth Risk Behavior Surveillance—U.S., 2001," U.S. Department of Health and Human Services Centers for Disease Control and Prevention, *Morbidity and Mortality Report* (MMWR) 51 (2002): SS-4.

112 *Nearly forty countries now report eating disorders* R. Gordon, "Eating Disorders East and West: A Culture-Bound Syndrome Unbound," in *Eating Disorders and Cultures in Transition*, ed. M. Nasser, M. A. Katzman, and R. A. Gordon (London: Brunner-Routledge, 2001).

112 *Long-held Fijian traditions valued large female bodies* A. E. Becker and R. A. Burwell, "Acculturation and Disordered Eating in Fiji." Presented at the 152nd Annual Meeting of the American Psychiatric Association, 1999.

113 *Women who grew up with an eating disorder sufferer in the family are more likely to fall victim themselves.* R. Rende, "Liability to Psychopathology: A Quantitative Genetic Study," in *The Developmental Psychopathology of Eating Disorders: Implications for Research, Prevention and Treatment*, ed. L. Smolak, M. P. Levine, and R. Striegel-Moore (Mahwah, N.J.: Lawrence Erlbaum Associates, 1996).

120 *Responding to starvation cues from our restriction, gastric secretions in the gut slow down.* B. D. Wadholtz, 1999.

121 *I'm in recovery from my bulimia* Personal communication with Joe Kelly, July 1999.

122 *In fact, The Voice gains power by making them feel like they can't survive or succeed without it.* For a good illustration of this phenomenon, see Dina Zeckhausen, "What's Eating Katie?" Eating Disorders Information Network of Atlanta, www.edin-ga.org/shopping/shopdisplayproducts.asp?id=3&cat=Play+Scripts.

122 *[E]ven now, years past anorexia* Knapp, *Appetites*, 87.

126 *The most influential tables* Gaesser, *Big Fat Lies.*

126 *Forty-two percent of girls in grades one through three* M. Collins, "Body Figure Perception and Preferences among Preadolescent Children," *International Journal of Eating Disorders* 10 (1991): 199–208.

127 *Forty-five percent of children in grades three through six* M. J. Maloney, J. McGuire, S. R. Daniels, and B. Specker, "Dieting Behavior and Eating Attitudes in Children," *Pediatrics* 84, no. 3 (1989): 482–87.

127 *Half of nine- and ten-year-olds* L. M. Mellin, C. E. Irwin, and S. Scully, "Prevalence of Disordered Eating in Girls: A Survey of Middle-Class Children," *Journal of American Dietetics Association* 92, no. 7 (1992): 851–53.

127 *Nine percent of nine-year-old girls* Ibid.

127 *By high school, 70 percent* C. Ferron, "Body Image in Adolescence in Cross-Cultural Research," *Adolescence* 32 (1997): 735–45.

Chapter 6. How Family Shapes Us

136 *One study shows that anorexic mothers* A. Stein and H. Woolley, "The Influence of Parental Eating Disorders on Young Children: Implications of Recent Research for Some Clinical Intervention," *Eating Disorders: Journal of Treatment and Prevention* 4 (1996): 139–46.

138 *Social historian Joan Jacobs Brumberg* J. J. Brumberg, *The Body Project: An Intimate History of American Girls* (New York: Random House, 1997).

141 *My father and I were very close* Kelly, *Dads and Daughters*, 112.

148 *The rules in a family with an alcoholic* C. Coniglio, "Making Connections: Family Alcoholism and the Development of Eating Problems" in *Consuming Passions: Feminist Approaches to Weight Preoccupation and Eating Disorders*, ed. C. Brown and K. Jasper (Toronto, Calif.: Second Story Press, 1993), 237.

150 *reacted as most partners of sexual abuse survivors do* For example, see Laura Davis, *Allies in Healing: When the Person You Love Was Sexually Abused as a Child* (New York: Harper Perennial, 1991).

150 *Father Hunger* Margo Maine, *Father Hunger: Fathers, Daughters and the Pursuit of Thinness* (Carlsbad, Calif.: Gurze Books, 2004).

157 *But we are called "human beings" not human "doings" for a reason* I first heard this statement from my dear friend Reverend Dr. Steve Emmett, who points this out frequently.

166 *she needed to temporarily back off from their sexual relationship while she worked through her feelings about the abuse* For example, see Davis, *Allies in Healing*.

Chapter 7. The New Extended Family

170 *In some present-day Arab countries* Gautam Naik, "Western Habits Fueled Weight of Women Prized for Size; Some Girls Are Force-Fed; Ms. Mohammed Tries a Diet," *Wall Street Journal*, sec. AP, December 29, 2004.

171 *In an earlier book, I coined the term Body Wars* Maine, *Body Wars*.

173 *This cause is not altogether and exclusively woman's cause.* Frederick Douglass (1848), in *Against the Tide: Pro-feminist Men in the United States, 1776–1990—A Documentary History*, ed. M. S. Kimmel and T. E. Mosmiller (Boston: Beacon Press, 1992), xxxi.

174 *Renoir once said* Knapp, *Appetites*, ix.

176 *60 percent of these young women fit a key diagnostic criterion for anorexia* C. Wiseman, et al., "Cultural Expectations of Thinness in Women: An Update," *International Journal of Eating Disorders* 11, no. 1 (1992): 85–89.

176 *Pageant contestants average fourteen hours of exercise* K. D. Brownell "Dieting and the Search for the Perfect Body: Where Physiology and Culture Collide," *Behavior Therapy* 22 (1991): 1–12.

176 *In the 1970s, the average fashion model weighed 8 percent less than the average American woman.* Wolf, *The Beauty Myth*.

177 *A booming consumer culture requires that women want* Gloria Steinem, *Moving Beyond Words* (New York: Simon and Schuster, 1994), 252.

177 *By the late 1990s, shopping malls made up over four billion square feet* Juliet B. Schor, *The Overspent American: Why We Want What We Don't Need* (New York: Basic Books, 1998).

178 *While women still make about one-quarter less than men* The ratio of female-to-male earnings in 2003 for full-time, year-round workers was 75.5 percent, a decline from 76.6 percent in 2002, because of a decline in the earnings of female year-round full-time workers. See www.census.gov/hhes/income/income03/prs04asc.html and www.census.gov/hhes/www/img/incpov03/fig12.jpg.

National Women's Law Center analysis (www.nwlc.org/details.cfm?id=1986&section=newsroom) shows: Poverty among adult women reached 12.4 percent, 40 percent higher than men's 8.9 percent poverty rate. The poverty rate for women and girls increased for the third year in a row, to 13.7 percent from 13.3 percent in 2002.

The poverty rate for single-mother families increased by 5.3 percent, to 35.5 percent in 2003 from 33.7 percent in 2002. The poverty rate for married-couple families with children increased by 2.9 percent, to 7 percent in 2003.

Real median earnings for women working full-time, year-round fell to $30,724, from $30,895 in 2002. The median earnings of comparable men were essentially unchanged at $40,668.

Households in the bottom 20 percent of the income distribution—disproportionately female-headed households—received a smaller share of aggregate income than at any time in the thirty-seven years that data has been collected. The bottom 20 percent of households received just 3.4 percent of income; the top 20 percent received nearly half (49.8 percent).

The number of women and girls without health insurance rose to 21.2 million, an increase of 927,000 over 2002. The uninsured rate rose more sharply among women than men between 2002 and 2003 (4 percent for women, 1 percent for men).

178 *We feel compelled to buy products with no proven* Wolf, *The Beauty Myth.*

178 *cellulite creams that cost U.S. women over $10 million in 2003 alone* For example, see "US Food and Drug Administration Warning Letter" http://www.fda.gov/foi/warning_letters/g4511d.htm; *Chicago Sun-Times*, October 15, 2004, www.suntimes.com/output/lifestyles/cst-ftr-cell15.html; and Austin (Tex.) *Chronicle*, May 3, 2002, www.austinchronicle.com/issues/dispatch/2002-05-03/cols_health.html.

179 *In her book Can't Buy My Love* Jean Kilbourne, *Can't Buy My Love: How Advertising Changes the Way We Think and Feel* (New York: Simon and Schuster, 2000).

179 *The average Western woman is exposed to as many as three thousand ads a day* J. B. Twitchell, *Adcult USA: The Triumph of Advertising in American Culture* (New York: Columbia University Press, 1996).

180 *Meanwhile, marketers are subliminally "imbedding" products and name brands into regular programming and editorial content* Scott Donaton and *Advertising Age* Books, *Madison and Vine: Why the Entertainment and Advertising Industries Must Converge to Survive* (New York: McGraw-Hill, 2004).

181 *psychological research showing that the self-esteem of women and girls drops markedly after only a few minutes* D. Then, "Women's Magazines: Messages They Convey about Looks, Men, and Careers," paper presented at annual convention of American Psychological Association, Washington, D.C., 1992.

181 *the producers of Pretty Woman did not consider the body of box-office superstar Julia Roberts thin enough for the film's nude* Kilbourne, *Can't Buy My Love*, 123.

182 *throughout Madeleine K. Albright's autobiography Madam Secretary* M. K. Albright, *Madam Secretary: A Memoir* (New York: Hyperion, 2003).

182 *For example, a Web site that promotes itself as* See www.ivillage.com/ivillage/support/pages/0,,606141_614685,00.html.

184 *For many years, legal correspondent Greta Van Susteren* Greta Van Susteren and Elaine Lafferty, *My Turn at the Bully Pulpit: Straight Talk about the Things That Drive Me Nuts* (New York: Crown, 2003); abcnews.go.com/sections/GMA/GoodMorningAmerica/GMA020205susteren.html; and www.washingtonpost.com/ac2/wp-dyn/A45269-2003Aug25.

184 *While we spend (for example, $20 billion annually on cosmetics)* See www.itds.treas.gov/cosmetics.html.

185 *If women suddenly stopped feeling ugly* Wolf, *The Beauty Myth*, 234.

185 *In an age when more than 80 percent of women say they are dissatisfied with their bodies* C. Steiner-Adair and M. Purcell, "Approaches to Mainstreaming Eating Disorders Prevention," *Eating Disorders: The Journal of Treatment and Prevention* 4, no. 4 (1996): 294–99.

186 *By 2003, 16 percent of cosmetic surgery patients in the United States were people of color* American Society of Plastic Surgeons, "2003 Cosmetic Demographics," www.plasticsurgery.org/public_education/loader.cfm?url=/commonspot/security/getfile.cfm&PageID=13323.

186 *Women of African and Asian heritage face unique plastic surgery health risks* Maine, *Body Wars*.

186 *One of every forty women in the United States has risky silicone gel-filled breast implants* Greer, *The Change*. See also, "Draft Guidance for Industry and FDA Staff: Saline, Silicone Gel, and Alternative Breast Implants." U.S. Food and Drug Administration, 2004. www.fda.gov/cdrh/ode/guidance/1239.html.

187 *A tragic example is Olivia Goldsmith* R. Gardner, "Looks to Die For," *New York*, February 16, 2004, 51–56.

187 *Investigations have shown deaths associated with liposuction and other cosmetic procedures, as well as autoimmune diseases from bursting or leaking breast implants.* Maine, *Body Wars*.

187 *A Fashion is nothing more than an induced epidemic.* G. B. Shaw, in *Simpson's Contemporary Quotations since 1950*, ed. J. B. Simpson (Boston: Houghton Mifflin, 1988).

187 *It takes on a tone of "fashism"* Maine, *Body Wars*.

188 *With the media focus on deterioration rather than vitality* Betty Friedan, *The Fountain of Age* (New York: Simon and Schuster, 1993; and AARP, www.aarp.org.

188 *Fair-skinned blacks invented passing* Steinem, *Moving Beyond Words*, 252.

190 *Steps for Aging Beautifully* Rita Freedman, *Bodylove: Learning to Like Our Looks and Ourselves* (Carlsbad, Calif.: Gurze Books, 2002).

Chapter 8. The Shape of Recovery

194 *Pain festers in isolation* Knapp, *Appetites*, 158.

195 *Many women who have recovered found it helps to break down recovery into smaller pieces or stages* Adapted from J. O. Prochaska, J. C. Norcross, and C. C. Di Clemente, *Changing for Good: A Revolutionary Six-Stage Program for Overcoming Bad Habits and Moving Your Life Positively Forward* (New York: William Morrow, 1994).

198 *Eating disorders expert Dr. Anita Johnston* A. Johnston, *Eating in the Light of the Moon.* (Carlsbad, Calif.: Gurze Books, 2000), xvii.

208   *Some eating and body disorder treatment programs incorporate 12 step*   C. L. Johnson and R. A. Sansone, "Integrating the Twelve-Step Approach with Traditional Psychotherapy for the Treatment of Eating Disorders," *International Journal of Eating Disorders* 14, no. 2, (1993): 121–34.

211   *All suffering is bearable*   Isak Dinesen, cited in Judith Rabinor, *A Starving Madness: Tales of Hunger, Hope and Healing in Psychotherapy* (Carlsbad, Calif.: Gurze Books, 2002), 63.

Chapter 9. Thinking and Coping in New Ways

219   *The solution is a technique called cognitive restructuring*   A. D. Domar and H. Dreher, Self-Nurture: *Learning to Care for Yourself As Effectively As You Care for Everyone Else* (New York :Viking, 2000).

220   *Unless you feel beautiful inside*   Marcia G. Hutchinson, *Transforming Body Image*, Freedom, Calif.: Crossing Press, 1985, 14–15.

224   *Using these limited criteria, studies find that about 40 percent*   American Psychiatric Association, "Practice Guideline for the Treatment of Patients with Eating Disorders (Revision)," *American Journal of Psychiatry* 157, no. 1 (2000, January Supplement): 1–39.

229   *I'm stuck with this idea that I need to be authentic*   N. Griffin, "American Original," *More*, March 2004, 83–84.

229   *Publisher Katherine Graham is another great example*   See Katherine Graham, *Personal History* (New York: Vintage Books, 1998).

230   *Sure, he [Fred Astaire] was great*   See Rosalie Maggio, *The New Beacon Book of Quotations by Women* (Boston: Beacon Press, 1996), 451. "Widely quoted and most often attributed to Ann Richards, although she has always disclaimed authorship, this remark apparently first appeared in a comic strip by Bob Thaves. In *Ginger: My Story* (New York: HarperCollins, 1991) page 137, Ginger Rogers says: 'a friend sent me a cartoon called "Frank and Ernest" from a LA newspaper. It showed Fred on a sandwich board announcing a "Fred Astaire Festival." A woman was standing near the sandwich board, talking to Frank and Ernest. The balloon coming from her mouth said, "Sure he was great, but don't forget that Ginger Rogers did everything he did . . . backwards and in high heels!"' The cartoon was copyrighted 1982."

Chapter 10. Embracing Our Selves

236   *"What is REAL?"*   Margery Williams, *The Velveteen Rabbit* (New York: Avon Books, 1975), 16–17.

238   *Through mindful breathing*   Thich Nhat Hanh, *Peace Is Every Step* (New York: Bantam, 1991).

239   *Buddhist teacher Thich Nhat Hanh calls smiling*   Ibid.

244   *Better Breathing Made Easy*   These techniques are adapted from Stacie Stukin, "The Anti-Drug for Anxiety," The Yoga Journal (March–April 2003): 108–13.

249   *the miraculous things every human body does on its own to stay in ongoing balance*   See Deepak Chopra, *AgeLess Body, Timeless Mind* (New York: Harmony, 1993).

250   *Twenty-five Ways to Love Your Body*   Adapted from Maine, *Body Wars*.

255   *Tibetan prayer*   Source unknown; shared by Carolyn Costin.

256   *Writing about her recovery from bulimia and body image obsessions, actress Yeardley Smith*   People magazine, April 26, 2004, 100.

Index